The Mud People

Chronicles, Testimonios & Remembrances

Patrisia Gonzales

CHUSMA HOUSE

Chusma House Publications

ISBN: 1-891823-05-1

Library of Congress Catalog Card Number: 2003102201

Cover Art Rendering
Deborah Vasquez

Graphic Design and Typography
Orange Frog Design • www.o-frog.com

Editor
Margarita Maestas-Flores

Chusma House Publications
P.O. Box 467 • San José, CA 95103
Phone: (408) 947-0958
Email: chusmahouse@earthlink.com

To contact the author, email her at patigonzaj@aol.com

First Printing
Patsons Media Group
Sunnyvale, California

Printed in Aztlán

Abuelita Vargas

The Diegueño people remember that Tu-chai-pai took some mud to make the people, "first the Indians, then the Mexicans."

– The Mythology of North America by David Leeming and Jake Page

> I never grew up Hispanic. I grew up Mexicana. Chicana, the granddaughter of Indians. My grandparents were Comanche, Kikapu, Mexican Indian, Mexicano. They didn't need to assert their Indian-ness. They just were. Being Mexican to them was just another kind of Indian.

One day, I asked my grandma about this. My grandparents had raised me. For me, her word was spiritual law. "Pues, somos Indios, mi'jita."

Receta pa' un libro
1 sacred mirror
1 earthen bowl for Venus
una olla for la moon
un metate pa' masar la palabra
13 lbs. of earth to wash in
10 liters of agua de un rio corriendo
10 bundles of reeds
un fuego
el aliento de la vida
cuatro vientos and a glass of water
two ears
a drum
52 dark moons & 5 lbs. of chile colorado
for the red, the black
a few drops of your own blood
to sacrifice
upon manuscript pages
flor de calabaza, a gourd of honey
open the blue door to the Cosmos
pero cuidado
you might get lost
so take some hilo
y la spider
And don't forget to feed the ants

Ollin–The Journey

A spirit sang these stories. A spirit called me. Not the kind that comes when people die or in ceremony, but a creation spirit. This book was called by a prayer. I want to write a book on México. I want to show the dignity of people I have seen from years of telling stories as a reporter. The stories called me. I am a gatherer of stories. As Grandma Emma says, sometimes the stories want to be told. "The story knows what has to be done. The story has a reason for wanting to be told."

I came to México in search of anonymous heroes, los heroes anónimos. I thought I was coming to write a book; instead I came to heal. Instead I found creation stories, and I emerged within them. Relámpagos y zoquete, my father, my mother.

Ancient México believed the wise had hearts that were picture books of knowledge – "the black and the red." Their hearts were recorded in the sacred black and red ink used by the tlaquilo or artist/scribe. El negro, el rojo referred to the knowing.

"Your heart lives in the painted page" – Cantares Mexicanos

I looked for the possessors of the red and black ink de las luchas chulas, bien canijas, of the fine struggles, the tough ones. They give a "heart and face" to that immortal anonymous hero, the People. A heart, a face–in yollotl, in ixtli–refers to character in Nahuatl, or the indigenous language of the Macehual. Like so many xicantlaca (Nahuatl for gente chicana), I found my own heart and face in what Mexican scholar Guillermo Bonfil Batalla called México profundo, deep México, indigenous México, campesino México, urban masses México, deep like red and black.

Xicano: xictli (the navel; ano–Spanish suffix for personhood) Person from within the center of the navel.

A sack of beans for a bed, a hiding place in the wind of a sacred mountain where calla lilies grow wild, here is what roots the people's hearts, in land fights and hunger strikes and long walks to history. The red. The black. The human spirit, the people's authority.

Their stubborn dreams are the moral history of México.

In México, those who do what they should, or what they must, often wind up as footnotes in reports of human rights violations: Fulanito de tal was last seen carrying two chickens. He was found dead. A militante of an opposition party…he was shot by pistoleros of the local cacique, a land boss fighting the peasants who the campesinos accused of sequestering others.

"For demanding restitution of their communal lands (5,000 hectares) still in the possession of caciques, 30 Otomí Indians from the congregation of Amaxac, municipality of Texcatepec, Veracruz were assassinated…." (From the newspaper Politica, June 25, 1992)

Often as I traveled México looking for anonymous heroes, people said, "They are already dead."

– They gave them a little piece of land.

For refusing to reveal the hiding place of Moctezuma's treasure, Cuauhtemoc got his feet burned with hot oil and a 50,000 peso bill, and a metro stop. Zapata and Villa got some bullet holes and monuments and were made the patrimony of the government. (I've dined at the Bar Opera with Zapata's bullet hole in the ceiling.)

Their anonymous armies got a grave and a jail cell, and some got bought off along the way. And some became the civic saints of barrios bravos with their own corridos.

el de Rubén Jaramillo
el de Lucio Cabañas
el de Carrasco

Ollin–The Book

On a bus in Mexico City – I'm tired, as usual. My three-in-the-afternoon nausea has hit, and I have the accompanying headache from too little oxygen. About this time, I usually start to wonder how they do it, how the women and men work all day and then go home to la chinga. A thin man gets on the bus and starts handing out fliers. He's wearing brown pants and a polyester shirt that has been wrung too many times.

The flier says something about a village under siege somewhere in Puebla. The "authorities" again. I always like fliers and handouts. People sell you poems for pesos to buy a Father's Day gift. Or you find out about some village that becomes "blessed" with a bloody sign of the cross. These fliers of teary ink function as los periódicos morales and tell of actions not found in much of the Mexican press.

It's the stuff that foreign correspondents ignored. Small uprisings and massacres are not important to the national security of the United States, as one foreign bureau chief for the Associated Press later told me. Until the Zapatistas hit.

I went home to my neighborhood, la Roma Sur, to listen to the viejito with the violin as old as the Revolution. It held itself together with horsehair and masking tape. I told el señor that my father loved the violin, and he tried to sell me his for $300.

The next week, it took me three buses and 48 hours to get to Colima to meet the children who protect the turtles from poachers. I watched the babies hatch, life peeking out of the sand in the light of night. Life returned to ocean. Then, a typhoon hit on a full moon while I was inside a hut. I went without a bath for a week. The village had no electricity nor a single eye patch for a one-eyed youth who protects the turtles; he wore sunglasses, even at night. As I left, the little brown angelitos of the turtles ran to wave good-by, chanting sacred words that are the sound of the universe.

You might ask what does too little oxygen, a man with a violin, a village asunder, and the children saving turtles have in common. In each of those tiny worlds, I saw the life-force of change. I witnessed the source of human spirit, how people respond to hard times, how they balance the surface reality with the unseen or the world that the spiritual creates. I found the latent potential for change and the chispas that make justice manifest. As life altered the lungs of Mexicans in Mexico City to survive the pollution, the village sends a son to Tenochtitlan para que se corra la voz, a ver si alguien nos escucha. Children, who likely will never learn past the third grade because there will be no school for them in their village, will swim with the turtles. Turtle will be teacher. And a viejito charms music through wood and masking tape, y chifla bonito.

These stories, and those you will find on these pages, are the subtext to what would occur in Chiapas in January 1994. A small part, moments in time. As it turns out, I have chronicled the foreground of change prior to the Zapatistas. While I have framed this book as one about the anonymous heroes of México's emerging human rights movement, I recognize that México has been engaged in a human rights struggle for more than five centuries. In moral time, they are all contained in the struggles of today. I like to think of struggle and suffering as information. They tell us about ourselves. Through struggle and suffering, we become "in formation."

I came across this passage as I looked for revolutionary journalism. It is by Práxidis Guerrero in Regeneración, a newspaper published during the Mexican Revolution.

> "REVOLUTIONARY EPISODES"
> There were other dead whose names I have not been able to find out; and in the moments of combat, they united with our own. It is said that one was from Zaragoza, the other lived in Las Vacas, and to experience the sound of the struggle and hear the exclamations of the combatants, it awakened in him the solidarity of the oppressed; he loaded his cartridge, took his rifle and went to the street to the cry of long live the Liberal Party. He lanced out in the open air before the soldiers of despotism. A spray of fire left him in the middle of the street.... Later, the name of this hero and those of all who took part in the action at Las Vacas will be heard when it is spoken of sacrifice and greatness.

My travels as a journalist taught me there was something missing in the ink of official history. Missing were the values, the threads to the soul, the medicine of people. A civilization has lost its ability to see the revolution within, yet it longs to hear the voice of that one hero of the world, the people.

I came to México to redefine our heroes, to bring them closer, to make them human-size. Atlas had the world on his shoulders. These heroes are of the everyday, all of the days, with names like "the ant" and "the little grandmothers." They are of us and within us. Joseph Campbell spoke of them in his book, The Power of Myth, "When we quit thinking primarily about ourselves and our own self-preservation, we undergo a truly heroic transformation of consciousness."

They make revolutions inside themselves, dying a bit along the way because a little death always accompanies transformation…el México despierto. Awakened México.

I did not understand why the face of a hero had to be so big, monumental like the colossal Olmeca heads. The Race of Heroes, the Race of Bronze of the Greek classics, those heroes are too far away. It seemed as if people were thinking in old codes that did not match the world that is here, but we are too close to see. People want to know how to master the will, how to defy suffering, how to find their power as human beings. The suffering of hunger, of too little love for too much of a lifetime, the tiny "slayings of the soul"–to change the world begins with these.

This journey began in different places. In 1991, mothers, wearing sepia photographs of "disappeared" loved ones pinned like sweetheart locks on their dusters, taught me where the heroes were.

Or did it begin two decades before, in the provinces, as I looked for dignity in contested spaces, in the cardboard homes of cartonlandia? Or when a man from Juchitán de la luchas floridas sent a message to North America to see the people beyond the pyramids–there in Oaxaca, with flowers the size of big hands. "Tell them we are all not charros (government-bought leaders); tell them that México is more than vacation spots, that we are fighting for a México that is true and free…." Or was I called by the whispering anima named Lucha?

Or did it begin with Jesus Maldonado, un indio from Guanajuato, who came to the United States at age six to escape the cursing years prior to the Mexican Revolution? This is my grandfather's México that Guerrero wrote of in Regeneración, about the time that abuelo left. "Children and women perished in Sonora; children and women have died in Veracruz and Tlaxcala; children and women, their backs bloodied, their faces saddened, their limbs made skinny, slaves and prisoners in Yucatan and las Islas Mujeres and…we have peace, dulce paz, divina paz…."

Or did my walk begin even farther back with the blood of my great-great-grandmother Mama Mencha, a Kikapua Indian, who saw Santa Anna ride. She strung tobacco and prayed with her hands to Grandfather Sun and died when she was 114. One of my great-grandfathers had an hacienda in Zacatacas, large enough to have "peons." It took three days by horse to cross. He lost most of it to the revolution. He lost his daughter, my grandmother, Carmen, to Texas, where she picked cotton. She was born near the pyramids of Chicomoztoc. She married a man named Jesus, and they built a home along a cattle trail and a great river. He fell in love with her at age seven–he loved "la lady" de la big house. These relations gave me las flechas of Kikapua, Comanche y los pueblos de la gran chichimeca. My ombligo is rooted in many places–en el Eagle, siete cuevas y nacimiento.

The abuelos gave Chicanos two countries and brought us their memories del otro lado, the Other Side, a scratched freeze-frame of the Revolution and legends of the people with a stairway to the sun. We made those heroes padrinos de la raza, godparents of my people. And we made heroes of our tías and uncles and great-grandparents, the sweepers of floors and keepers of memory and corrido song stories that said sometimes the good lose and sometimes the bad win. Hay que sufrir y hay que gozar. El pueblo sabe contestar.

The people know what to do with sorrow and joy.

I came to place myself within the stories of my antepasados. The geography I have explored is the "circle of memory" de los grandes. I came as an ancestor of my grandchildren. I must leave them stories, plant them in the barro. I paint las ollas, historias de olla. My chronicles and testimonios are how I heal the future. He limpiado los frijoles.

This is not an impartial account; I came to México as a listener. I came as a detribalized woman, not aware of all that I needed to recover. These are narratives filtered through the sieve of my perceptions. I don't tell all the sides of the stories. The people in these stories speak like a Xicana because that is how I heard them, even if that is not how they talked. Perhaps some scholars will call this romantic history. But I believe we need more love stories.

I plant these words for my mother and my father.

My father
Rosendo Gonzales
who made me seek.

My mother
Martha Eulalia Maldonado Dickinson
who always believed…for her prayers that kept us both alive.

My husband
Roberto
who heard my dreams.

He who sacrificed as much as I so this book would see the light, who moved with me to Mexico City. His life and wisdom helped shape my ideas.

Roberto
My husband
Tlazocamati.

La March de Xi Nich´

Table of Contents

Part One • Crescent Moon/Luna Creciente: New Beginnings, When Things Are Initiated 1

Crescent Moon 2
1. Las Costureras 5
2. Superbarrio 34
3. Los Chavos de '68 59

Part Two • Full Moon: Meaning Is Found 79

Constellation de las Mujeres 81
4. Madres–Tonantzin Coatlique 83
5. Las Abues, Las Benitas, la Coyol 125
6. Tlazoteotl–Guerra florida de Juchitán 165

Part Three • Morning Star and the Moon: The Guide, the Announcer 187

Mixe Legend 189
7. El Hue Guerrero–Mónico Rodríguez 191
8. Quetzalcoatl y el Relámpago–-Zapata, Quetzalcoatl 202
9. Jaramillo 216

Part Four • Dark Moon: A Time of Consciousness, Healing 227

Spirit Plate 228
10. Memoria de los Agravios; Becoming Time, Retoño 229
11. El Ombligo de la Tierra 243
12. The Offering of An Ant 251

Ollin: Movement, Not Endings 274

Acknowledgments 282

Part 1

Crescent Moon/Luna Cresciente

New Beginnings, When Things Are Initiated

Crescent Moon

Time of seed, energy is beginning, instinctive. Energy is inward. Time of initiation. The seed is challenged to evolve, advance; a time of struggle.

The costureras initiated the first independent union in México; they are challenged to move forward.

Superbarrio springs forth as the creative conscience of the urban movement that makes advances as a result of the 1985 earthquake.

The student movement and resulting massacre at Tlatelolco in 1968 mark a new era in the struggle for Mexican human rights.

La costurera

...La buena costurera: es artista
tiene mano de tolteca,
adiestra sus manos,
está dialogando con su propio corazón,
calcula, diseña, cose.
La mala costurera
que hace hilvanes
que revuelve las telas,
las enmaraña, soló echa puntadas sin tino,
se burla de la gente, la ofende

Códice Matritense de la Real Academia, as cited in Toltecayotl by Miguel León-Portilla

At 7:19 a.m. on September 19, 1985, an earthquake struck México-Tenochtitlan. Mexico City became a mass grave to 85,000 people, according to newspaper accounts, entombed by the greased palm of authorities who allowed hundreds of thousands of buildings to be built without meeting codes, who showed their disregard for life as people were left buried alive while soldiers guarded or rescued the valuables of proprietors. The earthquake revealed torture chambers in the attorney general's office. The aftermath: Almost 16,000 people wounded and 100,000 families left with damaged homes. The earthquake created a social tremor as well. The dead became an offering to Change. The costureras' union–Trabajadores de la Industria de la Costura, Confección, Vestido, Similares y Conexos "Diecinueve de Septiembre"–became one of its most public faces. I spent a year visiting them off and on while they were in a time of regeneration and regrouping.

Altar of the Costureras

September 19, 1991 memorial

Chapter 1: Las Costureras

Quiero trabajar con mis manos. Masar. Stitch. Sew. Bead. I can make my own enaguas. I learned to sew my own skirt with the women of Fuerza Unida, en su tallercito con la virgencita en el altar por New Laredo Highway. I want to make things with my hands. I want to make my own ribbon shirts, embroider flowers of ribbon and silk, cut my own cloth. I want to clean my own house and blow smoke and rezos in the crevices and cobwebs. Grow my own food. I want to know that my food and clothes come from my own hands…that the tortilla is a sacrament, round like the sun and a woman's skirts. Traditional. Traditional. I call it autonomy. Self-reliance. My spider in this woman.

I come from a family of seamstresses. My grandmothers made quilts and rebozos, tejían. They made trapitos into beauty. My mother made my quinceañera dress from her own wedding dress. When I married Roberto, she and my aunt Jerry made my wedding dress with a beaded quetzal on it. My tía Gerónima has made her living as a seamstress. Her arms always hurt. She looks like the seamstress sewing the Virgen's manta in Yolanda López's triptych of the Virgen de Guadalupe. Once, when I gave her a card of the image, she asked me, "Oh, Patsy! How did you get that lady to paint me?"

When we were little, my primas and I sewed belts for Justin Boots in our homes. Maquilábamos. Piece work. So did a lot of my muy girl friends on "the Southside" of Fort Worth, Texas. When the terremoto struck, I would not go to Mexico City to cover the ravaged dignity of the people there, nor learn of the costureras. I was in mourning. My father had died a week before, the night we went on strike at the Philadelphia Inquirer. His spirit called out to me, but I was too far away. I almost heard him. A faint thought to call "Daddy;" but oh, it's too late to call. I'll call tomorrow. My tío found him the next day, with the phone hanging off the hook from his desperate attempt to find help. I was torn between my luto and my longing to be there. As I watched the news reports, it was as if I could feel my father's lingering soul, acompañado en la miseria. My father died in the fetal position in my grandmother's bed. He died as he had lived. Alone. He had not wanted to go. I could not face more death, ni mas de la catrina, and instead stayed on the picket line.

My papá's death deepened my search to understand why people suffer, why some are poor, why some are never loved or are exploited, and why some become alcoholics and die of broken hearts. And so I met my own suffering and my spiritual renacimiento. My comadres Darla and Carmen were talking one day about how hard it is to sew zippers on a dress. "Sewing is really construction," Darla said. I looked at her and smiled because what struck me about the costureras was that their occupation should make them quite able to reconstruct their union. Years after the disaster, they sought to create a foundation that had not been solidified in the movement that spontaneously followed the disaster.

My abuelo was a builder. He laid concrete, he built foundations. He always said it was easier to build a foundation right the first time than to have to put a house on temporary blocks.

I came to know the costureras during this stage, around 1991-1992. At the time, the "current" or political faction, known as Colectivo Revolucionario Integral (CRI), was directing the coalition-based leadership of the union. The story before you is from aquellos ojos de lucha.

Retablo Vivant de Luto

The women with toltec hands stand in front of spirits. They make a descanso from iris, lilly, daffodil, and tears. They stop at a signpost along the thoroughfare as cars and combis speed by their ofrenda. They bow their heads and press their foreheads against a storefront window as they leave the roadside shrines to the dead. The dead spirits speak with the wind. The wind offers itself in circles to the grief. It consoles the grieving. Among them are women with holes in their hands, women who have seen others die on the factory line, women who make bra cups and cut pant legs for centavos and speak with scissors and thread. They gather like old flowers a gritar al mundo, GRACIAS VIDA, and remember the women who were worth less than a bolt of material and now speak the language of wind.

There is a priest at a makeshift altar at the locale of the September 19 Union of Garment Workers. I can barely hear him. The wind talks over him. Platíca con el luto.

– Mira no mas como ha engordado fulanita. Look how so and so has gotten fat.

– Dicen que esta todo amolado el sindicato. They say the union is all beat up.

– Pues ¿qué pues? What's with that?

The priest's sermon: "The compañera costurera represents Eva, Madre María, because la mujer brinda la vida. Working to take home bread is the first form of defense there is for a woman, that is, to provide daily bread for the children. But it should be a job with dignity. As a result of '85, we found that we have to organize in defense of life."

He tells the costureras "que no seamos agachistas."

He tells them, "Be organized, truly united. All those other threats can destroy and take our lives, but the lack of unity is a battle with ourselves. This union local of 1985 represents our life today."

Guadalupe Conde, who saw her compañeras die, stands at the descanso where many perished and tells the women that the greatest enemy should be the government. Instead, it has become the divisions, the mitotes, la falta de unidad, que fulanita de tal....

"Because we are seamstresses and workers, and thank God we survived with life, our lives are ignored. No one has ever paid attention to us or cared about us."

This year, 1991, no dogs are sicced on them like the year before, no pushing and hair pulling by goons the year before that. Nor the confrontations with the official and charro unions on May 1, when the independent unions always try to cut in and march with recognition. Siempre retemal.

This year, todo calmado. The calm is an omen that the union was weak, as if their constant gritos have no suffixes...revolu-, un-, vict-, their work interrupted and ruptured by the structural violence of free trade, the government's constant movidas, internal trampas, and the lack of unity and trust among themselves.

The Mud People

"Here many fell. We were able to save some, but the guards wouldn't let us through. Now the government wants to take away September 19 because we have been in an indefinite plantón. The government left us this locale. It was abandoned. There was no owner. Now they want to take it away. It is something we cannot permit," says la Lupe Conde.

"Compañeras, we should not be fighting ourselves."

The women become a sound inside their bellies:

Adelante, adelante	Forward, forward
porque la lucha es constante	because the struggle is constant
a luchar, a luchar	to struggle, to struggle
por un predio sindical	for a union lot of land

A moment of silence for those who fell at 7:19 a.m., when the earth moved her spine. Scholar Teresa Carrillo poetically notes that the mud deep under the island of México-Tenochtitlan moved for two minutes, bringing hundreds of garment-worker shops to ruins. The social tremor will leave aftershocks for years. Toci, "Our Grandmother," as Heart of the Earth, made things tumble. Y le dio una buena limpiada a la política mexicana.

The women's gritos can be heard under tons of rubble that will become a tomb; their voices are muffled and spiritlike. Women jump out windows or use bolts of material to return to life. Others who escape walk in circles around their nerves, not knowing that they are alive. Many could not escape because the doors were locked. Pinches patrones. Others were saved because they had the 8:00 a.m. shift. Like good workers, they report to work anyway.

News reports: At San Antonio Abad 150, eleven floors were flattened to three. In José María Izazaga 65, there were 50 clandestine workshops on eight floors. There were hundreds of clandestine shops and, in some, labored girls not yet menstruating. In those shops, there are no records, and many employers denied that there were employees working there that day. According to one study by la Universidad Nacional Autónoma de México in Nezahualcóyotl as reported in La Jornada, 80 percent of the shops were clandestine.

The smell of death is everywhere for days. The garment workers breathe in the dead and dying as they resume work in the damaged buildings, among buildings folded like accordions. Some

40,000 costureras were left without jobs. Three weeks later, 100 costureras still have not been rescued. One woman trapped inside of an elevator in the garment district is finally rescued 20 days later. Her body is still warm. The garment workers believe she died of madness.

Concha, la flaca, not the one who passed out a flier to boycott the union

"Nacho, me voy temprano," Concha Guerrero tells her compañero. Concha, who was on the 8:00 a.m. shift, had been asked to come in early to complete a task.

She caught a combi. Halfway to San Antonio Abad, the driver started driving funny. "The combi started jumping up and down. I was really mad."

"El chavo is just learning to drive," she thought. When the earthquake stopped, the air was on fire with the flames of buildings, flying electrical tentacles, and vapors. She walked the rest of the way to work.

"I've got to get to work," she thought. "What a sense of responsibility, eh?" When she arrived, she could hear los gritos de las chavas.

People started to dig through the escombros. They dug through Mexico City with their hands. When the army arrived, they would not let anyone pass or continue, though they could still hear the gritos. There was a gold store they were guarding. They raised their rifles and said, "Por favor, váyanse."

"Ya. Ya. Ya. Ya no hay gente," the army told the garment workers who had gathered outside the building.

"Es que están gritando." But they are screaming.

"No. It is only your nerves."

"Don't you hear them? Es que hay gritos."

"No. Not here."

"¡Hay gritos!"

"No hay nada. No más loquillas."

There is nothing. There are no screams, only crazy women.

The government told the people to stay in their homes. Pero el pueblo no se la tragó.

The government could not attend to the people's needs. At

first, it rejected international help. It told the people to stay home. The people were outraged, however, and refused to stay idle. "Human life is elevated to the rank of absolute good," wrote Carlos Monsiváis in Entrada libre (Free Admission). "During a brief period, society becomes community." A man nicknamed la pulga ferreted into the debris and saved people's lives. Monsiváis called it the "society of the ruins."

The reconstruction of Mexico City became a mass baptism into civil society as people organized to demand their rights as citizens, as they organized for food, housing, services. Days became months, then years. The aftershock became a social tremor–marches, sit-ins (the infamous plantón), and tent cities. To help yourself and others was an act of civil disobedience. I'm alive! The people's capacity to believe had changed. Héroes de las ruinas.

In his October 5, 1985, presidential address, Miguel de la Madrid honored anonymous heroes (he gave them greater opportunity to be heroic by rejecting international assistance). "The history of México–I have no doubt–will remember these heroes, including the anonymous heroes and the pages written by them will constitute one of the feats that has most honored our country. I repeat, I am proud of the people I govern."

Pero para muchos eran los refritos de siempre. For many, it was the same refried beans. "You know what? I don't buy that, that rap –'thank you, heroic people, and now go to sleep 'cause tomorrow you go to work.'" (Student quoted in Entrada libre)

On October 7 at the National Commission of Reconstruction, Dr. Miguel León-Portilla, the renowned interpreter of ancient México, receives a standing ovation after he reminded the gathering of a famous verse from the Aztec empire. "As long as the world lasts, the fame and the glory of México-Tenochtitlan will not end."

Lucha Puntada

Near San Antonio Abad, the Red Cross put up a tent to tend to the people. Soon, two encampments of costureras were established by feminist activists and women like Concha, who had been organizing in small shops since the 1980's. One encampment was near the site of las sepulcradas de San Antonio Abad 150; the other was downtown, in the historic district. The encampment at San Antonio Abad offered water, bandages, and food. As costureras received word of the campamento, they came; and a census was taken.

"What factory? Have you seen your other co-workers? What is the boss going to do?"

At first, the women did not want to make the dueños mad. Some 5,000 women waiting for their indemnification began to gather there for regular assemblies. Soon, costureras from the factory Dimensión Weld de México started to guard 30 machines with a plantón. They "planted" themselves in front of the factory, a common strategy of the workers to impede the owners from relocating their shop.

The feminists' networks played a key role in garnering financial, legal, and moral support. They also brought ideological differences regarding organizing strategies.

"Y ¿qué pasó con las muertitas?"

The women decided to block the main north-south thoroughfare of Tlalpan, which borders the encampment, in order to get machinery to rescue the bodies. They put up a banner saying, "We Demand Machinery to Rescue Our Families." It was a Sunday. Families riding on the metro could see the encampment. Whole families stepped off the metro to join them. When people saw it was not inappropriate to make these demands, "entonces la gente fue creyendo," recalled Concha. They formed a human chain to block machinery from being taken, threw nails so that the cars couldn't pass, and rocks so that the machinery couldn't move.

They marched to the President's home and to the office of the Secretary of Labor. Eventually, the labor department set up dispatch centers to process the compensations. The women made costurera dolls from trapitos, with names like Victoria Moda and Lucha Puntada. Victoria: "Quiereme. I am the hope of a new world." Lucha: "Sigueme. I am the hope of change." They did plantones in factories and outside the homes of patrones and posted wanted signs with their photos. SE BUSCA. BANDIDO. EXPLOTADOR.

When compensation was going slowly, the workers impeded the exit of supervisors and workers at the Secretariat of Labor.

Employers wanted to compensate them for only 20 days instead of three months, plus proposed further compensation for seniority and vacation.

"One patrón tried to leave from the window."

– Míralo por donde va.

– But he'll be late.

– Que se dilate.

Another hizo pipí out of the window.

"It was a spontaneous organization," said one advisor, Pati Nava, "that grew from the spontaneous resistance all the days of their lives. That combativity made us recognize the power in our meetings six months later. A year later, the encampment continued."

Some of the advisors saw the opportunity to create a women's project, while others set their minds on an independent movement against government-backed charro unions. Soon, it became apparent that what they needed was a union.

"The challenge was to create a legal instrument. We don't want to resolve the problems of today but an instrument, a legal instrument that allows us to defend ourselves today, tomorrow, and yesterday. The campamento became la base de fuerza that allowed them to fight for the union," recalled Nava. "It truly became un hormiguero."

On October 20, a month after the earthquake, they became México's first industry-wide union that was primarily for women and run by female leadership. It was known as a women's union.

"Las costureras representaba la ansiedad que tiene el pueblo de luchar por lo suyo. In the site of tragedy and destruction was born a courage to dignify a struggle and to rescue what was theirs," recalled Nava.

The union became a symbol of the role of women to change social conditions. That's why the mantas became so important as the logos of their combativity and democracy: la mujer wielding a needle-spear with a shield emblazoned with the Number 19 on a bandera known as ojos de lucha. Y más banderas: the women with scissors and the clock set at 7:19. That's why they came down when, they said, "el charrismo" later infected the union.

Evangelina Corona, madre soltera, mujer de chongo, emerged from the costureras' union organizing committee with pretty words of el evangelio. Era una aleluya. The costureras in the committee recalled that they hardly knew each other when they selected the leadership.

"Quien tiene más saliva, traga mas pinole," observed Nava. The person who has more saliva, downs more pinole, ground-up corn with spicey cane.

But according to Eva, "I spoke the language of the workers." So an evangelista would come to run a union with feministas, radicalistas y lesbianas, as she called them. Todas chupando de la unión.

"Los jalones began after we had the people," said Concha.

Mitotes, Relajos

– Que fulanita still had a sewing machine that was union property.

– Que Concha de la cocina popular did movidas on behalf of MAS (Mujeres En Acción Sindical).

– Que las banderas were held hostage.

– Que Eva would not release documents or the children's day care center, that she had a secret shop and ran another locale.

– Que las señoras del taller de mujeres grandes were not paid by Eva.

– Que Eva locked out members of the CRI and had them arrested while they were protecting the workshop for elder costureras, the one with the altarcito next to big spools of thread.

– Que Eva negotiated with the patrones and would not recognize the Congress of 1989. Se charrifico and would not recognize the congress vote that ousted her.

– Que CRI and MAS both accused each other of electoral fraud, of being anti-democratic and selling out the workers.

Teresa Carrillo writes in Gendered Unions: The Rise and Demise of the Mexican Garment Workers Movement that the group went from being a "disaster relief organization" to a union and one that was woman-centered, a hybrid entity–both a women's organization and labor union. Carrillo writes that the union survived by combining trade-union strategies with that of social movements. These differences in strategies also created tension.

From the beginning, there were ideological differences about the identity and strategy of the organizing structure. While initially there were several "currents," they eventually reduced to primarily a few. MAS, Mujeres en Acción Sindical, sought a cooperative; and CRI, Colectivo Revolucionario Integral, wanted a union. The costureras decided on a union but also organized cooperatives with machinery that was received as part of liens against employers. MAS, with the help of Patricia Mercado, oversaw the co-ops.

MAS emphasized negotiations and conciliation to avoid repression and the closing of shops. At different times, it backed Evangelina. Her corriente preferred not to mobilize. Worse yet, said Nava, "Eva began to negotiate with the government and employers on the backs of the costureras." CRI believed in strategic confrontation. As one CRI adviser told Carrillo, in organizing with the industrialists, union organizing must go through three stages: rejection, repression, and then respect.

MAS advisors were considered middle-class women who wanted to promote a women's project. They believed anyone could be a member and that the union contract was not the sole key to their survival. MAS felt that it was possible to develop "union life and have substance…to have a union life was not totally dependent on a contract," noted Carrillo. CRI members had working-class roots and viewed its purpose as a labor union that focused on women and that was "woman-controlled," Carrillo said. CRI felt they would lose their bargaining power without a union; it was the structure for their power.

MAS accused CRI advisers of making decisions for the union without the input of union representatives and rank and file members. Nava said MAS was more concerned with gaining control of the direction of the union. It was important to struggle within a union structure, said Nava, even if they did not always control the union apparatus. And it was important to have that instrument as a result of social movement. The currents became factions, and whoever won a factory gained the right to represent it in new negotiations.

In many ways, the various currents accomplished important projects. As one compañera told me, sometimes it was hard to tell them apart. Both negotiated contracts and established social projects that infused the union with issues and purpose, such as the day care, a popular school; a popular kitchen; and a housing program. These sustained the union when the indemnification period ended (and participation dropped) and as the repression grew once the union started fighting for contracts. A mere 16 contracts were in effect in 1992.

But in one congress after another, there were attempts, successful and not, to gain the direction of the union, which were usually accompanied by allegations of fraud and improprieties. A congress is a union-wide meeting where delegates vote on policy and union goals. At one point, MAS operated from one corrugated steel building and CRI from another. All the while, protestors from around the country often set up tent cities within those metal espacios de lucha, spray-painted with mannequins and the face of la luchadora Benita Galeana, for whom one of the locales is named.

In addition to these two divisions was Evangelina's faction. When she refused to relinquish her post as required by a union vote, they leafleted her church to pressure her to relinquish financial documents and control of various programs.

Evangelina

Her voice scratches in high pitch as she discusses her "administration." An assistant comes into her office, looks at her, and asks, "Why are you mad?"

To her, MAS wanted to negotiate and was opportunistic. CRI never negotiated and was radicalista. "Each of them wanted to make the movement private property."

"They transmit poison. If you don't see with the same eyes, they make you see with their eyes. I was watched, my every move, my telephone calls, to whom I talked."

Before the earthquake, Eva thought the patrón was the benefactor. She cut sleeves for 270 pesos a day. Three pesos for a pair of sleeves. She became a garment worker in 1952 when she moved to Mexico City from the provincia. A year later, Mexican women won the right to vote.

Just a few years prior, in 1948, un tal Jesús Díaz de León, a railroad worker known as el Charro, dismantled the railroad labor organization Acción Socialista Unificada, led by labor legends Hernán Laborde and Valentín Campa. Enrique Semo documented this in México un pueblo en la historia. El Charro and his followers, "los Charros," with the help of the army's bayonets, undermined the leadership of the national union, the Sindicato de Trabajadores Ferrocarrileros de la República Mexicana, and, for the most part, neutralized the ASU, leaving it in disarray. According to Semo, so begins the story of anti-democratic charro labor leaders and their charrazos within the labor movement.

Now it is hard for Eva to shake that epithet. As secretary general of the union, "I was a conciliator. The patrón and the workers must work as a team. I am not so abusiva that I would go and insult the patrón right under his nose. They call me pro-patrón. They criticized me because I embraced the authorities, the patrónes. If I am going to ask for something, I am not going to take your eyes out so you will give them back to me. You must be amigable."

"I didn't just have the support of the empresarios. I had the help of the people, of the authorities, of the people outside. I think they were just jealous."

Eva was criticized for meeting with then-Regent Manuel Camacho Solís, whose role was similar to that of a mayor of Mexico City, and for allowing her image and name to be invoked by President Salinas. Some say that Eva was not corrupt but that she did not keep a frank gaze on her allied union staff, who likely dipped into the union's coffers. To that she replies, "I can't say that it was fulana, mangana or sutana." Many of Eva's supporters were the older costureras, and she still held sway over a portion of the members. Many other costureras felt she was ill-equipped to head a combative movement and was more comfortable as the icon and public voice of the costureras. "Perhaps I lived the romance of the union."

Antecedents: False Labor

Concha became a seamstress at age nine. She met her first charro in 1979. She thought unions were good. She didn't understand why the charro told her to meet at a certain corner on tal día after workers tried to organize. She told him, "¿Sabes qué, Señor Usted? You cannot abandon the workers and take those machines."

The shop was secretly relocated. She never saw those workers again. Se metio en los chingazos in 1981 at Trajes, S.A., where the owner got a worker pregnant and then accused her of robbing him. He had married up, "con una chava de bien." He would bring mariachi, marijuana y chupe to the shop and bang on the machines and yell at the workers.

The workers there started organizing after he stopped paying Social Security. Carmen, the union representative for COR–Confederación Obrera Revolucionaria–told the workers to go on strike.

¡Sí, Sí.Una huelga!

"We didn't even know what that was," recalled Concha.

"I'll come back with the strike flag," Carmen told them.

Un grupito de seis stayed there to guard the shop all night long, and they let the rest go home.

"Nunca llegó esa maldita mujer." But the owners showed up with machine guns.

"Cómo es la ignorancia. La ignorancia no trae miedo."

Concha had gone home to check on her two little ones, Miriam and Julián. When she returned, she found the dueño Paco pointing the machine gun at el compa Agustín. His wife was pointing one at la compañera Mari, and the accountant had a pistol. One chavala was in the bathroom unaware of what was happening. Another was hiding in a tree. Concha told Paco that he was too much of a coward to shoot.

"Give me the gun, and you'll see that I will shoot," she told him. Concha called the police, saying that workers were about to be shot. El dueño Paco tried to get away, but all were caught and charged with carrying arms. Since one of the strikers was a prima del negro Durazo, México's feared police chief, he had them sent to Campo Militar Número 1, where they were jailed for two weeks.

Paco's mother-in-law came and pleaded for the charges to be dropped against her daughter, who had also been jailed.

– Go look in the jails where they keep delinquents. We are not delinquents. We are workers.

Y Otra Agarrada

Over time in their plantón outside the factory, the strikers made friends with the patrol officers, who would get them firewood and help them build a fire at night. Concha and the others would bathe in nearby homes. Many on the picket line would take turns carrying her children. The strike occurred during the rainy season, and they would sometimes have to sleep on beds of water and concrete.

One night, Agustín told Concha, "traeme un pulque." That's what he called his leche that he needed for his ulcer. When she and the children went to the store, a man approached her and told her, "Aguas, they are going to get you tonight." She tried to warn Agustín, but it was too late. So she went to the phone to call the alarm network of people who would come to their aid. Too late. She saw Paloma, Paco's attorney, with her long nails de gata coming at her. Concha breaks a bottle of Manzanita y órale.

She fought with some guys in dark glasses. "Y me lo eché."

They tear-gassed the strikers, put them in a van, and threatened to throw them in a canyon. They were taken to the police station and accused of "expropriation." They didn't know what that word meant, that they had no papers to carry out a legal strike. They eventually filed the documents through an independent union's registry, but by then the owner had changed the name to Maribi factory. Otra transa. They were in and out of that station house so often that the officers would say, "You again?" One time it was for kidnapping.

"There's no one in there. Go and see for yourself. And what a surprise," Concha recalled.

The accountant had snuck in and was inside; but because police found guns on the owner, they arrested him instead. The strikers did not let the accountant out for five days. They cut off water and refused to feed him. "Ponga una chinga pero bien buena."

They had a pachanga and broke out windows of the building. The dueño's wife had a perrita inside, too. Ay chihuáhua. She begged them to let her get the dog.

"No."

They threw it scraps, but none to the accountant. "The perrita came out skinny." One day, the charra Carmen started getting real friendly with Concha and invited her to meet with her, but "don't tell anyone." She and some other workers tell Concha that they are worried about her, her being a single mother (at the time) and all. They offered her a house through a federal housing program, a new job, and a salary where she could name her price. Pero deja ir a la huelga. And that's how they began to divide the strikers.

Out of 50, only 19 remained "de pies firmes, expuestas a las fregadas," Concha recounted in "Antecedentes del Sindicato 19 de Septiembre," a collection of oral histories by Fernando Talavera and

Francisco Muñoz. Two camps of strikers were created, while others took the bribes. Even Mari and Agustín went to the other side in the end. But when the vote was taken to be represented by an independent union, the strikers won. They even won the right not to have a supervisor, "because we know what we are doing."

Concha and Paco were always at it:

"Now we are equal," he would tell her.

"We are not equal. You are the exploiter, and I am the exploited."

"How much does Concha want so that Concha will leave?" Paco would yell out to the factory.

"Pues, I'm going to kill your children," he threatened.

"Well then kill them and eat them. Because with what you pay me, I won't have money to bury them."

The dueño thought he was being threatened by a drug dealer. The women would send fake messages to scare him. "Pronto voy a salir. Tenemos cuentas pendientes. Voy a cobrar."

"Concha, flaca, who entered here? Who left this?"

The factory eventually closed. The women tried to get severance pay, but with no luck. Paco had disappeared.

"Sismosas" or Reconstruction

In its reconstruction, it seemed as if the union was finally building a solid foundation for a project that had been born out of chaos, born out of life's need to organize and self-perpetuate, especially when it is threatened. But life only needs certain structures while they are useful. Contexts change and so, too, do the responses and purpose. For any foundation, one needs a strong base. All of us must construct a foundation for any endeavor, whether it is for a relationship or a social project. And yet what was the foundation for a union of workers in an industry that had been downsizing and still was trying to compete with global factories when global capital did not recognize the worker as the foundation of economy? In responding to economic violence or political economy in disequilibrium, the people, the human relations, are the foundation. And for that, one needs trust. But how does one gain social trust when the integrity of the union has been put into question because of factions, mitotes, allegations, and counter allegations?

Roberto Reyes Martínez, un compa on the union's executive committee, spoke of the challenge. "That we confront the problems justly is the problem, a concrete problem. No one trusts anyone."

"A veces el poder es muy cabrón y nos descontrola. No venden, no regalan y no dan la dignidad."

– In 1910, millions died for an idea. We cannot go against our own history.

"El pueblo es un sueño, una utopía," he said.

– But we are willing to reconstruct that dream.

What struck me about the union was how it became a living organism, how with all its victories and obstacles it became life itself. I respected those who continued to invest their lives in the union and could still believe in the ability of people to trust, to act, and to reason. Their commitment meant they still had hope, hope with action. They still had faith in the possibility of change. The union's evolution reminded me of the Buddhist belief that relationships change only through sustained interaction. The workers and advisors grafted this organism from their lives, including their fears, the trauma of loss and fear of more loss, their passions, and the subtleties of the mind. I've often wondered how change is affected by the web of our being; by what we bring from our lives; by the notions, filters and legacies that are passed on to us from our seven generations; by remembering that we are the legacy and fruits of past relatives and that we leave a legacy for future ones. Not only the legacy of institutionalized oppression, but also the spiritual and psychological legacy of revolutionary abuelos, an abused mother, or the builders of pyramids. And this energy that is each of us bounces off other beings. It rubs and repels–or embraces. Each relationship becomes a teaching about ourselves.

Once a friend and I were talking about love relationships. "I'm just trying to have a relationship with myself," she told me. Our relationship with our self is imperative for change to occur, learning about ourselves in relationship to others. We can only heal while in relationship.

All these experiences come together to create an organism called a project, a movement, a union. Life can either create or destroy. Constant crisis can force people to creativity. Or it can cause our energies to be all air and fire with no time to touch the earth and to see the ground we walk on. From a co-dependent relationship, each reacting to the other, co-dependent change evolves.

During a platica with scholar Teresa Córdova, she spoke of social change as the "outcome of a structurally conditioned interactive process of conflict." The costureras' movement was a good example of this process. The divisions and factions evolved in the context of the dysfunctional economic and political systems of free trade and Mexican corporatism, Carrillo noted. In effect, the union was organizing against global restructuring.

"The scale of organizing (within the context of free trade) is really daunting. No matter what tactical decisions they made, they were going to run into charrismo and the Mexican state desperately attempting to modify the charro union system in order to control labor," Carrillo said. Carrillo further explained the process. The union had more success in organizing the mid-size factories, but they were being gutted by free trade. They couldn't compete. The smaller factories were difficult to organize and the larger ones had greater resources to challenge the union in the corruptible legal system. With free trade, the garment industry became polarized between small factories that produced for the domestic market through subcontracting and big factories that exported their goods. American companies also capitalized on the sub-contractor phenomenon. U.S. factories could claim to be "clean" while Mexican companies subcontracted the work. At the macro level, the garment industry could also concentrate production at border factories or at certain production centers in the republic. These big factories did not want true organized labor to be present. It upset their competitiveness.

Nava observed, "After getting the union registry of a spontaneous movement, it developed into a live organization. One thing is to resist for six months to obtain liquidation (benefits)...another thing is to participate in the daily life of a union, participating and making decisions." To fight charrismo is one struggle, Nava said; another is to be satisfied with "el gesto," the gesture of negotiations, when a worker gestiona, or negotiates, with a patrón and comes away feeling thankful for "las balas que no me dieron" (the bullets they didn't give me).

Most costureras were experienced in el Charro de la gestión. They were accustomed to a paternalism that impeded them from taking responsibility and to thinking "that the union delegates are servants and me, only to come and work."

It was comfortable. Roberto said these workers were acting like sismosas. Sismosas were the women still operating with the attitude prevalent during the earthquake (sismo), when some could easily follow the union leadership without having to assert too much leadership.

When I asked Nava if the reconstruction of the union paralleled the reconstruction of the nation, Nava laughed, saying she had not heard this idea. Then she explained what the foundation of reconstruction should be. "It is the willingness to give and to participate in the life of the union…to construct, for all, better conditions. It is a process of education. Largisísimo. And this creates power. The social base must democratize their participation in power. The question is how to go from the intention expressed in a vote to a daily expression of power. They are working to recuperate the instances of democratic expression."

To Nava, the union's crisis was part of the process of a democracy. "The internal struggle of the organization is like all organizations and is part of the daily life of the organization. In a democratic organization, there exist various points of views…. This has not been an ideological struggle within groups where the costureras are spectators. It's been an ideological struggle where the workers have identified with one or another project and have fought for that project within the union."

I first heard this idea of reconstruction from Mercedes "Meche" Ramírez, the union's secretary general. Mercedes worked in a clandestine shop. Trabajo de hormiga, she called it. She earned $10 a week. She has a daughter. She was brown and small and reminded me of my mother Martha. She looked like she should be a Marta, so serious. She ended her silence in the union. "It is like going to school. The costureras have been our teachers. We live through each other, fight with each other." She came from a family of 12 and studied at night school to complete middle school. She went to work so that her brothers wouldn't be workers. She, too, would like to continue her schooling. Ironically, Meche was once mistaken for a charra before she started fighting on behalf of the union. Then she worked to unite it. With only 300 members left, where there were once thousands, she repeated the phrase so key to mass movements, la base. "It's time to return to the bases and reinforce the union, not stay up in the pulpits always," she said.

She was frank in her concern. "It's a return to the earthquake, everyone aligned with a current."

"We are living the charro stage of the union."

"We can't maintain the union thinking, 'that's her fight.' If we can survive to the next congress, it will be an accomplishment. We must fight not to lose the union registration."

She could not do it unless she went person-to-person with each factory. So she needed the costureras to speak to one another. "You must speak poco a poco to the people."

At Rosi Bras factory, five of the leaders were fired and dozens were laid off because of cutbacks due to the company's inability to compete with the coming North American Free Trade Agreement (NAFTA). Many small companies all over México started closing, just with the passage of the agreement. Four union leaders at Rosi remained "en pie." But there were rumors of more terminations to come. Many of the compañeras didn't get involved because of the fear of termination if they did. Mercedes says it's "la gestión que desanima," the negotiating of a union contract eroded morale. Union organizing was complicated by NAFTA. Even before NAFTA was signed, many Mexican businesses were already suffering its impact. Smaller enterprises were driven out of business. Much of the union's militancy was concentrated in the antiquated, smaller, mid-sized garment factories, the ones least able to compete with free trade.

"The (union's) executive committee made errors, but it's understandable with all the limitations and work to be done. But the base also made errors, and it's understandable," said Meche. "So many dreams were destroyed with the earthquake."

And she knew where the responsibility ultimately lay. "It is a seedling. We've planted it. If it doesn't grow, it is because of the fear of some of the compañeras. Each makes our image as we are. In this you must define yourself."

We all struggle in faith or with fear.

One day, I asked la compañera Gunda how the costureras viewed reconstruction. Gunda was a former costurera who always had her elementary reader at hand. She finally returned to school and in 1991 was studying to be a nurse. But she continued to serve on the executive committee, sleeping only about three hours at night in order to accomplish all of her tasks. She was a brown, quiet force in the union.

"The participation of the compañeras is the foundation to the reconstruction, that the compañeras return to make what is theirs, theirs," said Gunda. Que vuelvan. At the time compañeras, such as Concha la Flaca, were no longer active in the organization. Concha was learned in las luchas chingonas, how to organize in bathrooms or go undercover, or how to fake a fight with a compañera so that the patrón wouldn't know who were allies to unionism. But she had to earn a better living to help her children go to college. About a year later, I heard that Concha had returned and was working clandestinely as an organizer in a shop.

El Congreso

At the October 4, 1992, congress, or member-wide union convention, "la corriente luz," otherwise known as MAS, staged a boycott against the executive committee. Inside "el local revolucionario de Benita," as Benita called it, members of the CRI were desconsoladas:

– "If you don't fight to save the politics of all sections, there will be nothing left. The problem has to be resolved by the workers."

– "The boycott is anti-union. It only helps the patrón and the government. It puts the union at risk, as well as the compañeras."

– "Es una burla."

Guadalupe Benavides, an advisor: "It's an attempt at the life of the union. MAS has not participated in the life of the union. We have a responsibility to convene a congress to debate el año de lucha. The boycott claims that this is an illegal state of affairs."

The '92 congress needed two more delegates to constitute a legal meeting. Between Eva's faction and MAS, "They are boycotting the decision of the costureras and spaces where collective decisions are made and the democracy of the union!"

"We should be guarding against CROC and CROM (PRI-affiliated unions), not against those within our own union."

They recessed to see if they could round up the two delegates. In the end, they could not.

At Rosi Bras, many were fired; but Modareli factory was strong. Graciela of Rosi Bas laments the lack of unity. "Each year, there are fewer members."

La compañera Rosalba: "As a worker and a member of the 19 de Septiembre, I feel we are at a point of losing the union."

Meche: "The union is at risk, compañeras."

"They will tire, but that is not enough," said Pati Nava. "The challenge begins today. We have the conditions to hold a legal forum. We have to be creative and look for new forms of fighting...while there is the will to fight and the capabilities."

A Perder el Hilo

Once, I found this quote from Guadalupe Benavides inside the local: "Los grandes proyectos, las grandes ideas, son obras de los hombres (seres humanos) grandes porque los pequeños hombrecitos se ahogan en un vaso de agua. Se pierden en los pequeños poderes y se ven motivados sólo por las bajas pasiones." Great projects, great ideas are the work of great people because the small person drowns in a glass of water, loses him/herself in the small powers and is moved only by base passions.

I wondered how many of the women remembered that statement at the crucial moment when choosing whether or not to drown in those "small powers"–the hunger for control and titles, the arrogance of certain beliefs and righteousness, the smallness of mind. Often when supporters spoke of the costureras and their union, it was with sadness, as if already grieving a dream with a terminal illness. But it is important not to lose sight of the fact that the women were engaging female power, inmensa e inconforme, to transcend desperation. They thereby created an example and a space in labor and female history. Despite the drawn-out broncas of bad labor board decisions, of shops that closed rather than recognize the union, of ghost unions and charras, female powers emerged. I can't help but believe that somewhere in the universe all their moral anger, all their tears, all their good intentions, still wait to manifest in life.

The union is no longer in existence.

It was 1999. I called Professor Carrillo for a eulogy of the union. I remember the last time I visited the union in 1993, Meche was contemplating overriding the principle of "no re-election." Supporters had advised her to run again to save the union in the long run. The principle was considered inviolate and had guided the union after Evangelina's troubled reign. Slowly, the union crumbled and lost its legal recognition as a union with contracts. However, the locale still exists; and some of the pioneers in the union still participate in activities there. As a lasting legacy, Carrillo noted:

> The women became active and stayed active. Their activism kind of changed its face. The relationships among the people continued. The dysfunction of the union was not the divisiveness of the interpersonal conflict but the challenge of trying to organize within the context of free trade. It was not the lack of leadership skills but the context. The context of free trade, the context of the Mexican state trying to rebuild a more workable corporatism in the face of free trade–those are the elements of the difficult context that the union found itself in. How it happened is a secondary effect.

I remember reading in one of the popular memorias collected from the union that some of the pioneer union women, following union repression in an earlier campaign in 1968, went to pray after being released from Lecumberri Prison, crawling on their knees to the virgen at Tepeyac. They then went to thank la Virgen de San Juan de los Lagos. I remember other women told me how they made retablos para dar gracias for having survived the temblor.

This retablo, my own retablito, ends: "A toda las 'Diosas' y energías femininas, gracias por un poquito de vida. Que descanse en paz la unión de las no muertitas."

Ollas in Ollin

I carry a pot of tears on my head, una olla de lagrimas. I hear the pot moan and cry. La olla has a spirit. It must be used.

My pot of tears holds the sorrows and anger of our readers, both the sounds and words stuck in their throats and the ones let out. There are times when I feel like wailing for them or grinding them in my grandma's metate for pollen-soft powder.

The pot is telling. So I listen to its hum, throw a pot for tears welling; las lloronas, the women are weeping inside. Among my people, la llorona legends tell of the weeping woman. Perhaps presaging the Europeans' arrival, Moctezuma's sister went wailing in the streets, "My children, we are lost." Another famous llorona is said to have drowned her children when the Spaniards came.

Scholar Arnoldo Carlos Vento says many llorona stories of "historical or natural origins" were given negative interpretations by Spaniards. The original llorona, he notes, was a woman who cried all night when her children drowned in a fourteenth century flood.

La llorona tells us something is wrong with society, that there are many forms of madness–the Andrea Yates or the mamma in my barrio who lit Christmas lights all year for the son who took 20 years to come back from 'Nam. When he returned, she put out the lights.

Not all lloronas kill their children. They wander among bodies of water, like spirits; for water is cold like death and flows like emotions. They provoke us into right action, as fear of death often does. Some do not cry but rather cry out for justice, for "the disappeared" of the continent's dirty wars, for sweatshop workers. Some call us from the spirit world, like the missing and murdered women in Juarez, México. Others march and scold society and politicians.

La llorona is la madre tierra crying, a water spirit that announces the river of tears like the fearsome tzitzimime feminine spirits of rain, wind, thunder, and lightening, of which Alfredo López Austin has written.

The shedding of the tears–why is it I only see men cry in ceremonies? My husband says he can't cry but would like to–then maybe he can smile once again. Really smile. Peace-builder Roberto Chene says it hurts to see so many people hurting. "The daily expression (of injustice) forces you to shut down and numb yourself. If not, the daily anger would eat you up." The lloronas can't shut down, and a lot of people live and die from that rage.

I'm like my grandma Chenta. I cry when I am happy and I cry when I am sad. And I see red when I hear of genetically modified corn and terminator seeds. I do la llorona's bidding. I spill tears and stories gurgling from my pot's belly.

I've learned to balance my pot over years of walking through arrows of hate messages and expectations from people who project onto the messengers: militants, moderates.... "What is your theory, feminist or Freire?" Sometimes my hip goes out. My feet have grown wide and flattened from the weight of so many words and people on my head. Often, we women carry the burdens of our families, our beloved, and all things begotten thereof. No wonder we're tired at the end of the day.

From a dear reader of our syndicated column: "I see these stickers that say brown pride.... It's kind of like saying that you are proud to be retarded.... How could someone be proud to be part of the most lazy and stupid race in human history?...Do you think that white americans (sic) will stick around when the southwest (sic) is filled with nothing but your dirty peoples."

Dolores Huerta, a grandmother of the civil rights movement, sends us a message after 9/11 and asks us to write about how many abhor the Taliban's abuse of women but seemingly tolerate abuse and violence against women in the United States. Plenty of men, patriots or otherwise, still slap women around. Several families call us to say they were abused by police, one in Los Angeles and another inside a Wal-Mart in Colorado. Young men and women, survivors of every human horror, ask me, "How can I stop hurting?" Their pain and kindness heal my heart and straighten my back.

La comadre Ana Mora reads my story about a pot of tears and writes me an email titled, "Ollas in Ollin."

"She (curandera Elena Avila) helped me in México in 1996 for my first visit to the power place of Tlatelolco when my own olla broke, and I lay crying face down on the ground for Our Tata Cuauhtemoc. "...No fue derrota y no fue triunfo–era el doloroso nacimiento de la Nacion Mestiza." Al mirar esas palabras por primera vez, y sin planear, sin saber internamente exactamente porque, y sin poder parar, me deje caer un llanto tan profundo que !si! me desahoge...y Elena me dijo, "Aqui, aqui dejaras esas lagrimas por lo que hizo el Hue Hue por nosotros.... Aqui te vas a dejar esas lagrimas en México. Llora, llora, llora..." me dijo. Y I was healing with those tears, tu sabes, comadre ...letting them fall onto the sacred soil of México, where I left them. Y tantos estudiantes, también, que murieron alli el (2) de octubre de 1968, ¿verdad? tantos...uno se puede sentir todo eso alli...era aquel Rojo Amanecer, pues...o sea, era UNO de aquellos rojos amaneceres, mejor dicho.

"Dejate caer su olla de vez en cuando, como ya sabes hacer...y ayuda a otros a dejar caer su olla. Eso es mi deseo para ti...."

Long ago, the pots and pans rebelled against the people, el comal también. The moon has her own pot for healing. Tlazolteotl Ixcuina "es la senora del 'desollamiento,' de la fertilidad del campo."–Arturo Meza

In the codices, las ollas depict the future, abundance, fruits and flowers, or turbulent waters. Our most primal pot, says my comadre Martha Ramirez, is our uterus. It is depicted as the u-shaped glyph of the moon. Once, I dreamed my grandma Carmen had fallen inside the earth. I reached into a spider hole and pulled her out. I knew it was time to start throwing pots. Sometimes I dream my pot is broken or being mended. Long ago, I did break my pot. I've pieced it back together. Sometimes, I seep through its cracks. My pot is full.

The Mud People

Juan Ramirez's film, "Israel in Exile," depicts a mother who saved all her tears in a jar for the son who immigrated to Chicago. Tear by tear. At the right time, she sprinkled her tears to protect him.

I'm tired now. This pot gets heavy. Es tiempo a desollar mi campo. Someday, I'm going to break my pot–release its spirit and las lloronas. I'll sprinkle those tears in seven directions, let the winds carry their names. Then, we may all begin to wipe the tears and cleanse, again.

Hush. Shhh. Can you hear them?

Adelita

Inside the Costureras' headquarters

Superbarrio

> ...I imagined the justice of magical realism.
> If justice came to Guate, Rigoberta Menchu would be president. And a generation of leaders, some of the best of the country, would be alive to lead, not only in Guatemala, but also in Honduras, Nicaragua, El Salvador, México, Chile, Argentina, South Africa, and East Timor. The disappeared would talk among the living. And there'd be resurrection in the mass graves and among the masses. There'd be no armies.
>
> I've wondered, what do people dream of in Guatemala? What if their dreams slipped outside their minds for all to see–dreams with cigarette burns and floating limbs, butterflies for dead ancestors, and bright red healing thread for stitching wounds and democracy's cloth.
>
> Then would a country find its reality so undeniable, so unreconcilable that justice would arrive, not because of a "democratically elected president" but because when the people dreamed, the dreams came true?
>
> From "Dreaming Guatemala" by Patrisia Gonzales, Universal Press Syndicate

As a result of the 1985 earthquake, numerous urban land movements emerged in its aftermath. One was Asamblea de Barrios, a creative urban land movement representing 80,000 families that converted itself into a political force a few years after the earthquake. It created a social movement with "the sound of a fiesta" and captured the sly parody; the magic; el popular of truth, justice, and the Mexican way. A hero in a wrestler's mask became their symbol for the power of people organized–a lo Mexicano. Superbarrio Gómez is a técnico or good guy in the ring. He fights the rudos, or bad guys, of injustice. He was one of the first people I interviewed as I sought to understand los heroés anónimos.

Chapter 2: Superbarrio

I looked for a fat man with a red and yellow mask, Superbarrio Gómez.

The legend "B.S." (Before Superbarrio): They say, it is said…in "el libro de los vencidos," the book that chronicles the last stand of indigenous México in the Invasion, there was a guerrero, big and strong, tall, who mocked the Spanish in the "Aztec" empire's last stand at Tlatelolco. The warrior taunted the Spanish conquistadores with a chicken bone, waving his bone and laughing. There was nothing to eat. He would hide and return to throw rocks at them. No one could catch him. He would laugh and hide.

And when the young lord Cuauhtemoc, "our grandfather," Descending Eagle, was tortured and his feet burned in the last defense, the Eagle Who Descends sent word to the people in all the homes to turn off their fires and to wait and guard the knowing within their hearts, for their sun had hidden. When México-Tenochtitlan, "the place of authority," was again in danger, his spirit guerrero would return to the Mexicans. And that defiant warrior with the bone vowed, too, to return.

Well, much time passes, almost 500 years. México again is threatened. And once again the guerrero returns to la gran Tenochtitlan.

In a barrio in Tlatelolco, where the torch of that presagio, or prediction, was first lit, that guerrero returns as a citizen, common and everyday, one offended by the crisis, a man with no face in this urbe of 20 million people.

He was a candy vendor, a victim of the 1985 earthquake. He walked home one day under the shadows of the jacarandas, wondering what he could do. He pondered how he could help his people. He arrived at his barrio, the "fundamental nucleus" where people preserve tradition. He opened his door. Suddenly there appeared a funnel of light, red and yellow. He is bathed in a golden beam of blinding light, encircled by wind and summoned by a grave, clear voice. "You are Superbarrio, scourge of greedy landlords and corrupt authorities."

"And when the wind cleared, I was dressed liked this."

And the guerrero incarnate, weighing 200 pounds without his mask, wanders into the ancient ruins of Tlatelolco. There in the plaza was a man named Cuauhtémoc, last name Cardenas, a presidential candidate in 1988 who spurred a political uprising for democracy. According to urban legends of the mass movement, the guerrero and the Eagle Who Descends were united.

The myth self-elaborates. Superbarrio debuts June 12, 1987, at a march of 10,000 people, demanding housing.

He catches a ride with a neighbor. He approaches leaders of the Asamblea de Barrios, saying, "I'm Superbarrio, social fighter. I offer my services to the people."

A news report, 13 June 1987, La Jornada newspaper:

"Superbarrio negotiated yesterday with El Fondo Nacional de Habitaciónes Populares, [the National Fund of Popular Housing or FONHAPO] and gained pilot credits to acquire 10 properties to build housing and to hold a meeting with the Secretary of Urban Development to propose the expropriation of vacant and idle land with fiscal irregularities in the capital.

"The agreement occurred yesterday after a march led by the new super hero." The super hero, reported the newspaper, is made up of renters organizations of the colonias Morelos, Pensil, Guerrero, and the Coordinadora Única de Damnificados (CUD). The super hero…will guard the city to avert evictions and arbitrary increases in rent, as well as to guard against corrupt officials and greedy landlords.

"After the spectacle by the march, which occurred–as always–during the comings and goings of plainclothes police…[motorists] looked with wonder at Super Barrio, standing on top of his old vehicle…in which he arrived to the march, as if asking themselves: why the big deal for a wrestler?"

The protestors impeded the entry and exit of anyone to FONHAPO. Finally they formed a commission of 60 representatives of each organization, which met with José Luis Cuéllar Garza, coordinator of federal housing programs. Superbarrio presented his business card to Cuéllar Garza, saying, "I'm one of the técnicos and you, a rudo?"

Shortly thereafter, sightings of a hero in a wrestler's mask are reported, wearing pulp–red leotards trimmed with a gold lamé bikini and a yellow cape. He wears banana yellow boots on his un-winged feet. A woman faces eviction in Colonia Romero Rubio, on Pequín Street. Superbarrio comes to her aid to negotiate with the landlord.

As his fame grew, when an eviction occurred, someone in the barrio would shoot three firecrackers in the air. And voices ran through the barrio. Spread the word! ¡Que buscan al enmascarado! Look for the masked man! And Superbarrio Gómez appeared. The people united around him in a brown, human chain. Superbarrio hindered hundreds of evictions–a deed punishable with 20 days in jail.

Who here impedes this eviction? authorities asked. It is Superbarrio. And who is Superbarrio?

– Superbarrio is all of us.

On June 17, 1987, 200 goons tried to evict a family in Asamblea's stronghold, the warrior barrio, Colonia Guerrero. But 1,000 residents fought back with sticks and stones.

He is a hero of many avatars–a former real-life wrestler whose persona was evil, a collective consciousness of the masses, a street vendor who sells M & Ms at the metros.

"Not to put cream on my tacos but…" the masked man says in a voice that is as soft as his big belly, soft like dough bien masada.

"To be Superbarrio is to defend a people dispossessed. It is to believe the problem of another to be your own. It is to be in solidarity–en las buenas y las malas–the good and the bad. It is to raise your voice in protest in intolerable situations that can no longer be tolerated. To be just, popular justice–justicia de la buena–righteous justice."

The people were alone no more.

Superbarrio dances with "mothers of the barrio," the women "married to democracy" who danced the waltz of democracy in front of the National Palace. Super as the godfather at barrio quinceañeras, coming-out parties for girls turning fifteen. Super visiting the railroad workers' protest and giving odes to heroes of the railroad movement, Jesús García and Demetrio Vallejo. Superbarrio and "the Adelitas" of all the struggles go to Sanborns restaurant (of the blue tiles) to ask for a cup of coffee "owed to them" for more than 75 years, when Villa and Zapata met there for a revolutionary embrace.

It was as if a guy in tights had stepped out of the comic books and into a revolution.

He ran for president in 1988, wrestled with "dinosaurios" and AIDS (he debilitated the virus by dangling a condom), and was once detained by "la migra" in Los Angeles, reportedly on a tip from the Mexican consulate that he had no papers. (He had been protesting the mistreatment of Mexican immigrants in the United States, meeting with Southern California mayors and Mexican immigrants.)

Gusano de la Manzana ("Apple Worm") tried to unmask Superbarrio. He was a wrestler personifying anti-democracy and a play on electoral block captains of areas known as "manzanas." The Mexican congress tried to unmask him; the governor of Jalisco personally tried. Later came trips to France, Germany, Italy, Spain, Central America. He was written up in the Globe and People magazine. The New York Times called him the "Poor Man's Superman."

Never has he lost his mask (except when the migra required him to privately prove his identification).

His plastic-trimmed mask revealed the heroic imagination of the Mexicans. Not the imagining of states, but that of peoples. Imagination because it is a power to create, born in the face of captivity, corruption, poverty, alienation, and vast untruths. Heroic because it dares to imagine a different world. Behind that mask is the culture of imagination, a spirit of creativity, a theater of hope.

In 1988, Cuauhtémoc Cárdenas challenged the then 59 year-old Partido Revolucionario Institucional (PRI), officially garnering 33 percent of the vote (a figure contested internationally). Cárdenas, "of revolutionary blood and tree with good fruits," is the son of Lázaro Cárdenas, the most revered president of modern México. "Tata" (Grandfather) Cárdenas expropriated oil in 1938 and is credited with far-reaching agrarian land reform that returned land to the campesinos. Fifty years later his son parted the waters of historical memory for the Cardenist utopia, when "the revolution was patrimony of the campesinos who made it," writes intellectual Adolfo Gilly. When Cuauhtémoc Cárdenas, himself a PRI statesman, broke from the party-state, which was named the PRI name by his father, and launched his independent candidacy, there was an organic surge of support from the people. The scrawls of campesinos in communal letters likened the son to el Señor Águila on México's coat of arms–the Mechica migration story depicted by the eagle landing on a cactus in the pictogram of México's founding.

"They say there walks a son of the general. We must support him," they wrote in correspondence reproduced in Cartas a Cuauhtémoc Cárdenas.

Cuauhtémoc's picture was placed on home altars next to the santos. Something had changed in the Mexican psyche.

Traditionally, Mexican popular social movements, largely anti-electionist and divided by ideologies in prior times, were forced to support Cardenas because of a groundswell supported by the "la base" people. In this fashion, many united behind Cuauhtémoc, providing the grassroots support "for the indio mexicano with an indio name and an indio face." It reordered civil and political culture in México, creating a centrist-left opposition party aligned with social movements, the Partido Revolucionario Democrático (PRD).

The Asamblea had endorsed their own candidate for president. "Because we are tired of being bribed and used. Now we must speak, the renters, the outcasts, the roofless, the jobless, the workers, the students, the campesinos, the Indians, the ecologists, the women in struggle, the children with minds of victors." Their slogan was: "People, vote for yourself. Vote for Superbarrio."

Superbarrio supported Cárdenas and remained at his side as his masked alter ego. At one point in the campaign, following a dance for the children of the barrio in Campamento de la Democracia, an open-air electoral campaign center for the barrios, the people are evicted and the camp destroyed by government security forces. The camp, organized by Asamblea de Barrios, is pitched again. Asamblea paints a sign: "Yours is the night, ours is the dawn."

On election day, Cárdenas votes for Superbarrio. Carlos Monsiváis commented in La Jornada on "el capricho" de Cárdenas and "el relajo que es también resistencia." "Cuauhtemoc's vote for Superbarrio is, at the very least, an act of defiance. It is the smiling homage to the emerging forces that no longer exclude from their propaganda tactics a sense of humor, to the new urban culture whose antics also are resistance."

Then came the June election irregularities. The computers

went down for about a week. A half million people gathered in the Zócalo to protest. Many told Cardenas, "Just say the word." In the state of Guerrero, indigenous Cardenista leaders defended a municipal palace with bows and arrows. ("Well, they had a few other things.") Many believe President Salinas de Gortari won through fraud and tacazos–ballots stuffed like tacos.

August 13, 1988 – On the 467th anniversary of the heroic resistance and fall of México and on the heels of presidential elections embroiled in accusations of fraud, followers of "la tradición" charged with preserving pre-Hispanic or "pre-Cuauhtemoc" ways invite Super to place flowers at the iron and marble monument of the young Cuauhtemoc, "supreme hero of México." Amid the dancing plumes, Super is placed in a circle of prayer dances to the forces. Five thousand people watch.

From news accounts:

The danzantes cry out words from the final battle before the fall of Tenochtitlan. At the monument carved with the torture of Cuauhtemoc, an orator's words found their place amid conch shells and copal. "Facing the Great Threat...a new will has emerged among us, the will to fight...and, in the long run, the defense of our country's sovereignty, of democracy, of freedom...it remains with us to defend the consequences and significance of our actions...they (the government) will not be able to go against the popular will. The sale of the country and the corruption cannot consume us. No one can stay neutral in this fight."

Before the statute of the Mechica Cuauhtemoc, the orator spoke of conquerors and the false dawn.

> Each day it perturbs the Mexicans more and more the attempt to impose a government and governors that we did not elect. They submitted all of the people bit-by-bit. They made us impoverished quickly. They have wanted to yank us from our roots, erase our culture, break up the nation.... We all said no, but they did not hear us; they do and they say and they do not understand the peaceful voice in which we told them no and elected our own true representative.
>
> In their palaces they remain alone, and now no one believes nor listens to their lies. The truth comes in waves from below, from the huts and the neighborhoods, from the factories and the workshops, from the schools, a new presage of what has occurred....

Superbarrio placed a flag at the foot of the monument, inscribed, "In memory of Quauhtemoc and the warriors who heroically fought in defense of their fatherland MDXXI."

He spoke. "On a day like this, Cuauhtemoc left a lesson for all of us Mexicans to defend what is ours, come what may...¡Viva Cuauhtemo! ¡Viva México! ¡Viva Cuauhtémoc Cárdenas, México's president!"

From 1988 to 1993, more than 250 Cardenistas were killed in political assassinations. Super remained close to Cardenismo but distant from the PRD party that became dominated by strongmen with former PRI ties, who diminished grassroot's participation. "The people have to put the party in order," Super would tell me.

El Grito-Exvoto

The march of two flowers, one for the dead and one for those who survived, the ones la Huesuda–the Boney Woman–did not take.... Death carries the bones of the heroes in a black carton coffin, across from the building of the official Holy Inquisition, past the clack-clack-clack of Plaza Santo Domingo's letter writers on their Remington uprights ("Mi querida..."). The life-and-death march spills into the barrio of the brides and jacarandas, streets of bride bazaars, dreams that spin inside music boxes, charanga at the Bar León, and private baths for two.

"Let the champion pass to the front! Superbarrio has arrived!"

Firecrackers explode on the sidewalks. Roman candles drip along the city's floor as the "monumental offering" wends its way through the heart of Mexico City on the Day of the Dead, that particularly Mexican embrace with death that makes her part of life and la burla. After all, we are all common mortals at death, without masks or power.

Santo Domingo Hotel. Flor Baños. Los 15 Libros. Baños Mirabella. Instituto Cuauhtemoc Primaria. La Mexicana Dulces y Galletas. Café Restuarant China. Restaurant Nuevo León Bar. ¡Qué Viva the Mexican traditions! ¿Petacas? los de Miguel el coco de las peluqueras. El Rendevuz Café/Restuarant/Baile. Hotel Ambos Mundos.

"Well, we have to take the Zócalo, el ombligo-corazón of México-Tenochtitlan." It was always imperative to take back the public spaces from the government for dissent, theater, and negotiation. This is how democracy is created, heard, and seen. Calaveras (skulls), variously of sugar, cardboard or rhymes, dance around the Superbarrio mobile, a '63 Ford delivery truck, red and yellow with the urban tatoo: "SB."

Cantan las calaveras, "¡Qué viva los vivos!"

The mask speaks, "This is not only to remember our dead but all the universal dead and to recognize the valor of the 1985 earthquake, when millions of anonymous heroes risked their lives for people they didn't even know."

"We are going to take the palace door!"

People melt candles on the plaza, making a path of flor de muerto–marigolds–roses, tangerines and candles to the presidential palace. For the dead cannot see, but they can smell; and in the black eye of the night, the dead will return on the path of petals until the guards close the presidential doors with a dull THUD of "NOoooo."

Little boys get close to Superbarrio to touch his cape. Surrounded by an ellipse of children, he recalled the heroes of the ruins, heroes of el populacho. The plebes. "And the people continue being heroic and anonymous."

"I've seen things in moments of outrage when people are not attended. People know who is the good guy and who is the bad guy, and they choose sides.

"They are capable of sticking their face–or their mask–out for someone in the metro or to help a street vendor, who is constantly targeted. They may not know who is being attacked, but they do know the repression of the authorities and public security. But they can't tolerate that this happens all the time without doing anything. And they stick their noses where maybe they don't belong, which is risky, and join in solidarity. And when it is over, the people go on their way without ever asking for fame or renown because all they want is not to suffer injustices."

At the plaza's edge, campesinos festoon Zapata's face in marigolds or cempoalxochitl, the ceremonial flower of the spirits; and the Asamblea torches an effigy of el pinche gobierno. The Damn Government.

The Birth of a Hero

"When historians write of the urban popular movement 20 years from now," said Marcos Rascón, Asamblea leader and the mastermind of Superbarrio's many legends, "they will divide it in two periods, Before Superbarrio and After Superbarrio. With Superbarrio, the city stopped being so gray and indifferent."

"It is a myth of the Left that the masses tire," Rascón said. "When they are tired, it is not a physical tiredness, but tired ideas. They tire when they run out of initiatives, when they run out of opportunities."

"Superbarrio is a symbol of the collective conscience, that even if a leader tricks the people, the movement will not surrender," said Rascón, who also is a leader in the PRD. "As long as he stays with the people and linked to common sense and popular sentiment, if he doesn't separate from the people, which happens to all leaders–some believe you can reproduce power by yourself alone–if he doesn't fail to have direct contact with people in all these movements, as long as he struggles from the very bottom, with the people, then there will always be a Superbarrio."

According to the document "Asamblea Has Life Because of Its Struggles and Its Gains, "The red and yellow light that illuminated Superbarrio in those days in June of 1987 came not from heaven or the mystery but out of the collective, political will dwelling in the social struggles prior to the 1985 earthquake."

Difficulties ensued as struggles of daily survival turned to voter rights, citizen rights, and political killings. "El compadre" Superbarrio became more than a symbol of collective force.

"He turned a culture of defeat into a culture of victory," says Angélica Cuéllar Vázquez, a political science professor who wrote a book on the Asamblea entitled, <u>La noche es de ustedes y la amanecer es nuestro</u>. The Night Is Yours and the Dawn Is Ours.

Why was it a culture of defeat, as Super often called it? "Because they always lose." The Mexican Left, say intellectuals, venerates the tragic. "Even when they win, they don't believe it." Plus, they could use a sense of humor and la burla pa' sobar the cynicism.

"Asamblea recaptured the experience of triumph following the earthquake. But now it was not just the victims of the earthquake. But, as Super says, people who are victims all of their lives. They dignified themselves in the social struggle...and "Asamblea restructured the hierarchy of symbols." Dignified people don't have to be humiliated by officials or humiliated by a landlord in evictions. "Asamblea recaptures barrio culture, the age-old tradition of firing shots in the air when there is an eviction. They take on the city as a whole, a collective space that we all have to protect, and not just in housing, but also in ecology and education."

"Symbolically he seeks to break that unequal relationship and to present himself as an equal with authorities," Cuéllar wrote in the book, adding that they are equal on a moral plane. Sometimes we need to "perform" justice to experience it in our bodies, rehearse the imagined to make the magical real.

Mil Máscaras

"The mask," wrote Ariel Dorfman (and Manuel Jofré) in Superman y sus amigos del alma (Superman and His Soul Mates), "becomes the point of contact between the reader and the super hero." Now there are others in the legion of super heroes: Supervoto, defender of the vote (in a black-and-white costume; black for mourning that the vote is not respected and white for the hope that the people would be able to protect it); Supercívico in Tijuana, who protects the maquiladora workers and immigrants; el Águila Descalza of Guadalajara, a play on México's Aztec Eagle warrior clan; Superecologista, who protects the environment; and, even Mop Man of Justice for Janitors fame in Los Angeles. Later Mop Woman swept into the janitor's movement. It was as if the imagination walked out of the mind and into the struggle, faces of the imagined.

"The reason I use a mask is that we are a collective identity," explained Superbarrio. "Our face is the masses. If I lose the mask, I lose the collective identity. What matters is not who's behind the mask, but who believes in the mask." Super says he is not the hero in the true sense.

He speaks, his words clipped by his mask. "People don't need heroes," said Superbarrio.

"They are the heroes." They are heroes in the Latin sense: to serve. Or as the root Greek meaning defined heroes: to protect.

Soon there were five of him, but there was only one that truly embodied and defined the spirit. The others were to protect the identity, to make him everywhere. He became culture. Pues la cultura cura.

"You have reached el barrio cueva of SUPERRRRBARRIO GOMEZzzzzz. Please leave a message after the tone."

Fashioned after El Santo, a real life wrestler who made it to the Silver Screen fighting vampires and extraterrestrials, Super brought humor to the theater of Good versus Evil. Laughter is good medicine. When I was a kid, I had to suffer through Monday night "wraslin" on TV with my dad. He said it was no more absurd than politics. But wrestlers were never loved in the U.S. like they were in México. Back then, the wrestlers were real in both countries. But in the United States, anyone who watched them was considered backward folk. Then in 1990, I found myself interviewing Super. The humble mask understood that in the Theatre of the Oppressed, we have to change the ending.

In la lucha libre, la lucha la hacemos todos.

El Round–The Theater of Hope

18 July 1987–The fight of the century. The fight between good and evil. Catalino Creel, El Parchado, a character borrowed from a popular TV soap opera, symbol of greedy landlords versus the true paladin of justice, our popular hero Superbarrio Gómez, representative of the People. The match results in the first seizure of a wrestling ring in Mexican history.

News reports announce that at last the hated rival arrives.

"Here he comes, Catalino Creel.

"[C]ulero...[c]ulero...[c]ulero." Ass.

"¡No me vale madre!"

"Coward! Muy sacalepunta. You with your agents and your goons!"

"If you lose this fight, your own goons will disqualify you because you count on the force of the public hate and I count on the people's force.

El Parchado threatens him: "You, the Poor, you have always lost to the landlord." To the mat.

But wait, they STOLE the ring?

"Where is the ring that our compa (el compadre, Regent

Manuel Camacho Solís) lent us? Stupid us. The regent took it." Mexico City security police had removed the ring on wheels to parts unknown. The Asamblea retreats to a meeting where they are holding an open air forum on housing. Following the meeting, they demand the return of the ring and that it not be tortured.

The newspaper Uno Mas Uno reported, "In Mexico City yesterday the ring was stolen from two fighters, landlord Catalino Creel, and the other, the representative of renters, Superbarrio."

Carlos Monsiváis, a spectator, in an interview regarding "el rapto del ring" said, "The abduction of the ring is one of the saddest abductions in the history of twentieth century México. They have stolen the voting urns, the Angel of Independence, but this is the first time they have taken a ring."

People go to their camping tents and get quilts and blankets and throw them on the floor outside the cathedral. The multitude form a makeshift human ring. "To the Zócalo, to the Zócalo!" the crowd demands. "Take the fight over there!"

Creel tries to move the match to Las Lomas de Chapultepec, barrio of the high brows, telling Super, "You have too many of your people with you."

"Nos robaron el ring, carnal." They stole the ring, bro.

Weeks later the ring was recovered, and the fight was held in the Plaza de las Tres Culturas at the sight of sacred Tlatelolco, where blood ran in the Aztecs last stand and during the heroic stand of 1968. One spectator called it the plaza of the sepulchers. Several wrestling events later, 100 Superbarrio plastic dolls would be sold here.

The calavera Catrina–Posada's Lady Skeleton and a play on city slickers–is on the side of evil, delighting the enemy with the death grin of La Huesuda.

In the crowd, there is "little Superbarrio," a boy of seven or eight. Super Vecina, or Super Neighbor, Superbarrio's mythical girlfriend (in real life, he is married, father of two), takes the calavera Catrina in a headlock.

Women chant. They sing a politicized version of "Las Mañanitas," a song usually reserved for birthdays and anniversaries. "Éstas son las mañanitas, Superbarrio, for you in this time of struggle we support you…."

"Awaken, pueblo, awaken

It is time to fight
for a dignified home
of popular character."

– Voy a rompersele a su madrecita santa al parchado del Catalino Creel. I'm going to tear his holy mother's face!

– We're not a bunch of valemadristas-que-nomás-yo, I-don't-give-a-damn-only-me kind of people.

They will fight two to three rounds, time unlimited. The two come out, eye each other, study each other, and take their places. Super gives a headlock.

"Kill him! Finish him off!" from the mouths of children.

Creel flattens him on his back and twists his head like a piece of chicle.

"Look out!"

Super's mask is almost lost.

The Good Guy wins.

"That is theater," shouts El Llanero Solicito. "Long live theater!"

The mask: "In the Asamblea the struggle is collective. There is good, and there is bad. But our foe is a social enemy and you must defend it symbolically, inside the ring."

Ánimo, mi raza.

Over the years, there were other matches against Nucleosaurus, Apocalypse RIP (that's PRI in disorder); and Johnny Motto, representative of Free Trade Agreement and a play on Ya Ni Modo. English translation: "It doesn't matter." When the city held a plebiscite in 1993 to see if people supported converting Mexico City into the state of Anahuac, Asamblea sponsored another wrestling match between the Plebe and Chucky the Demonic Doll, the nickname of the regent's Number 2 man, Marcelo Ebrard Casaubrón. Years earlier, Superbarrio also handed then-Regent Camacho Solís the white glove, the challenge. He never got a match. Later emerged the PRI pseudo hero, Superpueblo.

There were other actions, other defeats. On June 17, 1987, 30 people were wounded by security goons who disrupted a protest meeting of renters. Most of them were women. In another confrontation, 60 were injured when goons came with tear gas. Now, certain barrios known for their resistance have been targeted by police forces, according to Super. Police know they must employ violence to dislodge Asamblea de Barrios members, some of who have been known to oust their assailants by stripping them of their clothes.

"When we lose, it makes us reflect," said Super.

He left the ring for the real fight, "the social fight where the public is not spectator but protagonist," says Super. "People have to be protagonists in their own world, become more humane. We have to feel like another's problems are our own problems." He dreamed of being star of la lucha libre.

"I was a rudo, a bad guy, in the ring, very explosive. I was a dark fighter." He said he was excellent theater. His name was Black Prince. After playing the wrestler's ring in villages offering earnings as little as 5,000 pesos, times were tight. He lost his mask for money.

But as Superbarrio, he's turned down offers to return to professional wrestling and to make films. "Those super heroes are commercial products, but they are totally false." Super is only plenty of flesh and bone.

Meanwhile, Superbarrio began to change. His wife did not want him to fight again. While still a professional wrestler in 1985, he injured his back when he was thrown into the spectator stands. The doctor told him if he ever received another blow like that he would never walk again. He became a candy vendor and sold M&Ms. "Then I was converted into a hero who defends the people." He had to study. He has only a fifth-grade education but is asked to speak on topics ranging from nuclear waste to human rights and initially found himself going to the Asamblea's political commission for guidance. "Hey, I don't know a thing."

The man who was anonymous with the mask off began to see the man behind the mask, his temper, his compassion, how he treated his wife. People who followed Super have seen him grow into his persona. He is wise and doesn't speak in domingueras, fancy Sunday-clothes words. I've often wondered if he tires of the mask. He is a big, kind, and gentle man.

"I've had to adapt to the character. When I take the mask off, it's a break. When you put it on, you don't know when you are going to take it off."

"It's no use to say I'm tired. It's no use to say that I won't come anymore. This is now a commitment greater than myself."

Y Otro Round

One lady had the boots in a bag. Another had the cape around her waist. He changed in the office of allies in the Mexican Assembly. Suddenly someone arrives in a mask. The security guards go for him.

– No one enters with a mask!

– It is Superbarrio. Leave him alone.

Pushing and shoving.

"Let him enter.... Let Him Enter...LET HIM ENTER!" shout people packed to the doors of the Mexican Assembly.

The security guards unmask him. "He's an impostor!" shouts Marcos Rascón. "Superbarrio has already entered!" ("We contemplated putting a mask over a mask or putting tiny faces on the mask, so when it was pulled off...choose your mask!")

Super is later escorted out brandishing a "V" sign.

News report: Accustomed to the figure of el tapado, the PRIistas were irritated yesterday by the presence of a masked man who interrupted the electoral college of the assembly of representatives of the D.F. yesterday....

Months later, when he was about to testify at a housing committee, congress told him to take off his mask. He retorted, "Take YOUR disguises off." And the Mexican opposition threatened to leave in solidarity. Finally, the masked man was permitted to speak in congress.

"Only when you lose, do you take off the mask. You lose your pride behind the mask. It is a moment of reflection. It is another person, another reality," he said.

Super greeted me at the door that day, wearing his mask and a pair of red sweats. Few know his real name and face. Many encounters later, he let down his mask.

"The mask is the last thing I put on. When I take off the mask, I take off the courage."

The Mask of Things

Superbarrio speaks of those who stir the dust of history.

> In the greatest changes of humanity, they have been made by the thousands and millions of anonymous heroes. Hidalgo, Morelos,

> Juarez have nothing of the anonymous. As you know, we pay homage to them. But who really made the changes, who suffered perhaps more than anyone, are the millions of anonymous faces whom no one remembers, but, however, were the force, the motor, that made humanity change. There are always caudillos; there are always famous ones in the struggle. But there is also that immense army.

Someone plays a scratchy record of Vicente Fernández in the downtown apartment unit where we are chatting. Someone wrings a mop. Someone is frying lunch, and a bit of water causes the oil to revolt. "For us, a hero is a Morelos, a Zapata, or a Cuauhtemoc, a personage of history who convinced himself of the struggle to the point of giving up his life." And yet, there is something inside of us that makes us all heroic. "Most assuredly we all have an anonymous hero hidden, and sometimes it comes out without us noticing it. Sometimes to survive in this city is an act of heroism."

Heroes Without Witness

In August 1992, the intelligentsia wrote epitaphs for the popular historical conscience of México. Literati wrote that history had been remade by the force of ideas rather than the force of people. El Pipila, an anonymous hero in México's war of independence against Spain, was "disappeared" from history. It was said he used himself as a human battering ram in the determining battle. It is written that he crawled on all fours covered by a slab of stone and set fire to the gate of the enemy's stronghold. But his story would no longer appear in the revised government history books. Mexicans sent a burro to then Secretary of Education Ernesto Zedillo. Teachers sang a popular nursery rhyme used for learning vowels, "a-e-i-o-u, the burrito knows more than you–Zedillo." Popular heroes had been erased from history: el Pipila, the Indian Canek of the rebellion in Yucatan. Several intellectuals debated whether el Pipila had ever really existed.

Mexican mystery writer Paco Taibo II wrote in <u>La Jornada</u> that on the 28th of September, 1810, "as the sun set," Miguel Hidalgo was desperate because he could not penetrate the Royalist fortification in the Alhóndiga de Granaditas, from where enemy fire had caused at least 60 deaths. "Miguel Hidalgo, general of the plebs, picked up a rumor that a miner was going about saying he could beat down the main door and calling him, he gave him carte blanche to try...that is how El Pipila entered into the history of México, abandoning it a few hours later to return to the anonymity which he had left when the rabble entered and sacked the Alhóndiga."

One of the alleged omissions that drew the most debate was of "los Niños Héroes" who died in battle in 1847. Symbols of native resistance to U.S. intervention, they leaped to their death. People were outraged that these symbols of national resistance against U.S. intervention had been left out of history.

On September 16, 1992, at the 145th anniversary of their deaths, it was front-page news. President Salinas stressed that the nation would always honor their legacy of patriotism. Later reports recounted how PRIista Idolina Moguel turned to page 50 of the revised books and said "Los Niños Héores sí están..." But an opposition candidate said they were just a mention. Reports followed that México had been encouraged to clean up its history for its new trading partner. A September 9, 1992, report in La Jornada quotes Ifigenia Martínez, ex-PRD senator, who alleged that a U.S. diplomat had informed a group of Mexican politicians that their history was "aggressive" against the United States. She said the government filed a formal petition with México's Secretary of Education. As many opponents noted in México's new master narrative, the Inquisition didn't happen. Porfirio Díaz fueled progress. There was no mention of why the United States invaded México, and President Salinas' presidential term was made history before it had even ended.

When the Revolution became institutionalized into a political party, the PRI, the revolution of the "bronze race"–of mestizo progress–became an ideology, as well. As communism swept México in the thirties and forties, the "martyrology" as Monsiváis calls it, became part of the civic religion of the Mexican Left, "man" confronting authority to make history. The blood of the workers would clean history, as well as the steps of the Palacio de Bellas Artes, near where various marches bled. Symbols were reversed. In the murals of Diego Rivera, the workers are the heroes; and it is the People who carry history forward on the burden straps of time. They became art. In the portrait "The Alameda," Rivera included in the rendering of pre-revolutionary high society the anti-hero of el gendarme, a guard to protect "decent people" from the masses.

"The Mexican Revolution, if anything, was really a collection of heroic deeds because it was a disregard for death. 'If you are going to kill me, kill me once and for all.' It demanded a high level of altruism and personal disinterest," says Monsiváis.

Between phone calls from friends and followers, Monsiváis talks of his chronicles of Mexican life. The phone rings. "Have you seen the Seventh Victim? It's a picture that has me crazy."

Click.

"Heroism, as I understand it in modern times, is heroism for continuing in extreme sacrifice in the name of an ideal or cause. Heroism implies a constant struggle with high risks."

At the time of the interview, in September 1992, Salvador Nava, a man fighting cancer, ran for governor of San Luis Potosí. He was the sure favorite backed by a coalition of various political parties, but he lost through fraud. He and hundreds of followers were marching hundreds of kilometers to the capital to demand that the vote be respected. Meanwhile, 30 female "Navistas" blocked the entrance to the governor's palace. Monsiváis considered the march "moral fury," but to him it was not heroic because international attention prevented repression. A new governor, but another PRIista, was appointed. Nava died about a year later.

"Now the episode of '68, to me, is heroic." In 1968, untold numbers at a student-led protest were massacred at Tlatelolco. "It's one of my obsessions. They knew they were going to confront a superior power. They knew the risk. They were aware of the criminal intention of the government; still they persevered. They resisted in the protests, in the taking of academic facilities, in the jails, in the interrogations. Above all, the legacy of '68 is something I link to civil heroism, its respect for social and civil human rights, and its confrontation against authoritarianism. That is heroic."

Maria Felix's eyes in black and white gaze over his study. Couldn't everyone be heroic? Couldn't we all have a hero inside? I ask him. "Few of us have them or, in that manner, there would be many heroes."

But if people are called heroic, why are they not heroes? "That is just a metaphor. It is a way of describing exemplary character. We have to distinguish, or everything would be heroic. At any given moment, heroism is provoked, as was proven during the earthquake."

Vox Populi, Voz Anónima

> "...the Mexican people are heroic all of their days: the eating poorly, the living poorly, the sleeping poorly, that is the daily heroism...This very moment, fancy hotels are full. The airplanes are full. That means there are many people earning lots of money. In turn, the workers' salaries are limited and they are the majority of the people who keep this country going. That is the everyday heroism, not just of the earthquake; and it is even bigger because it is cold, conscious heroism." – From Nada, nadie: Las voces del temblor (Nothing, no one, the voices of the earthquake) by Elena Poniatowska

There are heroes of high risk, heroes of action, moral heroes. The Mexican artist Felipe Ehrenberg speaks of the daily life "micro heroes." Why was there not greatness in confronting daily life–heroes of the spirit? Heroes of our dailyness?

"Malraux makes the observation in Anti-Memoirs that there is not heroism without witnesses. What you are talking about is popular heroism, not the individualistic heroism of the bourgeois that Carlyle proposed...and in popular heroism there is the idea that you cannot reach the rank of heroism until you've passed through martyrdom," said Daniel Molina Álvarez.

– "They call me the spokesman of the sentiments of the revolution."

Molina and I are drinking rum Potosí from the land where the Mexican Revolution first raised its fist. Molina writes a column on popular history for Mexico City's "moral newspaper" Corre La Voz. (Spread the Word).

"In the bourgeois concept of heroism, the heroism is individualistic, self-sufficient. I believe it's more complex. We need to look for a heroism of collective valor, a social valor, and not necessarily associated with martyrdom. We need living heroes because dead heroes don't do us a bit of good."

"But in heroism without witness, it is people who never want recognition, who never want fame, who never want to be recognized on the pages of history...it is a heroism that vindicates life and anonymity."

I once asked Super why so many people stop fighting after they obtained a home or electricity. Many popular movements have seen that to change the government or to get people to fight for land was not enough. In their struggle to keep people in movement, they had begun "projects of life." And they take a lifetime, many.

Superbarrio observes, "There are people who become convinced of the importance of their action, of organizing, of the struggle. And there are people, unfortunately, who sell their dignity or who sell themselves or cross to the other side."

"Sometimes we content ourselves with so little, so easily do we lose our dignity and easily lose the reason to fight. There are people…when the government or a political candidate offers them a solution that is unrealistic, and they know it is unrealistic, the people go and believe them. And they trick themselves, and I believe they lose their dignity. Here in the Asamblea, here, we don't resolve your problem. If you don't move, if you don't fight, there are no magic candles that are going to save you."

We talk inside an apartment in historic downtown, where many were left homeless after the quake. "In the greatest endeavors and the greatest tasks, the common people are capable, even to make revolution. I've read your Luther King…. It really makes me mad when people say it can't be done. I believe there are no impossibilities, no matter how difficult the problem may be. My enemy, no matter how powerful, cannot defeat me. There is no greater force than a people organized and determined to conquer its future and well-being."

Patria

A procession of little children walked to a remembering stone, a stone with candles dripping at its feet in waxen falls. Superbarrio walked in the middle of tiny hands, each holding a single carnation. He carried a little boy on his shoulders. Boy Scouts formed a people's guard around the march of young ones. The children brought flowers to the stone.

The stone had 20 names of warriors inscribed on it. The warriors died on October 2, 1968. This was their 25th anniversary. The poet and writer Leopoldo Ayala spoke to the crowd in a high pitch and fervent stilleto voice. "Get this. When we were walking over here, all of a sudden someone asked me, 'What's going on? Why are there so many people?'"

"I told him this was an important meeting. They are going to learn history. They are going to learn a most beautiful lesson, that is, the lesson of life, and the lesson of life is not taught in classrooms. The lesson of life is not taught in schools. The lesson of life is taught precisely in the streets and then in a street as important as this one?"

"And who is the teacher?"

"Well, the teacher, the teachers are many."

"But who here is the director?"

"It occurred to me to say the director is called Superbarrio."

"Superwhat?"

"Superbarrio."

"And who is Superbarrio?"

"Where are you from?"

"We are from Lomas de Chapultepec."

"Well, no wonder you don't know Superbarrio. You know Superbarrio, but you don't like him much. You see him as bad because Superbarrio told all of you that you are robbers, and we are going to return what you took."

"They looked at me funny. Well, it occurred to me to talk about who is Superbarrio. Some will say, 'Superbarrio, no I don't know him. I don't know what he looks like, Superbarrio.'"

"Well, I want to ask you now because Tita, a former 1968 student leader and teacher, has already given the lesson. As the teacher of truth that she is, she told us how we have to speak up. Who can tell me who is Superbarrio. Does he exist? Is he real? Can we touch him? Is he like us? Or is he different? A ghost? Because the rich fear the mask of Superbarrio? He arrives and the PRI jump. 'I didn't do it. I didn't do anything. No, No, No!'"

"Who is Superbarrio? What is his name? Is his name Juan. Is his name Pedro? Is his name José? You, what is your name?"

"Gladys."

"You, what is your name?"

"Mike."

"You, what is your name?"

"Jorge."

"You know what, Miguel? I'm going to tell you something. Superbarrio is called all of those names because you know what? Superbarrio has a lot of names. He has my name. He has your name. And who is the papá of Superbarrio? The papá of Superbarrio is called Pueblo. The papa of Superbarrio is called México, that generated the life of Superbarrio. And who knows who is the mamá of Superbarrio?"

"¡PATRIA!"

"Exactly. It is the motherland. It is the struggle. It is the revolution, freedom. Our friend is called struggle because it comes from the light, and it is called liberty. You know how Superbarrio grew up? He grew up thinking; he grew up studying; and he grew up in the movement, like the movement of '68. And there, there was the germ of Superbarrio. Let's give a cheer to this Superbarrio that is México, this Superbarrio that is our country, this Superbarrio that is our people, this Superbarrio that is our ideals. To him, to his father, to his mother, which is all of life."

I finished writing this chapter in 1993. On January 1, 1994, the volcán exploded. The National Zapatista Liberation Army rebelled in Chiapas. Tomorrow had come. México's future was changed, forever. Indigenous guerrilla soldiers with ski masks became etched in the mindscape of México. Among them emerged the mask of subcomandante Marcos–and later comandante Ramona, el Tacho y otros. México obsessed over him. Who was he? Where did he come from? Was he Superbarrio? Marco Rascón? An insurgent Jesuit priest? His name, Marcos, was symbolic, like his mask. He took it from a compa who fell. He told the people to look in the mirror to find him. In a communique from the jungles, he sent this message, "About whether Marcos is homosexual: Marcos is gay in San Francisco, black in South Africa, an Asian in Europe, a Chicano in San Ysidro, an anarchist in Spain, a Palestinian in Israel, a Mayan Indian in the streets of San Cristobal, a gang member in Neza, a rocker in the National University, a Jew in Germany, an ombudsman in the Defense Ministry, a communist in the post-Cold War era, an artist without gallery or portfolio .... a pacifist in Bosnia, a housewife alone on Saturday night in any neighborhood in any city in México, a striker in the CTM [the powerful but puppet union of the government], a reporter writing filler stories for the back pages, a single woman on the metro at 10 p.m., a peasant without land, an unemployed worker...an unhappy student, a dissident amid free-market economics, a writer without books or readers, and, of course, a Zapatista in the mountains of southeast México. So Marcos is a human being, any human being, in this world. Marcos is all the exploited, marginalized, and oppressed minorities resisting and saying, 'Enough!'"

We are all Marcos, or "we are all Ramona."

Permiso

Aliento de la vida
de los cuatro rumbos
pedimos permiso a
entrar aquí.
Abrenos las puertas sagradas
so that we may return....

October 2, 1968, government forces fired into a peaceful demonstration of thousands at the ancient ceremonial site of Tlatelolco. Untold numbers died, and this act became known as the massacre at Tlatelolco. It became an international symbol of the student uprisings of the 1960s. Prior to the massacre, students from all over México and Mexico City, from high school students to college students, had been engaged in a democracy movement and student strike that gripped the country. Today, Tlatelolco remains a sacred site.

Tlatelolco

Raúl Álvarez Garcín and Tita Avendaño at Tlatelolco

Chapter 3: Los Chavos del '68

Throughout the day, the people come to the past, as if summoned, to make the ritual walk. My heart is moved by memory, a place is made sacred by memory. It is the time of appearance. Women bring death flowers. They make an altar, of silence, of passage, on the stones where blood ran long ago in the time of broken spears, when the arrow splintered and the obsidian shattered in the Aztec's last defense of Tlatelolco. But on the floor of the Plaza de las Tres Culturas, in the barrio of the warriors, the people come all day, students after school, students with teachers, mothers of the disappeared, walking in revolutions and counterrevolutions around the ruins of Tlatelolco. And the plaza is filled with the light of candles, black and white photographs, tombstones of paper and tiny lights that scrawl upon the day–for the warriors who fell in '68. Our wounds are flowers; our wounds are jewels. A mass from a nearby church echoes in the ruins.

– To the task, my Jesus. To the task, mi Señor. The Father kisses the church floor.

In México, the past breaks through the earth.
They carve a great stone, their song is in them.
"My heart shall live, it will come back,
my memory will live and my fame."

-Cantares Mexicanos

As Gordon Brotherston writes in Image of the New World, from the memory of painted stone and wood, my heart comes back.

This is a sacred site. It has been made so by the ánimas, the spirits of a long time ago. This is a ceremonial place, a place of obligations, of prayers. It is a place made sacred by all those who died on October 2.

When you go to Tlatelolco, the dead walk with you. You can

feel their breath in the silence. The silence is a container for their memory, for all that was carried with the dead. It is here that the government made human sacrifices. The land has left a story here, a story to tell the children. The land has given me many stories. In Laredo, Texas, there is the hanging tree that still grows. At San Pedro Park in San Antonio, Mexicans were hung near the sacred spring, where my ancestors and other indigenas prayed.

Along the border, there are descansos, roadside altars of plastic flowers for those who have died trying to cross a line that doesn't exist. I've often said we need a place to heal the border. There are few places for us to pray at the border, to leave offerings to the Río Bravo, grande río. But here and there are people who leave cantos a la tierra y el río. These are the teachings of a place called Tlatelolco.

Once, as Doña Rosario Ibarra de Piedra stood in the rain with the other mothers of the disappeared, I lamented that so few people had attended the protest shrine that year. In her passionate counsel, she told me not to look for what wasn't. Still they come, she said.

And so I sought to understand Tlatelolco's power, how I walked with the spirits there. Tlatelolco is a sacred site–the people have made it so–and it called me inside of its stones to live the mistica of the place, to understand the "mind" of the land, the living, the breathing spirit of Life. Chief Joseph once said, "The Earth and myself are of one mind." The mind of the universe, of life, of animals, minerals, matitas. We become the piedras. This land calls forth its own "sacred geography," to borrow from native scholar Vine Deloria. The land is made sacred by its stories. History and geography become one with what is sacred. There are rituals to attend to; to walk circles with the ancestors, the dead, the sacrificed, los abuelos. They breathe through us.

In Tlatelolco, I see the appearance of time. Past, present, and future in a single moment, we are there, we are them…the white gloves of the army's Olympia Battalion, the bullets' white fire, the green Bengal lights. And I think of the epitaph of Mexican intellectual José Revueltas, "Gray is all theory; green is the golden tree of life."

A crown of flowers, candles in jelly jars, woeful conch shells that breathe the sea. They say it is the sound of Quetzalcoatl, y era nuestra herencia una red de agujeros.

¡es cercado por la guerra el tenochca;

es cercado por la guerra el tlatelolca!

When the army fired its anointing bullets upon the students, the professors, the housewives, the families, the young people protesting for democracy, in their desperate flee, they left their shoes, they left their lives. When it was all over, corpses and empty shoes were left on the plaza. The government in the initial chaos confirmed that 35 died. Some foreign press estimated more than 300 were killed. The government later said more than 20 died. Of course, the government has never been good at counting the dead.

Tlatelolco became the scar, the divide, between what México was and what it became, from what it wanted the world to believe it was and what it is–a yoke of violence and unfettered power cloaked in rosa Mexicana, the familiar domination all people have fought over all the world. "It marked the conscience of México," says the noble, respected Raúl Álvarez Garín, one of the principal leaders of '68.

The great siesta was over.

Every nation has a Tlatlelolco that is the defining moment in how it responds to truth–the assassination of El Salvador's Archbishop Oscar Romero, China's Tianeman Square. In 1968, the youth around the world seared convention; and, in México, los chavos heroés roared. Popular heroism is contagious, the writer-activist Daniel Molina likes to say. Much of México became consumed with a fever for justice. It stood and walked with los chavos rebeldes for two-and-a half months shortly before the summer Olympics–students from high schools and vocational schools and universities, intellectuals, professors, parents.

The people walked with the future–700,000, 400,000, 300,000 protested. In Mexico City. Oaxaca. Veracruz. Villahermosa. Yucatan. Chihuáhua. ¡Presente! The army took over schools. Government-backed student "porras" provoked confrontations. Thousands of people were arrested in peaceful demonstrations and school strikes; hundreds were wounded. But on October 2, 1968, the bullets tolled. For exactly how many, no one knows.

What did they want? To speak freely and frankly, the freedom of Demetrio Vallejo and Valentín Campa (two leaders of the railroad strikes jailed in 1959), the release of political prisoners, and the dissolution of the government's goon force. They wanted what all people want: to stop living lies, to live a life that is equal.

And people come on October 2 to fill the shoes that were left, to follow their footprints in the universe. Throughout the streets, past the vendors and businesses, you will hear the mantra, the echo of the coming people: 2 de Octubre no se olvida. October 2 is not forgotten.

"Who makes history?...History is made by the men and women who participate in it, la gente. But what people? All of the people? Do they do it, let us say, en bola, enmasse? We well know that Hidalgo gave el Grito de Dolores, but do we know what the anonymous mass thought when they were hearing it?" said ex-guerrilla Hugo Hiriat, speaking in 1991 at the 20th anniversary of Elena Poniatowska's book, La noche de Tlatelolco (published in English as Massacre in México). The book recorded recollections of the people jailed and persecuted in '68.

This "conversation with ordinary heroes" defied what the government said had not happened. Álvarez Garín tells the packed, screaming university audience attending the commemoration, "Twenty years ago we had the streets."

"In our country, I believe the biggest fight is the fight for the truth."

Los Vientos Dan Permiso

As we walked through Tlatelolco with a murmuring wind, Raúl tells me, "What is the truth behind the heart? What is the thing that creates sympathy for other human beings? It is social relations."

We enjoyed several philosophical platicas like this, while riding in his truck or visiting his mother. "Raúl, you spoke of personal valor with the students," I told him. That night, commemorating the book, he stated, "Personal valor, in this situation that we live, this is required in the battle for truth."

I asked him to explain la valentía of those days. "There are acts of heroism, acts of exceptional valor in respect to the '68 movement. One of the first questions that resulted is the inequality of forces. The concept of inequality is so great, people absolutely unarmed and the use of armed force against defenseless people."

Moments of said valor: Rector Javier Barros Sierra of the Universidad Nacional Autonóma de México flew the flag at half mast July 30 as a sign of mourning following numerous confrontations between students and police, the occupation of school buildings by armed forces and the destruction by army buzooka of a colonial-era door of Prepatoria 1 (1,700 were arrested and up to 400 wounded); the rector heads the first massive protest, with the army tanks in front two blocks away; and the rector resigns at the end of September. "His resignation reveals that (President Gustavo) Díaz Ordaz is responsible for everything."

"If acts are measured by consequences, by actions, one person who confronts the system absolutely alone but with the decision to protect or denounce and raise the denouncements or aspirations of thousands of other people…the acts of personal valor are also acts of heroism. The decision to confront oppression to protect other people."

He recalled how the students were preoccupied with preserving the equipment, the mikes, the mimeograph machines. They would confront the police to regain their confiscated equipment, or they would enter a hospital where the wounded were detained and free them.

After the university and school facilities were closed, riveted with bullets and occupied by police and army forces, the student brigades took over the streets holding "lightening meetings" in buses, parks, street corners. The streets became a battleground. Rocks and molotov cocktails against tear gas and guns. Luis Gonzaléz de Alba, a jailed '68 leader, writes in Los días y los años (The Days and the Years) that Mexico City was under an undeclared, illegal state of siege.

"During this time, there was an historic re-evaluation of Tlatelolco. Everyone was reading the book, Visión de los vencidos (an account of the Conquest from native sources)," recalled Raúl.

Vocational School #5 in the housing complex of Tlatelolco was the historic site where the Tlatelolcas went for final refuge from the Spaniards. There fought a warrior known as El Otomí Tzicaltzin, whose defiance is recounted in the Visión de los vencidos. He became a metaphor for the students. He was feared, and the Spanish could not catch him. He was always changing his clothes, disguising himself in plumes one day, in his white clothes the other. The Spanish could not recognize him. "Voca 5" also was the sight of serious and continuous skirmishes with authorities during '68. "Among the students (from many schools and universities), those students of la Voca 5 saw a lot of combat, confrontations with the police. They would change school sweaters like el otomí," said Raúl.

"In that same exact site, hiding within the Tlatelolcan ruins that the modern excavation had left discovered next to the buildings of the vocational school, el otomí reappears dressed in suit and tie, then in a sweater, a different colored shirt," writes Gonzaléz de Alba. But it is almost certain, he concludes, that those younger students did not know of el otomí's tale or how the Tlatelolcas had used that very spot for refuge.

"It is interesting how history repeats itself," Raúl mused.

He speaks calmly. He gazes into the stones. We gather inside his pauses. We walk in our own silence for a while. In Tlatelolco, there is never really silence. The winds and the birds talk. Los muertos dejan huellas.

Raúl remembers: In the first seconds of the siege, the people screamed "the council, the council." They ran to the steps towards the student leaders, and from the Chihuáhua building they were machine gunned. Thirty people were shot there. And the crowd retreated into a wave of chaos as if sucked in by the muscle of an ocean.

"When the initial shots began, the reaction of the masses was to protect the leaders. It was the multitudes that went toward the Chihuáhua Building (where the leaders were), and that is when they are machine gunned. Dozens and dozens were killed."

Raúl ran towards the church but backtracked towards the Chihuáhua building to look for a friend when he saw another 30 people gunned down by the side of the church. The barrage lasted all of 10 minutes. Then the soldiers rounded up 700 people behind the church. About 2,000 were jailed that evening.

"One month later, November 2, the Day of the Dead, it was important to express the pain of the people," he continues. The plaza was still occupied by police. "The first people who entered the place with candles and flowers were two university students, two compañeras, Maricarmen and Soledad. Then a multitude of people came to make their offerings and the plaza was filled with candles, votives. This is very significant." (On November 2, jailed students performed a simple act. Félix Lucio Hernández Gamundi read the poem "Vamos Patria a Caminar" by the Guatemalan Otto René Castillo.)

Raúl's eyes water. He looks into his coffee. It is our moment of silence. He mentions, too, the march of silence, when up to 400,000 people walked in silent protest–the counter silence–the threat of the army very real and the sound of only their shoes hitting the wet ground.

In the climate of terror that followed the massacre, students were hunted down; some left the country. At the end of October, following the summer Olympics, students from"the Poli"–the nation's poli-technical university–held a meeting. Thirty thousand of them are surrounded by the army and the soldiers shoot into the air in hopes of terrorizing them. But no one budged.

Eight years later in Tlatelolco in 1976, Tlatelolco was still closed. No acts were allowed there, he said. The students from the Poli organized a march of 5,000 students. They were blocked by police. "There were lines of riot police. First there was a generalized silence, then the students started yelling October 2 will not be forgotten. They forced the police to retreat and to open the way. Since then Tlatelolco is open."

On June 10, 1971, Corpus Christi Day–when children dress up like little Juan Diegos and Indian girls and pass out straw burros–another student protest ended in blood when students were fatally attacked by paramilitary forces known as "los halcones." At least 11 killed, perhaps even 30; 50 wounded. That day, student leaders jailed following the massacre had been released.

The year 1968 turned los chavos heroes into men and women who had made a decision. They assumed responsibility for the future.

"It became very clear that there were a series of tasks, moral obligations, determined by the social, economic and political situation. And it was worth dedicating all of our might to overcome the situation with profound convictions that were not intellectualized convictions or utopian acts but strictly from direct experience and direct conviction," said Raúl.

"This experience, we lived it, thousands of youth. It left us with a new attitude toward life. That generation continues to act in all the important moments. It is the same during the earthquake. It is the same in '88. And it will be the same in '94."

The apostles of '68 spread throughout the country like the wind upon a wave as they went on to participate in popular causes and spread that decision among the people. That wave spread to the Chicano movement, both by example and through student leaders who fled to the United States and played key roles in the movement there. Los chavos heroes continue to be in the front lines of the democracy fight they marched for in 1968. Raúl became a PRD assemblyman in 1991. Raúl spent 18 months in jail because of '68 and went on to found the now-defunct, hard-hitting Punto Crítico magazine and Mexico City's popular "moral newspaper," Corre La Voz, which is maintained through donations and distributed in the metro, political acts, and THE STREET.

The old warriors, Campa and Vallejo, were freed in 1970. They said the students freed them.

"Let's walk, why don't we? I like to walk," Raúl tells me. Raúl is a man of undisciplined graying and curly mane. When he enjoys a topic, he roars like thunder announcing a typical Mexico City afternoon rain. He carries a sense of playfulness that, perhaps, has kept cynicism at a distance.

We walk around the plaza and listen to its choir, the church organs, the fountain that is nearly dry, a dog lapping up the water, children hopping and cricket-screaching, and el ku-ku-ru-ku-ru dovesong. The nearby neighborhood of Nonalco is where the railroad workers lived and worked, where the army raided their homes when they stopped the trains to create an independent union. The union is still run by charros.

A child is scolded for falling down.

We walk around and around Tlatelolco. In Spanish, they call this place the plaza of the three cultures–indigenous, Spanish and "modern"–the great mestizaje, or racial mixture, born from the marriage of invasion and slavery. The ruins bear this sign: "In August of 1521, heroically defended by Cuauhtemoc, Tlatelolco fell into the power of Hernán Cortés. It was not triumph nor defeat. It was the painful birth of the mestizo people that is México today."

In Tlatelolco there are three rings of time: Tlatelolco, the ancient ruins; Tlatelolco, the plaza of '68; Tlatelolco, the complex of housing units where the government committed what Mexican intellectual Carlos Monsiváis calls the collective homicide in the 1985 earthquake. They are three. And they are one.

We look at the ancient stones that surround the plaza. Raúl points to the Convento Santiago Tlatelolco, the church where castille roses fell and left an image of the dark virgin on the mantle of the

Indian Juan Diego, after he told the bishop that the Virgen de Guadalupe had appeared to him at the hill of Tepeyac.

The Convento Santiago was built with the stones of Aztec pyramids. Like most churches in México, it was built with the destroyed memory when all of México became a holy inquisition. Pancho Villa also escaped from this convent when it was a prison during the Mexican Revolution. Many people who fought for justice landed inside these prison walls. And it is here the green Bengal lights flashed on October 2, 1968, the signal to at least 2,000 soldiers and police to start the carnage. The church closed its doors. The church did not open its doors.

They didn't hear.

They didn't hear.

How many people were there? "The plaza was full," says Raúl.

Some say 30,000, 80,000, up to 200,000, or really just 10,000. How many? "The plaza was full." How many died?

"The plaza was full," says Raúl.

Hundreds? Thousands? Conjecture.

> ...En los caminos yacen dardos rotos.
> Las casas están destechadas.
> Enrojecidos tienen su muros.
> Gusanos pululan por calles y plazas.
>
> Golpeabamos los muros de adobe
> y es nuestra herencia
> una red de agujeros.
>
> Esto es lo que ha hecho el Dador de la Vida
> allí en Tlatelolco.
>
> – Excerpt from the poem "October 2, 1968" by José Emilio Pacheco (published in Tlatelolco, Mi Amor, edited by Daniel Molina) based on Nahuatl texts describing the Spanish Conquest

The Chihuáhua building no longer has a name posted. Nor was there a sign for October 2 in 1992. Tlatelolco's housing units have names for dates in Mexican history: Febuary 15, September 16, April 2. That October 2, some of the buildings were hung with black bows. "We'd like to put up a sign someday, something simple that says people died here on October 2," Raúl said at the time.

There are long silences as we talk. Raúl drifts away. His voice becomes soft. "That's the way it was." He says October 2 is like any day for him. When he speaks of the people of '68 his eyes say something else.

"When does a spark become big?" I ask.

"How difficult. Who knows? What I do know, no, no, I don't. But it does happen at a given movement. It is a question of time."

I tell him, "Buddhists believe the time for something to occur can be created, that time can be controlled, or better yet, created." We spoke of understanding time, political times, times of legality.

"Well that is what I was going to say. I know how to create the conditions. It is a problem of conscience. That is how things change, when things are no longer considered normal," he responds.

Consciousness: the flow of time. Time: A Buddhist journalist once told me that time is the difference between the action of the cause and the appearance of the effect. In the shadows of Mt. Fuji, where the mist is so low you walk on whiteness, a Buddhist leader said to me, "The past is what is in your mind. What is in your heart is the future. But there is a constant, you, your very life." The time, then, is created by our actions.

"Everyone knows that students were massacred here. They don't know the details, but it is done. It is indelible," says Raúl.

I think of the student who underwent electric shocks to the tongue, the testicles, the anus, as he listened to his mother screaming from torture; of the youth found with a bayonet in the back; of the women in the Tlatelolco apartments who heated water and poured it over the heads of the goons when they attacked the youth and provided heated water for the soda pop bottles converted into molotov cocktails in pre-October 2 confrontations.

"Look," Raúl said, "the most important thing that has changed is the popular political action. If we think in the rhythm of things, the form of taking consciousness, and the role of concrete experience, from, let us say a hundred years ago, the change is immense. What could be done then when elections were stolen? There was no other option but armed resistance."

We spoke of decision, of making up our minds. For every external cause and effect, there is an internal cause, among them being decision and volition. They are both a cause and an effect. We spoke of guerrilla resistance. "Guerrillas, what they have is the decision to fight," Raúl said. And then, there was the PRD's constant fight for legality. "It is an extreme, dynamic confrontation, and strong."

That year, there were 140 deaths (of PRD members), "more than fell in the Berlin Wall," he noted. "But there no longer exists the violence of Tlatelolco. If they did that one more time, this government would end forever. Forever."

A year later, at the 25th anniversary of Tlatelolco, 250 PRD members had been killed. Before tens of thousands of people gathered at the plaza, Raúl remembered the continuum of violence against popular expressions decades prior, and his words prepared the people for more violence.

"We are immensely interested in ensuring that the great conflict of 1994 (presidential elections) does not erupt in violence," Raúl said at the time. "What we want is to tie their hands so that they cannot find conditions to use violence. We are developing everyone's sensibilities so that they can perceive when violence is a threat."

What is the difference between nonviolence and armed warfare? Raúl's consejo: "It is not a question so much of violence or pacific deeds but the meaning that each has.... The message of Gandhi: I'm convinced of the weight of my reason that I can withstand violence. It is absolute weakness confronting absolute force. That moral sentiment can destroy physical force. Moral force is absolute; it is tangible." Tangible, he says, is a school. "It completes hope for Mexicans."

"A Gandhi, a (Salvador) Nava, they only have human valor as their flag or their shield; and they have been able to prevail and will continue to prevail."

What does it take to transform? "Hard work, a lot of hard work."

And like resistance, great intelligence.

Buddhism calls it the mystic function of concentrated mind, determination. Our minds reach out across the universe to create external effects. The life of our mind becomes one with the mind of the universe.

I have pondered why on the face of things we do not always see the effect. But in the law of the universe, the law of cause and effect, at the given time there will be the appearance of things. A cause can be so great it speaks directly to future generations.

The law of cause and effect is like the law of gravity. It is strict and non-judgmental. For too long, we have understood cause and effect from the western scientific mind. The law of the universe is scientific; and it is spiritual, beyond a linear temporal understanding. Cause or effect can take centuries to materialize.

Tlatelolco is more than ruin. It is ritual. It is a place where people imagined, a place with different languages of historical moments. As Molina writes, it is the people condemned to fight always, the people without a face or a name, warriors, gritos, silence, love, the people who have always fought in Tlatelolco. They complete what Native American scholar Greg Cajete calls the "ritual landscape" of the abuelos of long ago.

A poem by Molina:

"No somos nadie, no somos nadie.
Somos la tribu sin rostro y sin nombre
Solo somos los que hemos peleado siempre en Tlatelolco."

There are years when there are marches, in tens of thousands, or scattered like rain, and still they come. There are times when there are no organized rallies, and still they come. I have seen students claim the streets and the walls that day, torch the presidential palace door, and write: October 2 will not be forgotten. I have seen people perform elaborate Aztec rituals in prehispanic clothes and European skin. And I have found great truth in the spontaneous ritual of the students who come with a bunch of carnations and place candles to the four directions–in the rain. And still they come.

Rojo Amanecer

For the 25th anniversary of Tlatelolco, a truth commission was created, calling on the government to disclose national archives on the '68 massacre. It got nowhere because the government wouldn't open its archives. Classified information…in the name of national security. Even the institutional party supported the march that year. Police said 4,000 marched; some news reports said up to 100,000. A silent march also was held. As it meandered past Solidarity Plaza, past the plantóns of teachers and workers who had been in permanent sit-ins for years, a heretofore secret film was playing at a video street festival. It showed three minutes of actual footage from '68: the people being shot like a flock of doves in a gruesome killing gallery. The march walked by as the rat-tat-tat-tat of gun fire scratched the silence.

A day after a quarter century, old men and women in canes gathered in circles on the plaza.

"Here! Here were the army tanks. Until the earthquake, there was a big hole in one of the buildings. They hid the bodies in the basement, and then they took them to a crematory at Campo Militar Número 1; and they were never seen again. And years later, when the earthquake hit, they kept finding bodies."

When the earth was broken to install the modern stele, a mass grave was found. It was believed to be the bones of the warriors who at this very site fought in the Aztec's last defense of their nation. Press coverage was discouraged, and some people believe among those bones of eagle warriors were those of the warriors of '68.

A procession of small children brought flowers to a great stone carved with memory, a stele with the names of the 20 identified dead, built in honor of the 25th anniversary.

"Hi, my name is Tita." Aka Roberta Avendaño.

"Do you know what is here? Who can tell me?"

"Why did you come?"

Stares and whispers.

"Did you know that here people died?"

"Let's see, another. Let's see...you."

"Ok, someone else. How about you?"

"The army killed them," says one boy.

"Do you know why?"

"No."

"Ok, you."

"Do you know of the people who died? Do you know people died here? Do you know why?"

"You there. Speak up!" Tita the teacher still thunders like Tita the student leader of '68.

A child speaks. "They asked for their rights."

Another. "They asked to live in peace and that they respect their rights."

"Do you think for painting signs, for asking the president to give the people what they needed, that we have enough to eat, that we have where to sleep, do you believe it was just that they had us killed…?"

NOOOOOOO!

"So he decided the best way to shut us up was to kill my compañeros. Here, like yesterday, we gathered, many, many, united and strong. There we were, peaceful and happy, like now, listening to what the people said over there. The speakers were there on that floor." She points to the third floor of the Tlatelolco housing unit.

"All of a sudden the police arrived and from here…have you seen fireworks that the church fires? Like this, zoommm. Those lights, unfortunately, were the sign for the soldiers, the agents, to begin shooting at the people gathered, as we are. So they shot at children, women, students, all the people who were here. Many of us got away. Many of us were shot indiscriminately. They gathered the people in the pyramids, their guns aimed at them so they wouldn't move. Then, in the early morning, they began to throw the bodies in buses. Some disappeared; others died…."

"You, with the passing of time, will continue living in this country and it is important for you to study. It is also important for you to understand what the problems are of the country; so when you grow up, you can find solutions to the problems. Always defend her. If you do not understand, then ask. It is no use that the big people talk, and you don't understand.

"Let's see. Who can tell me what they understood of what I said?"

No one answers.

"Because they wanted something."

"For whom?"

"For the rich?"

"No, for the poor."

"And who did this killing?"

THE GOVERNMENT!

"And did they have the right to do this?"

NOOOOO!

The children were told that when people do something grand, the Mexicans erect great stones so that the people will not forget.

"When a Mexican does something important, does something courageous, the others recognize him. That is the meaning of these stones that they call steles," said Molina, whose brother-in-law's name is on the tall, simple slab. "Our country is full of steles of Mexicans who did something for others. It is important that we remember those who have done something for us."

The poet in white, Leopoldo Ayala, tells the procession of little ones holding single carnations, "When this stele was just a hole, for those of you who do not know what was down here, for those of you who do not know where we stand, here, under this monument, here was blood, here were dead, here, here, were defenders, defenders of ideals, defenders of life. More than 500 years ago, here were buried the Tlatelolcas. Here, they found a cemetery that guards the remains. There, with those stones, are buried, with all the glory, those who defended us against Spanish barbarians, who in those times were the gringos of today...."

"Pablo Neruda said they can assassinate the flowers, but they will not be able to finish the spring. The spring arrives, and many flowers come with it."

Molina tells the students that Tlatelolco is the heart of México. The wash of a helicopter drowns his words.

"Tlatelolco is a place very important to us. More than 800 years ago, we didn't live here. In a march that lasted 100 years, we Mexicans arrived here to this valley, full of lakes so pure that there were fish; and we ate the fish from the lakes. A group of Mexicans came to live here on the island of Tlatelolco. This is all our past. Important things have happened here. At this church appeared the Virgen de Guadalupe. This is another sacred root of Tlatelolco because Juan Diego went to the hills and received the roses in Tepeyac. But when the Virgin of Guadalupe really appeared was when he came here and showed his tilma."

"In a while, we'll visit the church. You'll see on top of the mural is a saint, San Cristobal. They thought that if you asked this saint he would save you from violent death. The first mural painted by the Spanish was San Cristobal–in that church. We're going to see the mural and ask St. Cristobal to protect us from violent death. Still, when the army shot at us, the doors of the church were shut on us."

"They didn't hear."

"They didn't hear."

"We are going to ask that the doors of the church be open for everyone."

In Tlatelolco, the victims wrote history, says Monsiváis. They also received the death sentence, he says.

In 1992, revised elementary school books mention Tlatelolco and the '68 movement for the first time. La Jornada published this excerpt: "On October 2, days before the inauguration of the Olympic games, a student meeting was broken up by the army in Tlatelolco. Blood ran and the city trembled. It is not known how many people died." The book was later discontinued.

But people didn't need history books to tell them what happened in Tlatelolco. And they don't need a commission to tell them the truth. It is written in the memory; it is recorded in popular remembrance. They need truth commissions to know that their government can be held accountable. It allows people to trust their government. It is a concrete manifestation of a democracy, an antidote to cynicism. Mahatma (the great soul), who was born 99 years earlier to the day of the student slaughter, led his fight against oppression with nonviolent methods he called Satygraha, literally "holding fast to the truth." It was not a truth often found in history books or official records. It was a truth found in the faith of people to create the conditions for change with their bare lives, the faith that something that doesn't exist can. The deeper the cause, the greater the effect–just as a great tree roots profoundly into the earth. Just as in the Mayan way, the Ceiba tree, the sacred tree of life, roots into the navel of the earth.

When people die, where does the mind go? Where does memory go? Memory, the mind, conscience, we cannot touch them; but we know they exist. Energy can neither be created nor destroyed but only transformed from one form to another. Every thought, word, and action is a cause; it is an energy. And on October 2 the concentrated mind of '68 is put in movement. It appears in the people who emerge to fill the shoes left on the floor of Tlatelolco when the memory makes the heart come back.

Those little children went inside the church at Tlatelolco, the church that shut its doors 25 years before. In a nation where churches are sacred, protesters painted on the walls: "God's beard is stained with the blood of students." And the children asked San Cristobal to answer their prayers.

With them they carry Tlatelolco of all of the times, and still they come to place a candle in the rain.

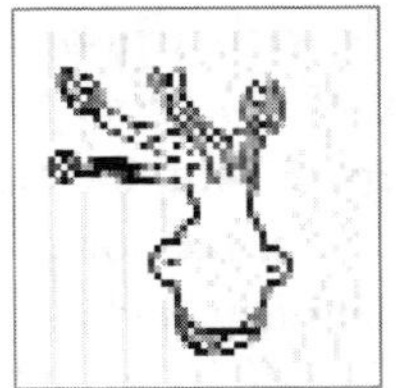

Moments of Truth

The inheritors of '68 continually attempt to force the government to commit truth–truth commissions, legislative commissions. Official complaints of genocide and criminal complaints are ignored and resisted by the attorney general. Their proposition is simple yet profound: that the guilty be tried in the judicial system, that the rule of law be honored.

How many died? Who shot first? Who gave the orders? Who shall stand trial for war crimes, state terror?

Some questions are answered, vindication, corroboration of what is already known. And always, the ommision of truth by the government. Each round of revelations is accompanied by a sense of performance by the few living actors who could clarify what really happened. Former President Luis Echeverría, military generals. A Theatre of the Absurd. U.S. documents declassified in 1994 estimated that some 200 people were killed that day. On the 30th anniversary of Tlatelolco, the legislative '68 Commission obtained declassified national archives, but was stymied in its investigation because few army documents were available.

International media in 1999 reported on the published memoire-like papers of General Marcelino Barragán, which suggests that the order to shoot was issued by President Díaz Ordaz. According to news reports, the general wrote a letter to his son entitled "The Truth for History." The documents were published in a 1999 book, Parte de Guerra. Tlatelolco 1968, by Julio Scherer Garcia and Carlos Monsiváis.

Over the years, other bits of truth emerged–tiny clots of tissue shed from memory's womb. La Jornada reports: There was another paramilitary unit of snipers (apart from the Olympia Battalion) that provoked the crowd, shooting even at the army from buildings surrounding the plaza. The massacre was preceded by a military order. For years, historians have agreed that the government orchestrated the violence to justify generalized repression of protestors, but for the first time more precise details were confirmed with documents from the military. Proof of lies, proof is the popular memory.

In 2001, México's National Human Rights Commission issued a 3,000-page report that concluded 275 of 530 people who were reported as disappeared in the dirty war that followed Tlatelolco were actually at the hands of government entities.

Government photos of Tlatelolco sent anonymously to Proceso magazine show that there really were men in white gloves or white handkerchiefs tied to their wrists. Photos of detained men stripped to their calzones. Email Proceso if you recognize anyone, the magazine exhorts.

Proceso magazine published declassified U.S. documents in January 2002 that linked Echeverría to the dirty war via telegrams from the U.S. consul in Guadalajara, relaying a promise from his foreign secretary that "as long as he (Echeverría) is president, the United States doesn't need to fear any communist threats from the southern flank."

Another document dated January 1974 stated the Mexican government had informed all authorities that they were "authorized" to ignore due process of law in dealing with the "terrorists." In other declassified documents, the January 27, 2002, Proceso reported that several police sent by the commander of the paramilitary "Halcones" were trained in Washington D.C. under an agreement with the Nixon administration.

Raúl has led the fight to criminally charge ex-President Echeverria with genocide and homicide, particularly for the Corpus Christi Day carnage.

In November 2002, a mechanic with the Mexican Air Force testifies before a military court that some 200 campesinos wrapped in bags were dumped during 33 flights over the Pacific Ocean from 1975-1979; he implicates two military generals.

In response to the human rights report, President Vicente Fox appointed a special prosecutor for the disappeared. Later, he released the declassified documents of the national archives, but one general said they were only "confetti." The special prosecutor was greeted with skepticism by the families of the disappeared. They refuse reparations. "A son has no price."

El sueno llega dentro la humedad de estas palabras. While writing this, I had a dream. I saw rows and rows of stones sitting upright, as on a monument, a stele of their footprints. The dead do leave tracks.

La Sangre de Tlatelolco

Part 2
Full Moon

Meaning Is Found. Completion.

Doña Guille

Constellation de las Mujeres:

Tonantzin - The mothers of the disappeared become the mothers of Mexican democracy.

Coyolxauhqui - Women in the urban land movement redefine the role of women in social change.

Tlazoteotl - The fearless Zapotecas and my testimonio explore healing from violence through life's cleansing, regenerative powers.

La madre

La madre de familia: tiene hijos, los amamanta.
Su corazón es bueno, vigilante,
diligente, cava la tierra,
tiene ánimo, vigila.
Con sus manos y su corazón se afana,
educa a sus hijos,
se ocupa de todos, a todos atiende.

Cuida de los más pequeños.
A todos sirve,
se afana por todos, nada descuida,
conserva lo que tiene,
no reposa.

From Códice Matritense de la Real Academia, as cited in
Toltecayotl by Miguel León-Portilla

The 1968 massacre at Tlatelolco radicalized many youth. Some turned to armed struggle, while others pursued social change through nonviolent movements throughout the country. But in response to the guerrilla activity, the government repressed numerous movements and activists; and many were disappeared. The Mothers of the Disappeared, formally known as Eureka, were one of the first groups who emerged in the 1970's to challenge the institutionalized terror and culture of impunity.

Chapter 4: Madres–Tonantzin Coatlique

In the sorrowful mystery of the mothers of the disappeared hay un rosario de testimonios.

The rosary of testimonies, the first sorrowful mystery: Cuando Lucio Cabañas se lanzó de guerrillero, los días se pusieron gruesos aún para gente acostumbrada a no comer, a no rendirse y a no estar agachada....

The name Cabañas became a death sentence in the sierra of Guerrero. And there were a lot of primos and compadres by the last name of Cabañas. There was a lot of corn that year. Había harta milpa, harta milpa había. Aquí todo se da quien trabaja.

The army threatened to burn the fields and orchards, and many were. No one could find people to work the land that was untouched. El susto had appeared. Los guachos–the army–came in the thousands, up to 20,000, and put roads where there were none to catch the guerrillas. They installed telephones, built clinics, and opened grocery stores. In what became known as "operación limpieza," the army starved the people to starve the guerrillas. Even women's breasts were searched for money. Residents resorted to smuggling bread and tortillas inside dirty diapers. And the children "mamaron la leche del sufrimiento," they suckled the suffering in their mothers' milk. And the Doñas say that is when el susto came, and it never left the children. El susto. Fright. Trauma, the bad spirit of fear, the unsettled spirit of the dead, or perhaps, the disappeared.

You hear all of the Doñas speak of how el susto made their families ill, how they lost their souls. How they got sick because of el susto and so much coraje, rage, and shocks to the soul. Whether in the costa chica or the costa grande in Guerrero, whether in Sinaloa or el D.F., the susto that Mexicans still live with had taken hold. And no spoons of sugar or limpias could cure it. Nor all the velas. When the

Las Madres de los Desaparecidos

people are ill, the land will be ill. Years later, they found corpses of children in the fields. The dogs would bark when they saw the guachos. They saw death in their eyes.

The campesinos were easy cover for Cabañas, the former school teacher who founded the guerrilla movement "la Brigada Campesina de Ajusticiamento del Partido de los Pobres" following a 1967 confrontation at a school over teachers and uniform fees that ended in a gun battle between government forces and campesinos. Lucio was forced to the mountains, and for a few years, his guerrilla movement operated in the mountains at the same time as that of Genaro Vázquez Rojas and the Asociación Cívica Nacional Revolucionaria. They were forced into illegality after the army shot peaceful protestors in 1960 and again in 1962. Vázquez was killed in 1972; Lucio died December 2, 1974–several days before his 36th birthday. It was one of his own men, El Chabelo, who betrayed him, said Doña Margarita. The traitor Chabelo was allowed to carry a gun at all times, in return.

"¡Están matando al pueblo!" ¡Contestamos con la guerra!
"¡Venguemos la sangre de nuestros compañeros campesinos!"
– A final November 1974 communique from the mountains (Published in Luis Cabañas, el guerrillero sin esperanza by Luis Suárez.)

In 1974, Lucio kidnapped then-Senator Rubén Figueroa, who later became governor of Guerrero (and whose son was governor of Guerrero during the massacre of campesinos and Indios in 1995). Elena Poniatowska writes that his kidnapping led to the most reports of disappeared–255 out of more than 500. When Lucio was negotiating with Figueroa for the freedom of political prisoners, he estimated there were 400 in Guerrero alone. "…porque cuando dicen vamos a perseguir a Lucio no vienen a fregarme a mí, vienen a fregar al pueblo," Lucio said to Figueroa in tape-recorded conversations by the guerrilla. Some say the disappeared numbered close to a thousand. There are no numbers for the dead and wounded.

Even after Cabañas was ambushed in December of 1974, los guachos were determined to destroy and disappear the resistance. And anyone who would not conform themselves con atolito con el dedo. Boys were killed and disappeared for carrying a chicken, a pig, a bag of rice. To have corn was revolutionary.

Los Apagones en el Alma

Years later in 1992, the Doñas have come down from the mountains–though it is the time of corn–to speak to me. I listen to "the stories in their wrinkles"–like Cecilia Rodríguez says–as a caldo of beans stew in the kitchen and honey goes bad on the shelves. They sit like las sierras madres.

Doña Amada's great uncle was accused of taking a liter of milk and a kilo of meat to Lucio and her brother was disappeared at age 14 while carrying a bag of bread. "Ya, ya, ya no llores."

Doña Chela went to a bruja who said her disappeared son was dead, but still she prays, "God, only you know."

Doña Cerrita, "Yo ya no rezo."

Doña Téodora, "Yo sí rezo."

Doña Humberta, que saltó llanto, "Yo me rezo llorando."

Doña Margarita, piedra que no llora, "Not even tears do I have. I have to use artificial tears. Se acabó las lágrimas de tanto llorar." But she never cried in front of the government.

Even as they speak, there is a tension among the Doñas. They speak of the repression as if it was in the here and now. There is still fear, especially of the bandits. Some people say the bandits no longer have a rebellion to keep them busy. But still, some of the mothers are afraid. "Why are you afraid?" asked Doña Margarita. "If the guachos didn't hurt us, why be afraid now?"

Why, some men were freed from so many complaints de tantas mujeres. "Acuerdate. Acuerdate bien."

I look for the faces of the mothers who held the first hunger strike in 1978 in Mexico City, which marked the first public action by the loved ones of the disappeared. I looked for the viejita who sold her marranita to go. There were eight Doñas sitting with me that day. They are the council of elders, the council of listeners from el pueblo de Guerrero. They speak for the Doñas who no longer live, who died young or of hunger, que ya no aguantaban la tortura moral, the moral torture of the soul. Los toques al alma. They speak for the ones who died with hope of seeing their sons. Doña Elisa would say it didn't matter if she went hungry, if she knew of her son's whereabouts.

"We are the ones made of strong wood," Doña Margarita says.

Many say they know their husband, their son, their brother is still alive because they sent a letter or two from prison hidden in the frames of santos. Most of the letters stopped coming after the 1970's. "¿Dónde está mi papelito?" They show tattered letters, worn and shiny from being opened and reopened by hands, lavados en sudor, tierra y lágrimas.

Letter 1: This is to inform you that I find myself detained in el Campo Militar Número 1. But I am completely fine. 30 August – Miguel Nájera Nava

Letter 2: Don Miguel, I would like you to do me a favor and send me only two things, two batteries and Colgate toothpaste, the biggest tube you can find. If possible, send it to me with this boy tomorrow.

Margarita Cabañas shows me five letters from her husband Miguel. She says she knows he's alive because someone said they were with him in prison. Letter Number 1 was published in the local newspaper after the military denied that he was in custody.

Miguel sent letters, naming people who were disappeared and among the living in Campo Militar Número 1. He also wrote her, reminding Margarita that fulano owed their store money for 100 cans of coffee. And did the cow have her calf? "Can you send me newspapers with good news?" And why have you not sent the things I asked for?

Sorrowful Mystery Number 2

The message came in threes. Tres tepalcates, trastes de loza, three plates. Three knots in the napkin. Three utensils. A plate broken in three.

"Señor, me faltan tres." Lord, three are missing. "Estos cabrones must have three outside." That's how Luciano Rentería Estrada knew that three political prisoners had been taken from a Guadalajara jail in 1977, in repercussion for a political kidnapping. "We want to know who was taken. We know three are missing," he and a grassroots committee told the warden.

He had told Armando, his son, to send messages if he was in trouble. His son was a member of la Liga 23. At one point, he saved his son as he was being placed into a vehicle and taken to a place he likely would not have returned from. When Don Luciano's son fell, his compa told him, "If we leave them alone, they'll disappear them."

So the family members of political prisoners staged a march, many marches, to the house of the governor, to the penitentiary, to prohibited plazas. Guns were shot in the air to scare them away, and guns were pointed at them as they marched to the prison. At one point, an attorney supporting the protesters asked the women if they wanted to go. ¡Sí! "Bien aventadas todas."

The attorney marched with the women and children. People were so afraid of their actions that taxis refused to go near the march. Children marched in the back with phone numbers to call in case there was violence. When a functionary told the group that he knew nothing of the three missing prisoners, Doña Felicita grabbed him by the collar and said, "¿Cómo, hijo de la chingada, qúe no sabes nada?" Era una señora fuertotota. She was a strong woman. "Se encabronaron las mujeres." They saw their sons two hours later, and the missing three resurfaced.

The parents won the prisoners the right to bathe, to get some sun and to eat food without maggots. Later came rock concerts, mariachi and conjugal visits. They won a street block for protests. Moral victories. And when chacales, government-backed prisoners, were given bombs to attack the political prisoners, the general prison population came to their defense, having witnessed their tortures in a room among the common prisoners. No guerrillas died, but 20 chacales did on October 10, 1977. They were going to make it look as if the guerrillas had planned the attack, but the mothers visiting the jails were warned. They received a letter saying that following the visit with a functionary "the combat will begin."

"The dog will finish the robbers." In other words, the chacales would finish the guerrillas and frame them as the instigators of the attack.

On May 17, 1978, Don Luciano was part of a group who met with President José López-Portillo. He told them, "We needed to create a force. The counterinsurgency is forcing us to repress them. We need a counter force to confront it."

Says Don Luciano's son, Armando, "The government needed the excuse to cleanse the political community."

Don Luciano was often followed home. He would hear knocks at the door and find notes saying, "viceras de uno" (a prisoner's organs) or "so-and-so is no longer in the penitentiary." When some of the political prisoners escaped, the mothers, wives, girlfriends and sisters were detained and submerged in water, recalled Don Luciano. The baby daughter of the political prisoner "Guaymas" was not fed for a day-and-a half.

They won espacios, the spaces where democracy is created, sitios of discontent, to borrow from Chicana scholar Emma Pérez, such as the plaza near the University of Guadalajara, for hunger strikes and plantones that lasted three years. Don Luciano's son was released, arrested again, and finally won amnesty after spending six years in jail, instead of fifteen. "We broke the impunity," he said.

Says Don Luciano, "All the political prisoners are our sons."

Sorrowful Mystery Number 3

Doña Licha's son Eduardo had been missing for about a month. He was disappeared. She went to the jails. She went to the hospitals, to the army facilities. "Yo ando buscando a mi hijo," she would tell them. No one knew anything. She retained an attorney. She received word her son was in a clandestine jail. "Vaya usted y hable con la señora Rosario. Se llama Rosario de Ibarra."

Doña Licha lived in a sheltered world. No sabía de nada. She did not even know how to get to the Zócalo to the first huelga at the cathedral in Mexico City. When she did arrive, she still had the bolsita of clothes she was carrying for her son. Doña Rosario said she would take the case as if it were her own. Doña Licha stayed the day. That was 1978, and she has been con la Doña Lucha ever since. To this day, her husband blames her for demanding her children's freedom. "No he dejado de buscar.... Aunque duele, aunque me duele."

Jesús Piedra Ibarra took the family car to the store to buy some cheese and a bottle of cooking oil. Rosario Ibarra de Piedra never saw her son again. Police called her and told her he had been in an accident. When she arrived at the police station, she saw the family car with the cheese, the bottle of oil, and four bullet holes. Her son was accused of being one of two guerrillas who were in a shootout with police. But he escaped. Her home was searched, and posters of Zapata and Che were taken as proof of guerrilla involvement. Her husband, a well-known doctor, was detained and tortured. They damaged his spine and dunked him in urine. When the media reported his hospitalization, Jesús called to see how his father was. It was the first news of Jesús since he went into hiding four months before. Later, Rosario started to receive phone calls. "Wrong number." She knew it was Jesús. But one day the men watching her house disappeared. She knew this was bad news. A few days later, the press reported that Jesús had been detained April 30, 1975. He was reportedly tortured and transferred to Campo Militar Número 1 in Mexico City. Rosario immediately went to México, eventually renting an apartment in her still-unsuccessful search for her son. It is decorated with the names and faces of the disappeared.

So began the sorrowful mystery of Doña Rosario and her son Jesús. She intoned the same words of women all over México, many who died with this prayer on their lips. "Quiero saber de mi hijo." I want to know of my son.

Doña Rosario knew that there had to be other mothers like her, and she started placing ads in the national newspapers. On August 28, 1978, more than 80 women went on a hunger strike in front of the cathedral at the Zócalo in what would become the first unified act of a movement for the disappeared, the persecuted, and political prisoners. Among them were Doña Margarita, Doña Licha, Doña Guille, and Doña Celia. The mothers of the disappeared, as they are informally known (though there were fathers, brothers, sisters, wives, and compañeras), shocked the "decent people" of México. In fact, they were outraged that algunas locas were so atrevidas. No se deben meter en asuntos no suyas como encimosas.

"Mujeres viejas," they called them.

"¡Mujeres metiches!"

"Ay vienen las mitoteras."

"¡Pinche viejas!"

They were women who enlisted the help of others to read government documents that spoke of their loved ones, women no muy barrigonas ni gordis because they were too poor, worried too much, and lived too hard. Mujeres who in many instances were padre y madre to the disappeared.

As a result of the one-week hunger strike, 1,500 political prisoners were given amnesty. Numerous orders of apprehension were canceled and exiles who fled the persecution following the '68 massacre were allowed to return home. To the Doñas, this could not have happened without some degree of political reform.

But few among them were the disappeared of these mothers. The mothers continued to hold hunger strikes all over the country–in Monterrey, Sinaloa, Chilpancingo, Acapulco (up to 300 women starving "like cows without food"). They were tear-gassed, "with only a little rag to protect them." They walked down el Paseo de la Reforma in Mexico City, blindfolded and in chains. They made mandas to the shrine at Tepeyac on December 12 (the feast day of the Virgin of Guadalupe and Lucio's birthday), near milagros for sale, icons of the virgin in crystal ball lights, and creyentes who walk on their knees for 42 miles as an offering and manda to the insurgent Mary. The mothers celebrate this day because the Virgin, like them, was a persecuted mother whose son was tortured and crucified as a rebel.

When the mothers assumed this social responsibility for their loved ones, they assumed it for all Mexicans. The struggle became a manda for life, which did not end after offering the pain of their knees, their bones, the tiredness of leaving their life in the struggle, ni los huecos en los corazones. This is how female energy was released inside México. "Los actos nos desahogan," they would say. The energy of sadness and loss transformed into strength, into dignity. It willed itself hope, the greatest prayer.

Women are good at moving energy. Tonantzin–Our Venerable Mother Earth–she has so many faces. Coatlique: la madre tierra, the energy that accumulates inside the earth. Tlazolteotl: feminine healing energy that recycles what is no longer useful, works on all of life. We women do Tonantzin's work.

The actos became the graves, public rituals of grieving, ofrendas; the streets an altar, a space made sacred by their lives. This is the nature of life. Nuestra madrecita absorbs our wastes, takes our ills, and makes a nice, rich compost that is transformed into life again. She regenerates herself. She is the regenerative power of life.

The mothers sent telegrams. "Señor Presidente: Why don't you free the people? We want them the way they are, however they are."

President López-Portillo granted the amnesty. President Salinas de Gortari escaped out another door rather than face them. He would become very angry when the madres would shout at him that "freedom has been disappeared." President Salinas on the 10th of May–Mexican

Mother's Day–"nos dieron en la torre." When one of Salinas' children was ill, the mother's sent a telegram. "Your pain is the pain of the country. What has happened? Have you given us the kiss of Judas?"

Then, on Mexican Mother's Day in 1991, the mothers tried to deliver a card to the First Lady at los Pinos.

> Señora Cecilia Occelli de Salinas,
>
> We have always considered that the solution to the painful problem of the disappeared Mexican políticos is in the hands of the president of the republic. In actuality, it is in those hands of your husband for being the universal inheritor of the acts of all the functionaries of his government, and because, in this presidential term, the practice continues of forced disappearance of people, and because he gave his word to the madres de Eureka (the name of their organization) on April 17, 1990, the day he granted us an audience.
>
> Aside from that, we consider that, in this presidentialist system as is México's, he is the only person with sufficient power to order that this great injustice be corrected. Nevertheless, we, with the spirit engraved from the pain y con la sensibilidad a flor de piel, never put aside the human factor in our struggle. As such, this Mother's Day 1991, after wishing that you pass it filled with happiness at the side of your husband, (we hope you) help incline your husband toward being disposed to a favorable response to our demand so that we, too, will have the happiness of returning to embrace our sons and daughters.
>
> –Signed with 15 signatures

About 50 police and soldiers roughed them up, including the crippled compa Guaymas, aka Mario Alvaro Cartagena López. He took seven bullets in a confrontation between la Liga and armed forces in Jalisco, was disappeared, tortured, and now uses a wheelchair and drives a taxi. "Yo soy compa de los desaparecidos." (I'm a compa of the disappeared.) After the shootout, he did not receive medical attention for days. When he did, he was given a colostomy.

–Yo era guey combate, a tachero, a good military man.

But it was his mother, who fought for him "como una perra," one of the mothers who initially didn't want to get in trouble and who helped gain his release. So after he was released from prison as part of the amnesty, he supported the mothers. His compas asked him, "Oye, compa Mario, why are you with that señora media burguesota, that bourgeouis lady?"

"I am alive because of Doña Rosario," says el Guaymas. "Esa vieja es vieja heróica." That old lady is a heroic old lady.

"The Doñas are more brave than the men. They gave us the example of tenacity."

And the Triqui Indians saved their cadavers in petates for the mothers to show how they had been massacred in violence.

Mexican human rights activist Mariclaire Acosta, then president of the non-governmental Mexican Commission of Defense and Promotion of Human Rights when I interviewed her in 1991, says the mothers took away the fear to speak out after the government repression following '68. Every Mexican Mother's Day, they are remembered for challenging the torture and illegal apprehensions of thousands of Mexicans in the 70s and 80s–and even still today. They are the santa madre, the mother courage, of the culture of human rights still nascent in México. Santas por ser valientes. While often it is said they helped foster justice, I believe what they really engendered was the healing of México by publicly articulating pain and truth. Trauma undermines truth. Yet once we acknowledge trauma, it can become the deepest truth of oppression. Democracy, human rights, when they transpire, are really a healing of the structures of human relations. Most healing continues for a lifetime.

María Jiménez, a respected human rights activist in the United States, says the mothers embodied how community becomes family and essential to all social change. "Their reproductive and nurturing roles were transformed from the private to the public, the biological to the political," she told a women's conference sponsored by the Foundation for a Compassionate Society in 1996.

"They did so, not to assert their prominence in the male-power structure, but to assert their moral rights as lifegivers, as mothers," she said in a speech later published as part of the Feminist Family Values Forum.

"To my mind, this movement of the Mothers of the Disappeared was the forerunner of all modern movements seeking democracy throughout Latin America. More significantly, it is this movement that redefined for me the essence of the women's movement. While this is the common vision for women throughout Latin

America, for me, a Mexican American living in the United States, this was a new perspective: this courageous campaign against totalitarianism broadened my vision of how women could achieve equality."

There are reportedly close to 100,000 disappeared in Latin America. Doña Rosario says that's why the mothers fought, so that México would not become another Argentina or Guatemala. She once told me that Mexicans take pride in el aguante de Cuauhtemoc, his ability to take the torture of the Spaniards. But, she says, we don't have to get our feet burned like him.

Doña Rosario at an acto in 1991: "We have been in a long and difficult struggle for many years against a powerful enemy who is false, is a hypocrite, and is vengeful, as is Salinas de Gortari. Many say that Salinas de Gortari was just a young student when this occurred. But Salinas de Gortari is the heir of the government, the repository of public power. He is responsible for all the disappeared and political prisoners of his presidential term and of terms before because, just as he is the inheritor of the political machinery as the supposed maximum representative of the government and the army, just as he inherited the money, he also inherited the clandestine prisons and the police."

"Don't stay holed up in your homes until your son is taken or killed or you suffer the absence of a loved one. Join us. Join us in the struggle so that not one more person will be disappeared."

"Vivos los llevaron. Vivos los queremos." They were taken alive. Alive is how we want them.

Descansos, Descancio

The road of the disappeared begins in Acapulco and wends its way through un reino del palmar, past stands that sell agua de coco. In Atoyac de Alvarez, known for its coffee, we continue on the road of the disappeared in a pesero to the mountain pueblo of San Vicente de Benítez to meet with Doña Margarita. The villages of el Paraíso and el Porvenir are up the way, places with names of cynical metaphors. El Paraíso (Paradise) is where Lucio was born. It became a nerve of the guerrillas when war came to paradise and the campesinada paid for it. It occurs to me that we are on a road that did not exist before, a road bloodied with the wounds of campesinos when the army hunted the guerrillas. All along this road, the animas of the disappeared travel, as the Doñas say, in purgatory. The road is hobbled with rocks. When it rains, most buses can't get through. Bare-chested old men con sombreros de paja mount the bus, sitting like old knives. The people are the brown mix of coffee and tamarindo. All around is the green light of wet hills, verdura, the vapors of the hierba, the lush plants that cloaked, "los que andaban por el monte." And you can hear the murmullo of the mountains fecund with struggle, murmuring, "aquí el gobierno los chingó."

These are the mountains "de tantas madres de miserables,"–the guerrilla Mariano (aka Lucio de abajo) in Ejercicio de Guerrillero by Carlos Bonilla Macharro.

As I smell the land, hear the whoosh of birds I have never seen before, I think I shall never see Acapulco like a tourist dancing in a neon seashell. In Acapulco, I shall remember that the women went hungry; that people were disappeared while tourists made love on their honeymoon; that in the mountains a 10-year-old niece of Lucio's was raped; that a señorita was raped shortly before her wedding; and that some muchachos were massacred at a ball court. La matanza en la cancha, the Doñas called it. I shall remember the people of the mountains, whose faces carry the dead, their stride weighted with the disappeared. It is like other places in México.

At the Bellas Artes, I see people marching and running for safety. At a metro stop, I see flowers for the dead of the 1985 earthquake. At the Zócalo, I see tent cities and the smile of Doña Licha with edges that disappear into sadness. Perhaps descansos, roadside shrines and altars where people have died in public spaces, should be placed on the road of the disappeared to put their spirits to rest. But the shrines of flowers incarnadas would compromise the hope. The dead come back as flowers, as Roque Dalton wrote, "only their names die."

"Mientras hay vida, hay esperanza," says Doña Margarita.

When Doña Margarita went to speak to President Echeverría, a functionary asked her why her husband was arrested. "Because I am the prima of a guerrilla, but he had nothing to do with the guerrilla's people. We are business people. (We were the only ones who sold sausage. We had cold cuts.) But not for cowardice will I deny my last name. I am the daughter of a Zapatista colonel in the Mexican revolution. Lucio's grandfather was a Zapatista general."

When the guachos came looking for Miguel, Margarita was holding her children with either hand. They threw Margarita against the wall and started beating her. Margarita called it their "manda de cobarde," coward's rule. Her husband had been a soldier.

"Hmmgh. They are brave with you, but they are cowards with the guerrillas. They killed chamaquitos in the back at the ball court," interjects Doña Chela.

"Do not kill him like a child," Margarita pleaded. "Take me; I am a Cabañas." That day, April 25, 1973, the guachos destroyed the store, taking all the medicine, everything of value, her wedding ring–de oro bueno. Someone left an old pair of guaraches for new ones. About a year later, they took her 11-month-old daughter, Berenice. Margarita went looking for her daughter. There were army tanks all the way up the mountains. "Todo eso allá estaba lleno de verde." Soldiers later returned Berenice, and she would often cry when people came near her. Cry and cry. Berenice, at age 12, shot herself twice with a .22 gun; but she survived and went on to college.

Other children tried to throw themselves off rooftops, and some still believe they are being followed by the guachos. "Perhaps some day the message will come. That is what I ask of my God, that he help them like the souls in purgatory without hope," says Doña Chela. ¡Ay, Señora! lament the Doñas.

Many mothers here have lost hope. And some turned PRIistas. Some of the disappeared were released and now work for the government. The Doñas turn rabid about this, but then they remember the others who were set free. One boy, who was disappeared at age three, reappeared when he was 18 years old.

"I believe the people have forgotten. Our people don't light them candles," says Doña Margarita.

– Hay hueveros de guachos, the offspring of the guachos, that I have run off my orchards.

Her hope for Miguel's return grows distant. "Todo de él ya se cabó. We're selling all the valuables." The property–an ejido of coffee and corn–the store, and the house were worth seven million pesos; now it's on the block for four million pesos. "Everything in the main house is destroyed, the refrigerator, the stove." She sold the milpa. She sold the cows. She is morena and speaks brusquely, and she looks older than she is. "I'm 55 and look at me."

"I closed myself off," says Margarita. "I stopped everything. And that is bad. I lost my happiness. I only spent my life working." She stopped going to family reunions and praying to the santos. Her only diversion was a telenovela from Chile, "Mis días."

Miguel's mother refuses to move from the house he gave her, though the doors are falling down.

"¿Qué tuvo la vaquita?" Miguel asked in one letter. Margarita never sold that calf in memory of him.

Elena Poniatowska, in her chronicle on social change in México, Fuerte es el Silencio, said Rosario gave México a social conscience.

Doña Rosario "arde," writes Poniatowska in her chronicle of the first hunger strike. She burns all night like a votive candle, and she wears the incense of struggle. Subcomandante Marcos calls her the mother of Mexican democracy. ("We cannot allow them to assassinate hope again," Doña Rosario tells the multitudes at the Zócalo in March 1995.)

When Rosario speaks, I hear raspas in her voice, which is sweet and raspy like a snow cone. She seems to be always hoarse from so much passion, from a mother's obsession, and from so many actos. It was the women around her, amoratadas y amoladas, whom I sought to know. Zapata had his army of the south; Villa had his dorados. All revolutions have Adelitas, the public heroes, and el pueblo heroico. They remind me of a passage from Andre Malraux's Anti-Memoires in which he quotes Nehru in his defense at the Gorakpur trial on November 3, 1940: "It is not me you are seeking to judge and condemn, but the hundreds of millions of my people, and that is a heavy task, even for a proud empire."

So I set out to walk the sacred circle surrounding Doña Rosario, women whose hearts had been parted like watermelon smashed open on the ground, women que no pueden hablar muy bien, pero que sí tienen educación. Tener educación, to be educated, does not mean schooling per se but to dignify one's life, to have honor. This is what Eduardo Galeano calls the thread of history. "The history of America, the true, betrayed history of America is a story of endless dignity," writes Galeano in We Say No. When the people do fight for dignity, he says, they are treated as delinquentes.

Sorrowful Mystery Number 4, Doña Celia

I looked for Doña Celia Piedra de Nájera of the huelga at the cathedral but did not find her. In 1978, Doña Celia mobilized many of the women in the mountains for the hunger strike. Doña Rosario had written to her because they had the same last name, and she had heard of the work they were doing there since 1975. The women thought, perhaps, they were distant cousins. She helped organize support for the disappeared and persecuted in Guerrero. Celia felt stronger then. The Celia I found had dried up at the root inside, part of her had disappeared along with the hope of finding her husband Jacob. Jacob Nájera was detained September 2, 1974.

I asked her what happened to the Doña with the pig. "¿O, la señora de la marranita? She sold her pig for 60 pesos. 'It's all I have.' She gets to Acapulco and is robbed of 50,000 pesos. Era una mujer de inocencia. 'Don't worry, I'll pay you for it,' I told her. 'You stay here and I'll go for you.' De la sierra era la senora. Tenia muchos deseos. She really wanted to go. She thought that if she didn't go they wouldn't free her son."

Jacob was an elementary school teacher, a good one, de los buenos, in San Jerónimo de Júarez, where he met Celia. He was involved in the Movimiento Revolucionario del Magisterio, headed by Othón Salazar. He knew Lucio and introduced Celia to him. Lucio went to their wedding. Celia recalled that Lucio used to say, "de algo se tiene que morir." We all must die of something. In 1965, seven years prior to launching the guerrilla movement, Lucio was forced, for political reasons, to go to another school in the state of Durango. Celia and Jacob never saw him again. But when Lucio's guerrilla detained Rubén Figueroa for a ransom in 1974, the ramifications would be felt for years; and they would destroy Jacob and Celia's life together. At that time, Jacob and his family were on summer vacation at the family home in Chilpancingo. In July and August, two relatives came to tell Jacob that "they" were looking for him, strangers who were not from their pueblo, plain clothes officers. Again a relative came, "They continue to ask for you. I don't think you should come back." Jacob said he had no reason to stay away.

When Jacob returned from summer vacation, his wife noticed a strange man watching them from behind a newspaper. She noticed a young man following them, 15 paces behind. Two or three days after returning to the village, she noticed a car. In their village there weren't many cars. At night, she awoke to a car. Jacob told her to go back to sleep, that she was worrying about nothing.

"Que eran cosas mías."

"Ay, duermete." Oh, go to sleep.

Even the school principal advised Jacob not to go back to school. Celia told Jacob, "I don't want you to go. I am afraid."

"El que nada debe, nada teme," he told her. He who owes nothing, fears nothing. I'm going.

The next day on the way home, Celia noticed a strange car, a black Galloxie. When Celia returned home, she found the children crying, "They took Daddy."

On the first day of school, Jacob was resting in his hammock in the afternoon before he entered his second job at a private school, when a group of armed men arrived asking for him. He asked if they had an apprehension order. "Here, there are no orders of apprehension," they told him. "These are our orders," they said, touching their guns. Jacob tried to resist, but they threatened to hurt his family.

Celia says he was taken by judicial police, un tal Galeana. Someone told her that Jacob was arrested and handed over to "la güera de dios," the Virgin Mary.

In Carlos Bonilla Macharro's account of his role as negotiator in Figueroa's release, Ejercicio de Guerrillero, he mentions visiting Jacob in search of Lucio. "You know I feel the poverty of our state in my heart and even invite to my table los zancas de Lucio when they look for me or pass by here. But I have never been to the mountains. I am not afraid, but I do have my children.... I don't know, I repeat, where he could be in the sierra," Bonilla Macharro quotes Jacob as saying.

His brother Andrés believes this is proof that Jacob was taken for political reasons.

Celia says someone identified Jacob, "as the teacher of a cousin," in Campo Militar. "We never heard of Jacob's fate since then," says Andrés. Jamas. Never. Andrés' family would not let him look for Jacob. There were cases where brothers looking for their fathers or brothers were disappeared themselves. There were rumors he was taken to a clandestine prison in Acapulco. There were also rumors he was thrown from a helicopter into the ocean, with lead and rocks tied to him. "Rumors. Only rumors," says Andrés.

The family has documents in which Andrés and Doña Celia ask for the whereabouts of Jacob. "Les Ruego"–I implore you–for information on him, writes Celia. The documents were sent to the state attorney general, the national attorney general, and Figueroa, who was governor by then.

In the 1979 government report on the status of the disappeared, the government–que no sabia nada–stated that Jacob had died in a confrontation with the army during the September 8, 1974 liberation of Figueroa–six days after Jacob was detained. The Doñas say they know of a señora, Doña Maria, whose husband was killed in front of her. She has two sons who are living with her, though "the book of the government" says they are dead. Sometimes, the only proof that remains is the memory of the loved ones.

Jacob was always helping the people, says Celia, helping them get financing for their crops. He was always reading a book. Celia only finished elementary school. "I'm going to explain this to you," Jacob would tell her.

"I burned it out of fear, fear for my son," she says. Her youngest son looks like Jacob. She says her sons are closed to politics. Andrés says she keeps them away from it so she won't have to go through this again. She sits in a rocking chair with her eyes full of la dulsura–the sweetness–of the land, mangos, bananas, agua de coco. She starts to cry. "The hope has gone cold," Andrés says to me discreetly. "When someone dies," said Doña Celia, "you know you will never see them again. But this is a martyrdom."

When she struggled, she said, it was "un aliento, un consuelo."

"Hoy me siento torpe, muy torpe (Now, I feel very dazed)," she says. "I no longer go out. I no longer participate in anything. I ask God why is this happening if I am a believer?"

Poniatowska has written that Rosario "has made an act of life from her suffering, un acto que nos enaltece, a loving act of giving of herself to others, an act of creation." She writes that regardless of the outcome, the struggle had ennobled the mothers of the disappeared. Watching Doña Celia cry, I realized she had created something valuable and concrete from her immense grief and suffering. She had become a fire unleashed by confronting the powers that inflicted this pain. But when she stopped fighting, when she changed how she responded to the suffering, that hope and sense of indignation for their beloved, the lifeblood of all the mothers, faded; and she did not know that she could find it again. The struggle had emboldened her. It was a pain reliever, a balm for a soul deadened from grief. Unlike Celia, Doña Licha and Doña Guille, women who hold up the sky of the movement, had chosen to live a continuum of struggle. Their lives were engaged–without sight of resolution or victory. This was their moral victory. The question is do our lives become value by creating value, becoming the struggle itself, or flesh hanging upon sorrow? Just as the guerrilla becomes the mountain, the river, a freedom fighter, becomes the struggle. Ordinary folk become the sorrow, the anger–if we do not make a conscious effort to fight and challenge what creates that suffering. This struggle becomes the manda in which we sacrifice our lives.

On Doña Celia's wall was a saying: "Vivir no es sólo existir, sino existir y crear, saber gozar y sufrir, y no dormir sino soñar. Descansar es esperar el morir."

Gustavo Hirales, an ex-militant of the Liga, says that México had its own secret war, from 1970 to 1978, in which 1,500 guerrillas were killed, including innumerable police, paramilitary and soldiers.

In April 18, 1988, the magazine Proceso published the transcript of testimony by a Mexican soldier, Zacarías Osorio Cruz, who deserted the army and applied for political asylum in Canada. Osorio testified that he deserted because he was forced to commit secret executions of hooded prisoners detained at Campo Militar Número 1. He was granted political refuge. The magazine gave this account of his testimony:

High ranking officials from the Secretary of Defense issued the orders with sealed official documents that could only be opened by the commanding general of the brigade, in Osorio's case, the Primer Batallón de la Brigada de Fusileros Paracaidistas at Campo Militar Número 1. The orders cited the cell numbers of the prisoners to be taken and were given to Osorio's lieutenant, Rubén Darío Zumano Durán, who would summon Osorio to get his arms for "special missions." Osorio, usually accompanied by his lieutenant or captain, would give the document to the commander of security at the military prison, who would direct them to the cells where hooded prisoners awaited them with their hands tied. They often took four to seven prisoners at a time and made 15 to 20 such "missions," and a couple of other brigades had similar ones. The prisoners were taken to the target range at San Miguel de los Jagüeyes during the night and were shot and "left in pieces." Someone else would dispose of their bodies. "What is really important is not to leave tracks of what happened. This is what the government of my country does; it leaves no traces; it doesn't leave anyone who can talk." Osorio also was a parachutist who was sent on special missions to pick up prisoners–hooded prisoners–eight to 20 at a time in Atoyac, Guerrero, Chilpancingo, Tapachula, Tampico and Veracruz. He transported them to Campo Militar Número 1.

Osorio deserted and crossed illegally into the United States. He said he feared for his life because others in the army who complained about these secret missions died under suspicious circumstances. Osorio worked in Kansas and Michigan as a farm worker and dishwasher and was deported back to México. But he returned, making his way to Canada.

Torturas

At first, the political prisoners in Guadalajara did not want their parents to visit them. While the youth wanted to destroy the system, the parents were working inside the system to protect them. "We had a more direct struggle. We wanted to bring down the system," says Armando Rentería. "For us, there was no compromise. We did not believe in legality. We didn't want anything to do with the system." When the families successfully pressured the government to show the prisoners (alive)–and it was televised–the cartulinos, or political prisoners, were impressed. "The committee is doing something important," they thought.

When Armando's parents started organizing the committee in Guadalajara, Armando found new respect for them. He had thought they lived insufficiently political lives. Don Luciano remembers giving his son books to read as a boy. "Bourgeoisie" materials, says Armando. At age 12, he was studying Che, which would serve him well when he later joined la Liga. A year later, he started running, and practicing target and painting antiwar slogans against the Vietnam War. He was part of the first group of communist youth in his barrio. By middle school, he was doing clandestine work. By age 17, he was detained for the first of a dozen times, many on trumped up charges, including bank robbery and homicide, even after he had stopped being a guerrilla. "To be a communist continues to be a crime."

Once, early in Armando's clandestine preparation, Don Luciano found some documents and read them, "¡Cabrón, estos locos!" He brought Valentín Campa to talk his son out of armed resistance.

But Armamdo would go on to militate with a couple of student groups, clashing with a government-backed student mafia. He concluded, "Esto sólo por las armas." The group he was in, Frente Estudiantil Revolucionario (FER), eventually merged with la Liga. Armando became the state leader of the guerrilla group, whose name is derived from a failed attack of a military installation in Chihuáhua in September 1965.

Jalisco produced numerous groups who chose armed struggle…and la gente whispered rumors about death squads from El Salvador and Nicaragua training in México in 1972 and 1973.

Armando often spent more than 23 hours in darkness in cells four meters by one and a half, two people to a cell, only arm-to-arm wide. "At night, they would take us to torture us, the cattle prod, false executions." There were numerous mock executions from 1974 to 1975. He remembers standing blindfolded and telling them, "If you want to blow me away, go ahead." Then came the barrage of fire. Someone grabbed him and said, "Now you really are going to die."

Armando says a prisoner was shot as he was kneeling next to him. And then there was the psychological torture of knowing his parents were being followed, or the nightmares.

"I know the clandestine jail of "el infierno"–the hell–in Campo Militar Número 1, the underground jails and manicomios," Armando said.

"But one of the worst tortures," says Don Luciano, "is the uncertainty of what is happening to them."

At first, the committee fought just to reduce the torture. When Armando's family saw a photo of him in the newspaper, they didn't recognize their "flaco." Don Luciano remembers when Fidel Castro offered refuge to the political prisoners and approximately 10 were freed. He recalls a television crew interviewing people about their opinion. Because he fought for the political prisoners, Don Luciano's friends mocked him, saying he was a communist.

"A compa died in torture," the prisoners would tell their families during visitation. "They are hanging Armando from his arms." Don Luciano would go home crying after seeing his son. Some parents couldn't take it, recalls Don Luciano. They thought it humiliating. Others thought it cleansed them.

Armando was the first on the amnesty list, but it took four years to get him released.

In 1981, he was summoned by jail officials. "Before, when they called us, it was always to beat us, interrogate us." This time, he was free to go. He tried to, but they wouldn't let him walk out–yet. There was a ceremony. "I only went to say goodbye to my friends and brought nothing with me but a cradle for my daughter." He walked into the outside world, and the streets looked wide. After years in maximum security, he had lost his sense of perception. His legs were loose, medio huangos. "I kept looking back to see if someone was following me." Two weeks before his release, a prisoner had tried to kill him. When political prisoners were freed, they ran the risk of being abducted again, Armando recalled. He stayed in his room for three or four days without leaving. In 1984, he was arrested on bank robbery charges and, he said, tortured and submerged in excrement, then freed.

Armando speaks inside of his father's panadería. When Roberto and I arrive, we are greeted at the door of the panadería and led down a large, dark hall, up some stairs to their home. Armando had just returned from Cuba a year before, after living there for five years. He is the father of two and enjoys working with youth. He is skinny and wears the veneer of a military man. And yet, I wonder, does he pull away from his wife or his mother when they see he is in pain, denying the memory, the vulnerability, that far-away look. It is a look I've seen in my own husband's eyes. Does he no longer remember his dreams? Or does he offer the pain up to some place in the universe where pain can be put to use for some greater good? "The psychological torture depends on your conscience," says Armando, coldly, as if he bore no wounds.

Armando says he knows a police officer. "I know he tortured me. I see a profound pain inside of him. I still talk to him. It was his job."

El Rosario

Doña Licha says, "La verdad no sabía nada." Ella era de costera. She sewed clothes. A relative taught her to read with a second-grade syllabus that belonged to one of the children. Fueron siete hijos. "All I knew was that they were studying. Sometimes my son would come home late. 'Hijo, it's 11:00 at night. Ay, mamá, una compa no tenía comida. Le compramos una torta.' The little money that I gave him, he would give to a friend who had none. Or he would walk home because he gave his bus fare to someone in more need. Sometimes he would arrive without his jacket. He had loaned it to a friend. When he was little, I wondered what he would be. Now I live with tremendous anxiety. Does he remember his mother? It is an agony that is going away poco a poco. I still have hope that I will find him. Hope is the only thing that has kept me going."

Doña Licha has a newspaper photo that she wears on a placard. It is the only photo that she has of Eduardo. The guardia blanca took all the ones she had when they burst into her home looking for him. The photo shows Eduardo and some friends when they were stranded on some mountains. Eduardo and his sister Rosalina loved to go hiking. Now they are gone. "Mis hijos, quisque eran comunistas, traficante de armas."

The family was watched and followed by police. When they came home, there were guards with guns aimed at them. Her son disappeared in 1978. He was abducted from school.

Doña Licha used to wash clothes for "la señora." One day, la señora Rosario called her and told her to come the next day. She had something important to tell her. She found out that Rosalina had been in a confrontation. "We'll ask for an amparo (a form of legal protection)," Rosario told her. But it was too late. A month later, the army said Rosalina was dead.

Her daughter Rosalina was reported killed in an ambush April 23, 1980. She was studying biology and was pregnant. Her husband, "he was from the movement, supposedly he was part of the liga comunista, la de 23 de septiembre," had been killed a year before. One day before the police came, a teacher of Rosalina's stopped by to tell her that she would have a test the next day. By the time the police arrived, her children had already gone to school. The house was surrounded by a hundred police. Doña Licha's 13-year-old son was beaten and interrogated. Doña Licha had not seen her daughter in months. Because Rosalina had already received threats and was being watched, she communicated with her mother through secret messages. The last message said she wanted to talk to her papá and would say where later.

In the confrontation that Rosalina was involved, one girl survived. Another, a teacher, died. "Nos llegan de platicar que no iban muertos. They were tortured in Campo Militar." The military waited 45 days to return her remains to Doña Licha.

Inside her china cabinet are amber glasses, porcelain dolls. She serves me with folded, pink napkins. In those folds, I see how entering the struggle helped give some sense of control, some sense that not that much has changed. The struggle becomes the grave to mourn with daily rituals, like folding pink napkins.

Poniatowska writes that women in México are reduced to handy appliances–stoves and washers. Trapitos. I imagine the struggle is sometimes like stirring beans, y a fregar con el quehacer: a planchar; el plantón; a barrer el polvo, sabiendo que el polvo regresa; a amasar la masa (que según mi abuela brinda buen pecho); a jalear orejas de "burrocratas" con sangre de chinche; a levantarse a las cuatro a preparar la comida con tiempo; a levantarse a las cuatro a llegar al mitin con tiempo; el no comer por tantas tareas; y el no comer por los niños. El aguante es el aguante, séa hasta la madrugada o desde la madrugada, séa sola o séa acompañada, a velar los chamaquillos que andan por quien sabe donde–while scrubbing the floors of evil. And sometimes the struggle helps people recover a small part of themselves that disappeared with los seres borrados–a pupil, a piece of ear, a finger, some small part of life that comes alive in the madre spirit, despite their scarred existence.

"Sometimes I feel una ansiedad." Anxiety. "I wonder where my son is. Is he in school? Something must be happening to him. If all my children are together and one is missing, I miss him because I know something is happening to him. I can feel it and that's why I feel he is still here. As long as I am alive, I'll fight."

The children of Doña Laurita, another Doña luchona, were released from Campo Militar. They said they saw him in 1979. They said they were in the same cell with him and that they saw him being taken blindfolded and placed in a car. Doña Licha said he was taken to

Oaxaca. She went there but could not get into the jails or prisons. Nadie sabía nada.

Young friends of hers made a special shrine: "Eduardo Hernández V. fue detenido y desaparecido el 28 de Abril '78. Hijo: 'Nunca te he olvidado. Siempre has estado en mi corazón.' "

I wonder if the Doñas question if fighting for a loved one may have sounded their death knell, as in Argentina.

– Remember, Doña Licha, how we would take their actions to the market, to the people in the mercado, las tablas, los talleres, el tianguis? asks Doña Guille.

Doña Licha recalls that Eduardo was in the second grade in 1968. He came home one day and told Doña Licha, "Oh, mami, you should have seen the way they were beating up on the students."

"You stay away from there. You don't go near there." She thought the youngsters were in trouble por andar de revoltosos. "Ahora, yo soy la revoltosa."

She fights alongside Doña Rosario, giving her strength. "Somos compañeras en el mismo dolor, entre la vida y la muerte."

For two years, her home was watched, her phones tapped. Sometimes there are strange men near the home. And a neighbor always is noticing her comings and goings. And her sons work so that she can militate como una loca. When she walks me to the pesero, she keeps looking back.

"Now it will be the struggle of the youth.They are the ones who will make the changes. They are learning to live another freedom. A nosotras ni nos pelaban."

And I imagine Doña Licha waiting for her son to come home, looking at the clock and drying her hands on her bata, waiting, and looking back and knowing, "Donde hay amor, hay paciencia."

Sorrowful Mystery Number 5, Doña Guille

Es una mujer rosada del trabajo, es pura calor de madre.

– I come from the time of el tren burro. I mopped floors on my knees with grass.

One day after selling candies at Mercado la Merced, she came home and found the house closed. Doña Guille was alarmed because a newborn grandbaby and toddler just out of the hospital were staying with her. She found them alone, crying. "¿Qué pasará, María Santísima?"

The police had apparently entered the house, ransacked it, and took her husband and two daughters. They twisted their arms, demanding, "Tell us where Francisco lives!"

She called her son Francisco. "I haven't done anything wrong," he told her. At 10:00 p.m., the police returned and took another son, "mi hijo Jesús."

"Tell us because you are the accomplice of your brother. It's best if you cooperate."

Doña Guille asked them, "But why, if we haven't done anything wrong?"

"Your son is a terrorist. He robs banks."

"If we were bank robbers, would we be in this misery?" The agents took a car, a bicycle and some money for school supplies that a cousin had earned through selling palomitas–popcorn.

Francisco had been working in a factory and was a leader in a union strike that led to salary increases. He started hanging out with friends who did solidarity work with a group known as "Union del Pueblo." His father didn't like his associating with them. Time passed, and they stopped coming. When a bomb went off at a bank, the police came looking for Francisco, whose car had been borrowed by a friend and implicated in the bombing. Jesús was released, but Francisco fled with 2,000 pesos from pueblo to pueblo.

Doña Guille went to Doña Rosario who told her, "We will fight until we find our children."

Doña Guille's house was watched. Her son, Adán, medio borrachito, lost his job because he also was accused of being a terrorist. "Do you know you have a terrorist working here?" the agents asked his employer. "That's when he got his beating." When agents came to her house, they threatened, You don't want to die in an accident, do you? Like your son? Another son, Fernando, was killed in a hit and run. "I felt as if the floor was breaking apart."

"¡Ay, mamasita linda!"

"I wanted to kill them, to deprive them of life."

Three men, grandototes, in civilian clothes, came to her house. They practically tore down her door. She told them to just stay there as long as they wanted. They watched her house for years. They followed

Francisco's wife, threatened her and beat up her father. Francisco's wife was threatened that they would kill her and her children. They accused another of Doña Guille's sons of making explosives, when, in fact, they were fireworks that were sold at Doña Guille's changarrito in front of her house during Christmas. Later, someone in her neighborhood came to see her, wanting to know if she wanted information about her son, que traía una carta de él. "I don't want to know anything about my son Francisco," she told the woman." You can keep the letter because he was not in any trouble that he cannot get out of." The woman never came back. Doña Guille knew it was a trick because spies dressed as nuns even dared to watch her house.

Doña Guille always thought you couldn't go against the government.

"I never went to school. I did not know things. If that is the incorrect word, you can correct me. I wish I could be young again and be able to go to school to teach all of those who don't know to become aware, to learn about everything that is happening. That's why I go with la señora, for humanity, for all of humanity."

"Que se rebele la joventúd, creo que está bien…if in a marriage there is a bad father and a bad mother, the children must rebel." Now she tells the youth, "I am with you. They should defend themselves. They should become aware and tell it to the rest who don't know, like I did not know."

"Para un matrimonio se necesita mucha concha. "A marriage requires lots of patience. Her husband blamed her for her son's fate. He called her bad names, telling her that she would look like a pendeja. "Él nos abandonó. Pues, qué bueno, que no lo siento. This is a struggle for humanity. That's why I don't feel I lost him. It was good luck. I am free."

She is as frail. Con el coraje de una madre, she hits the table and says, "Yo lo siento de deveras. Quisiera ser una bruja para embrujar todos estos condenados."

She even went to a curandero to find out if her son Fransisco was alive. He told her, "The star that guides you, guides your son. He will be fine."

– Ay, señorita, yo acudí hasta un pajarito que adivina.

She starts to cry chubasco tears; she sheds a monsoon. When another son disappeared for two months, she panicked. She went to a divining bird, pajarito que adivina, the kind that tells you your future for treinta centavos. You stick a piece of paper in its cage. It pecks on the paper, and out comes your answer.

"I have a son lost. I want to know if he is all right." The bird said her son would always be fine and that things would go well for him. A man next to the bird told her to say "three Our Fathers and three Hail Marys." The man told her to take the treinta centavos and buy a candle and pray to the Father, Son, and Holy Spirit. Her son showed up a few days later. A shoemaker, he had been working out of town.

– Ay. Ay qué dolor. I would walk the streets crying in silence because of all of these things. I wanted to go to school and teach the children all of these things. A school that teaches children their rights, not war, not arms. Since I believe in God and the santos, if God gave us land for each one of us as he did when they were taken out of Egypt, why fight with arms? I believe the children have to be shown that we are all brothers. Why not give them the land so they can maintain themselves?

"Pero, no. Sale un cabrón. Entra otro más chingón. Cada quien por si mismo. I don't think people should be that way, no?"

One day she saw a man by her house. She recognized him as one of the ones who used to come to the house to visit Francisco. "I am el Chino," he told her. He went with Doña Rosario, and Francisco was cleared. Francisco knew that his mother was fighting for him. He wrote to her in letters that arrived at the house of one of Doña Guille's friends. "My son is free because we fought."

She says Francisco is sick. He says not so much. His hands shake as he talks. He is handsome, prieto, with bad bottom teeth. She says he has susto, that he got his diabetes because of susto–his wife, too. "Diabetes comes from susto," says Doña Guille. Doña Guille is always sick and too poor to afford a doctor.

"We learned to live another kind of freedom to make the changes. I fear, I hope the changes don't take too long so that I can see them. Even if we don't see them, others will. This is what makes me young again."

In her candy store is a picture of Popocateptl and Iztaccihuatl, the two volcanoes that personify the legend about two lovers. "Como soy india..." Mazahua, she explains, adding that Moctezuma's headdress should be returned from Europe. "No niego a mi raza y eso me da un coraje."

"I want to return in people's hearts. I want to complete everything here in this life, all that is good. I was not aware; but having become aware of what is happening, it hurts me, even if they are not my children, because I truly feel a great love for the truth. Hopefully, los chavos will continue our work. So that when we are no more, they will fight so that no one will be disappeared or killed. My little grandson tells me he will fight when I am gone."

Consejo: "Like it or not, one must enter the revolution."

Doña Guille can't read or write. She can't count too well anymore, either. To get to her house, she'll tell you to take the metro exit with a certain color. When she goes to the panteón to visit her dead, she doesn't know where her mother and father are buried. But she goes there anyway, thinking, "if my abuela is here somewhere, then I'll pray."

"Ay que papá, help your grandchildren. Abuela, help them along the way, that they find work, un taquito. Protect us from the threats." On día de los muertos she offers them un dulce, una frutita, and fills the store with candles and panecito. "Sabiendo uno comprar…. If you know how to buy, you can afford it. A chicken's head is cheap and very good, patita de pollo, a chicken's foot in soup con arrocito…."

"I never liked to have friends. I do not like to hug people. I did not like to play with dolls." Her stepmother made her go to work as a girl. Her father said she didn't need schooling, "y órale a trabajar."

"No, I never liked to be hugged. But when the youths are released, I want to hug them and cry in their arms. I want to jump and scream." And for the others she thinks, will they return? "Qué no los maten, que los encontremos de deveras."

Moonsoon Mourning

At the 15th anniversary of the mothers' hunger strike, some of the madres stood near the Angel of Independence with black umbrellas. Doña Guille, who often has her gaze at half mast, looked me in the eye, her hair loosened from the bobby pins, and asked, "¿Cómo lo ves? ¿Somos malos o somos buenos? They say the youth were bad."

On August 4, 1992, Rosario published the following in the editorial pages of the newspaper El Universal.

> Those of us who joined (the mothers of the disappeared and Eureka) were united by la pena, la ira, the pain, the wrath, and the impotency.... In our homes had entered the "escoba del terror oficial" that swept our children, fathers and husbands, brothers, compañeros, and friends. The void of their absence hurt us, and we extended our hands in search of them..."la terrible escoba del terror official"–the terrible broom of official terror–stopped for a moment its sinister "limpieza" (cleaning) when our unanimous complaint echoed past our nation's borders and the obstinate insistence of the mothers in long hunger strikes rescued from the basement of Campo Militar Número 1 more than 100 disappeared. All the disappeared are the children of the mothers of Eureka; every mother of Eureka is the mother of each of the disappeared. The pain of all of them is the pain of one of them. All torture hurts us, all offenses wound us completely! ...The people know this and respect us, but, "the terrible broom of official terror" continues "sweeping" and we need much more than the respect of the people to confront this.

Motorists drive by and "disappear" the mothers as many people do the beggars and the homeless, thinking that by pretending not to see them they won't confront their own silence, their susto, or their "compromises with reality" of which Jacobo Timerman writes. Silence becomes the refuge of violence and abuse. And fear becomes a prison without bars, say the Mothers of the Plaza de Mayo in Argentina.

Silence. I have often said that communities don't fight because it is the only way they know how to survive the abuse. They are an abused entity. Like a battered spouse, they begin to think the abuse is normal and that they are deserving of it. And they stop smiling. And they begin to think it's ok for the Migra to stop them because they are brown.

María Jimenez calls it abused community syndrome. Others term this historical trauma. But when I think of the work of the madres, I believe their actions are a grand and painful naming ritual because they broke the silence. We must name the abuser and vocalize the abuse to set us free because the abuser feeds on our silence.

Paulo Freire says silence can be the sound of hopelessness. He writes that oppressed people must name their existence as a basic precursor to self-liberation. The madres named themselves more than the mothers of Juan Chanclas, grandmothers of María Pistolas, or madrinas de Maria Machete. They became the elders of the disappeared, the forgotten ones, and they assumed that role until death. They are some of the clan mothers of democracy. In our movement, with no elders to name us, we named ourselves as a people; or the naming appears to us as a result of the path we walk. Like when José becomes Joe. Or when the Spaniards put saint's names over Indian names. Or when San Jose, California, becomes San Jo and Mathis, Texas becomes Masas, and Joe becomes José, again–or is given his Indian name. Or when we return to the Indian place names of our ancestors. And the naming can be a painful journey through ourselves, to find ourselves so close to humanness, pelando espinas del nopal. It summons spirits that become a necklace of tongues, severed hands pinned to the enaguas of fighting women and other lost members of our ancestors who were punished for being defiers.

Having read Timerman's account in Prisoner Without a Name, Cell Without a Number, I am awestruck at his story of jail and torture during Argentina's Dirty War, how seeing his jailer's eye through a peephole helped him maintain his humanness. Yet it is the lesson of the Holocaust, of Central and Latin America's civil wars, of the Japanese internment in the United States, and our country's own dirty war to clean its borders of immigrants who are converting the nation into "foreign soil." How does a country arrive at such history and why don't people fight? At what point is there no turning back the violence? As an advocate on nonviolence, I have tried to understand what makes a people give up hope on the ability of people to peacefully change a political structure, so that the only answer is "sólo por las armas." And yet I understand that it is often an act of self-defense, that people take up arms to defend their lives and that of their people; sometimes they take up arms because they can no longer feed their children, because they refuse to bear more children to such conditions.

César Chávez believed you could appeal to the conscience of a nation, yet that presupposes a certain sense of morality. Or the very intention creates the morality. As Chávez once said a generation ago when he broke one of his fasts, how we live our lives determines what kind of people we are.

> Our struggle is not easy. Those who oppose our cause are rich and powerful and they have many allies in high places. We are poor. Our allies are few. But we have something the rich do not own. We have our own bodies and spirits and the justice of our cause as our weapons.
>
> When we are really honest about ourselves we must admit that our lives are all that really belong to us.... It is my belief that only by giving our lives do we find life. I am convinced that the truest act of courage, the strongest act of humanity is to sacrifice ourselves for others in a totally nonviolent struggle for justice.... To be human is to suffer for others.... God help us to be human.

The lessons of the Zapatistas and Central America's resistance movements show that the guerrilla movements are what brought the government to the point of negotiations. But it is the indignation of people such as the mothers who created the moral possibility for peaceful change.

¿Y el gobierno qué no sabe nada? I ponder what allows a government to be so capable of violence and a people so possessed of cynicism. Timerman writes that people try to destroy what they do not understand. But to disappear human beings says that your life is worth so little we will not produce a corpse or freedom. The act becomes more than the violence to an individual; it is a means to control a community by what is not there and by what is unknown. The message becomes the power it has over lives. The illegality is disappeared so efficiently, the act vanishing with the victim. They remain in a conjugation of to be, writes Analia Penchazadeh. "They are referred to as a state of being," she writes.

The Guatemalan resistance leader Raúl Molina once told me that to be disappeared is a "continuous crime," where the dead cannot die and their loved ones are eternally tortured. Then, what is worse? That no one believes you or that you are believed and the cynicism is so great, the lack of hope so vast, that no one acts; and they, in effect, become accomplices? The torturer becomes the judge, the police, the elite, and even ourselves. Great good may come from great evil–if action is taken. Otherwise, the potential for good lies dormant until sufficient action and stimulus creates its emergence. What is worse, I ask, a country's capacity for violence, or the people's incapacity to act? Cynicism is part of the susto; it is a symptom of the internalized oppression. The trauma functions as the daily oppressor. And I hear Neruda's verse from the poem, "World's End."

> "...we all go on living
> after the others are murdered
> knowing, perhaps, we have stolen the lives
> of the best of our brothers."

I had seen many of these women cry charcos, mujeres whose ojos brotan manantiales.

"Ya no lloramos," dice Doña Licha.

"Yo si chillo," says Doña Guille.

"Yo lo hago en la noche."

"Desaloje el corazón," says Doña Chela.

"Everything makes us cry."

"I stopped crying after crying all that time that my son was persecuted," says Doña Guille.

But then they always start to cry, "lágrimas de rabia, lágrimas de impotencia." I still feel their tears in my throat. And many times, I had to stop writing these words before you. Those tears became the agua bendita of México. Holy Water. And I hear los arrullos de las madres, "que de mi vida, que de mi sangre." To have stopped fighting would have been to abandon their children. Las dadoras de la vida, the givers of life, honored life itself with their struggle. They created. They named names.

The mothers of the disappeared have gone by different names over the years, the most recent one, "Eureka." "It means something found," says Doña Guille. They are las lloronas of the world, the weeping woman who cries for her lost children. We hear the march of these women in the remote corners, in the backwaters, and in the jungles. La llorona wails in the mothers against police brutality in New York, in the Mothers Against Drunk Drivers, in the Mother's Against Gangs in Chicago, in the Mothers Against the Incinerator in Los Angeles, las CO-MADRES of El Salvador, or the Mothers of the Plaza de Mayo in Argentina. In the mothers, as Roberto says, who struggle for our lives. As Rudolfo Anaya writes, all women are la llorona, crying when their children suffer.

After all, it was woman who gave the first gritos de dolores.

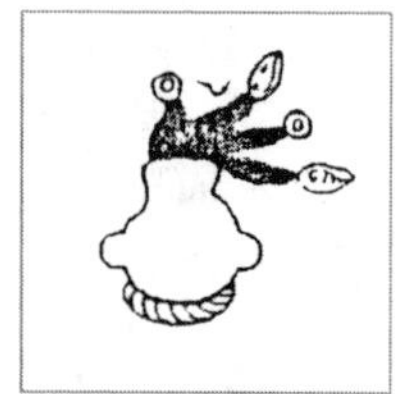

The National Human Rights Commision 2001 report on the dirty war:

532 cases of record; 544 testimonies

Soldiers, police, and other government security agents involved in at least 275 cases

At least 74 officials from 37 government agencies involved

319 cases from rural areas

225 cases of people from México's urban areas

Eureka presented 452 cases.

Informants T-115, T-237 and T-123 report on Jesús Piedra Ibarra's detention. They contradict the official version that he died in confrontation with police, instead, testifying that the presumed leader of la Liga 23 de Septiembre was tortured and disappeared by the Dirección Federal de Seguridad.

T-210 implicates Mario Arturo Acosta Chaparro, one of 24 military officers listed among those responsible for the dirty war. Testigo 210: "...que conocio a la pesona que responde al nombre de Jacob Nájera Hernández, fue desaparaecido por implicarlo en pertenecer al grupo guerrillero de Lucio Cabañas, que la detencion la realizo un comandante de nombre Isidro Galeana, quien estaba al mando de un general de nombre "Acosta Chaparro."

Benjamin Domínguez Trejo, an advisor to the commission on the psychological effects of the survivors, reports to the media one of his most difficult moments: "To find myself at Eureka with the mamma of Eduardo Hernández Vargas...and she asks me how her son ate...."

I kept thinking of México and the United States when I went to South Africa in 1999 and saw how people were seeking truth. They were telling their stories in South Africa. They said this will heal their memory as a people. The Truth and Reconciliation Commission says the people need truth to heal, and they need to tell their stories. Archbishop Desmond Tutu says that the commission is seeking restorative justice, not retributive justice, which focuses on prosecution. To him, retributive justice does not provide "permanent closure."

"We seek to do justice to the suffering without perpetuating the hatred aroused. We think this is restorative justice," he said in a January 11, 1998, Parade article.

For that, memory must be restored. Perpetrators are confessing the truth for amnesty. The people, who in Apartheid were not heard, are telling what happened. It is said to give new meaning to their trauma. The human rights community hopes this will change the meaning of their suffering.

Many wonder if this is sufficient justice. Can the balm of forgiveness assuage the need for vengeance? Tutu and others concluded that a spiritual solution is key to dealing with the legal and political ramifications of this legacy.

Most truth commissions are created because truth telling is the only weapon in the restoration of democracy, a trade off for prosecution of the criminals and state terror. Trade truth for justice, quicken to mercy. Perhaps a truth commission is what México–and the Americas–needs in order to heal. Yet, truth commissions usually come with a change in power. In México, the same institutions, extralegal and extrajudicial, still flourish. The question is, how do we remove the internal violence that breeds such suffering?

To tell our story. To witness and to be witnessed. Let the air heal our stories; let our breath heal the memory. In México, the stories have been told; they have been breathed into the aire. They are part of our oxygen.

How do we recover from economic violence, the psychological violence of poverty, the legacy of invasion, and the emotional violence we inflict upon one another as a result of all these historical wounds? We must face the potential for violence inside all of us. Restorative justice. To what are we to restore? We cannot restore what we have never had. You cannot re-cover or bury history. The bones will poke through the earth and trip you. In México, se cobra con venganza.

Must we wait, as an indigenous community healer once told me, until we "no longer want to hurt (ourselves or others) anymore?"

"Sometimes our hearts have to break–open," says my friend and Buddhist teacher, Nancy Ali.

As I went through a decade of files on '68 and México's dirty war, I found this poem by Rosario Castellano entitled, "Memorial de Tlatelolco." To my surprise, it invokes la Tlazoteotl, whom the Spanish called the filth-eating diosa. The poem was part of a flier promoting a homage to the student movement on its 25th anniversary.

> "...No busques lo que no hay: huellas, cadáveres
> que todo se le ha dado como ofrenda a una diosa
> a la Devoradora de Exremenentos.
> No hurgues en los archivos pues nada consta en actas...."

Earlier, I lit a candle, asking the ancestors to write through me. As I write this, I see red. For a moment, I think it is blood on my hands.

Lupe & the Buddha

In the name of the Virgencita de Guadalupe…I confess that I am a Guadalupana and a Buddhist. Bless me Guadalupe-Tonantzin, for I do not pray to you the way my mother does. I see you as the female face of sacred life, Grandmother Earth; the feminine presence of God, of Life, of Creation itself.

When Buddhist teachers asked me to relinquish you years ago, it was violating. I returned you, La Lupita, to my home. I could not break my mother's rosary. When I invoke your counterpart, Tonantzin–Guadalupe appeared with roses on Tonantzin's sacred hill in the 1500s–I return to you as did my ancestors. My prayers–whether they are Buddhist chants or offered with tobacco–connect with all my mother's rosaries and all my foremothers' prayers to Grandmother Earth when they prayed the "Indian way."

She who comes flying from the light like an eagle

While working on this "pot cript," I had a dream. I saw César Chávez, Dolores Huerta, and the Virgen de Guadalupe. César and Dolores were in oval frames, with Tonantzin ascended above them. The dream's message was that the United Farm Workers movement "matrized" the Chicano movement with the female power of the warrior Dolores, and with the male-female balance of César and Helen Chávez. When they raised la Morenita for nonviolence, a feminine energy in itself, they invoked the maternal sacred. For me, that energy is at once compassion and love. When Tonantzin Coatlique is joined with her, they represent the absorbing, writhing, fertile, snaking energy of Mother Earth. Coatlique. Tlazolteotl. Tlazohteotl.

Coatlaxope (la madre tierra, la que come el mal)

Women's circle: We are all given mementos. I'm given a picture of Guadalupe-Tonantzin. I look at it and begin to testimoniar. When I was a girl, my mother almost died. The official diagnosis was pneumonia. I diagnosed fear and abuse as the dis-ease. My mamma was shot at by a neighbor who thought she was a burglar as she hid from my father, with me in her arms. My father chased her with a knife as she ran with me in her arms. I was less than two; and my mama and I would hide in closets, her shushing me till daddy fell asleep and woke up nice. Shush and everything will be ok. When my mama almost died, she prayed to the virgencita that if she lived she would leave him. She lived.

The women murmur.

I looked at the prayer card, and my voice starts to shake. My dad never got over it and died with a broken heart.

Years ago, I realized what had happened to amá had happened to me. Her pain was mine, too. And the virgencita came and told me, "You have to let her go now." But I didn't want to. I was afraid she was going to die. "You have to let her go now," she told me again. And I saw some part of my mama's pain sucked into the blue-black swirl of the cosmos.

I grew up praying to a woman. I rarely prayed to God. I did not know him, though I stayed up many hours trying to figure out who made God. I remember my mamá and my abuela telling me, "Ask the virgencita. Pray to Her."

When my grandma was detained in México in 1950, she was separated from her ten children for 10 months. Immigration wouldn't let her return to the U.S. Despite letters from my grandpa's boss and ten birth certificates (and the fact that she was a Kikapu Indian), they wanted more proof she wouldn't be a ward of the state and would be a good resident of the U.S. She'd crossed into this country when the border was a dirt road and she had no birth certificate, like many indigenas of México. My mama was in charge of all the little ones. Everyday after school she'd go to St. Patrick's Cathedral and ask the virgen to bring her mamá home.

When vandals began defacing murals of the Virgen de Guadalupe in Los Angeles, it made me physically ill to see her tortured. I wrote these words: "Huetonantzin, ancient mother, they have painted your face white and beside your halo they have written the numbers 666 in dripping red. Perhaps they fear the feminine sacred."

Tonantzin (Our Most Venerable Mother) was known among indigenous peoples in México as embodying a feminine energy with many expressions: the earth's regenerative powers, fertility and nature's ability to destroy or create. For the survivors of the 1997 Acteal, Chiapas, mass killings, you became the Virgin of the Massacre, your broken image pieced back together as their shrine.

For many, what is sacred cannot have a bared body. In Santa Fe, New México, people mounted an unholy inquisition against Chicana artist Alma López, who shows "Our Lady" (Raquel Salinas) embodied in a two-piece bathing suit of roses. López was denounced as promoting a lesbian agenda, and Salinas as being of unholy body. Sacred images can separate or unite. Sometimes they become "false," fall out of favor, are destroyed, or inspire inquisitions and censorship.

Sometimes decolonization creates a divide between younger Chicanas and many elders. In the Chicanas' efforts to understand Her, to challenge colonization and the social construction of meaning, to "re-vision" the sacred and woman, they've made Her more physical–ironing clothes, sewing, carrying groceries, being a grandmother and wearing tennis shoes. It is also our elders' traditional faith in that Indian Virgin of the forgotten red-brown folk that has kept us alive as peoples of the Americas (or spiritually subjugated, in some people's eyes).

Is it our longing for the sacred feminine that creates these icons, that puts a body to the sacred, or incites moral outrage? Or is it that She appears to us because She pulses through our spirits, calling for us to know Her? As I followed the Taliban destruction of Buddhist images as false gods, I wondered what makes people fear icons that largely have become art; and when does faith turn inquisitory? Sometimes people confuse images with faith.

Buddhist elders say that images only have the power we give them. Like many Buddhists, I do not worship images of Buddha or even pray to him. We seek to fuse our spirit with Life itself, what others call God and what I understand as Great Spirit, to respect all of life and to bring out our "Buddhahood," an enlightened state inherent in the universe at all times, even in moments of anger.

My ancient soul yearns for the sacred feminine energies inside the earth, the moon, the universe, and I pray "the Indian way" of my ancestors for all these things. By honoring the feminine energies, I honor myself as woman. But when I pray to la morenita, I don't see her the way my mamá did. I see Tonantzin, madrecita tierra. I see my mamá praying in her hospital bed. I see my grandma braiding her hair with rosaries, seven in all, one for Uncle Sam and another just for me. I see the campesinos who raised her image for protection and asked her to ask God to bless them with justice. And all my prayers fuse and bead with my mother's and grandmother's thousands of rosaries, Ave Marias, and roses.

Bless me Coatlique-Tonantzin for I have....

Once, when I went to cover Superbarrio at the Basilica, I tried to pray. Hail Mary, full of grace, who art in Heaven....

Bless me Tonantzin-Guadalupe for I have...forgotten the words...so I'll just pray the way my grandpa did, to the four winds. He said God was on his shoulder, anyway. In the name of the Sun, the Moon, and the holy Mother Earth...amen. Aho. Hue Tonantzin. Ave Maria. Coatlaxopueh.

Patrisia Gonzales

La anciana

La anciana: corazón de la casa,
rescoldo del hogar,
vigilante.

La buena anciana:
amonesta a la gente
le da voces.
Es luz, tea, espejo,
ejemplo, dechado.

La mala anciana:
rincón, obscuridad,
pared, noche obscura,
se burla de la gente,
es afrenta.

From Códice Matritense de la Real Academia as cited in
Toltecayotl by Miguel León-Portilla

In the 1970s, the Mexican urban women's movement emerged to fight for land, food subsidies, and better ways of living as part of the larger urban popular movement. Eventually an umbrella organization of 60 neighborhood associations was formed by the popular urban movement–Coordinadora Nacional de Movimientos Urbanos Populares. With the onslaught of changes rooted in the 1985 earthquake, CONAMUP asserted significant leadership in the socio-political renacimiento that followed. Its women's council was in the forefront. In 1988 came el temblor del pueblo, and there came a great electoral opening that spawned the participation of numerous grassroots movements. Women from 19 union and neighborhood organizations and the Left and middle-class feminist groups founded a national coalition. Their focus: democracy, food subsidies, and an end to violence against women. They wanted a symbol that reflected their reality and

The Mud People

Las Abuelitas

turned to the revolutionary skirts of Benita Galeana, one of three female pioneers in the Mexican Communist Party in the 1920s. Benita was a woman, who like many in the urban movement, migrated to México from the provinces in search of a better life, a woman who struggled against society, who had been part of the backbone of a social movement, invisible like many women are in such fights, except that she wrote the autobiography Benita at age 33, saving her from the anonymity of popular history. In honor of her history, the Coordinadora de Mujeres "Benita Galeana" was created. Benita was grandmother of the Left; but, in particular, she became an elder to the working class women's movement and Mexican feminists.

Chapter 5: Las Abues, Las Benitas, la Coyol

In the time of purple fruit the heart of cactus, I met las abuelitas, the woman in the braids and the one who makes the sun hide. In that rebel trenza were mud and movement and heart of the earth, women with cactus spines in their hands, who know of things that woman knows, like chicle takes the spines out…hang your papitas in a stocking to keep them from going bad. Things woman knows, like yerba ruda, for bad spirits, and "other things" that whisper about late moons. Cosas que las mujeres de yerbas buenas, yerbas maestras, sell at the mercado La Merced, next to the long line to see the lady who cleans souls with a frog. Things…like being madre, vientre, creation, bearers of the barrio.

On a bitten moon, the movement women rubbed their hearts with the perfume of a rebellious woman and the fractured light of the celestial dancer with her brothers, the 400 stars. And dogs were sicced upon them as they marched down the streets of Mexico City, banging spoons on pots and pans. And they were punched in the face, stoned and baptized with hot water for being "mujeres ya otras," more woman.

If you look into the eye of movement, you will find them, tiny good souls who are mirrors, for every movement has its abuelitas, little grandmothers of struggle. Great mothers. Long women, the veins of Maguey Grandmother, who walk among rock, rubbled hills of the Sleeping Woman, and raise their skirts at Authority.

"Y órale compa."

Ancient México had a symbol for movement, ollin, also earthquake. In Nahuatl, the heart shares its root. As the Nahuatl teacher Delfino Hernández has written, Yolotl (heart) is literally "the movement" of persons. He says that life is movement, and movement is the symbol of life. In Latin, heart is the raíz of courage. Corazón, cor.

Ollin is chavas bravas because woman is life, especially old woman, and life has the power to give, if we let it. "Porque el corazón no se arruga," the grandmother Rosa Guerrero once told me. Yes, the heart does not wrinkle.

In 1978, archaeologists unearthed a stone disk while excavating the sacred remains of the Templo Mayor in Mexico City. They said it was a dismembered woman, the one with a mask of tinkling bells and snake skirt, Coyolxauhqui, symbol of the moon, the Milky Way, and the female energy of the universe. Warrior woman of the cosmos, the one who makes the sun hide. About the same time came the birthing of the great coalitions of mass movements in the late 1970s and early 1980s, and the women of the "National Coordinating Body of the Urban Popular Movements" (CONAMUP) emerged from the ball of The People, a puro golpe. Warrior women of the earth of their lives, regado con llanto y llama. They were leaven for the urban movement. The woman's alliance eventually became organized as the "Regional de Mujeres."

When the government implemented an austerity program during the peso devaluation crisis of the early 1980's, the People stopped the city, stopped the buses. And the women were in la bola.

Within eight years, they acquired subsidized tortillas, free milk, and people's kitchens. They took over government offices. "No one enters here!" The secretaries threw hot water at them, and the mujeres del pueblo began to create their own history. They became aware of their sex and their class, of what it means to be poor and a woman, as they fought side-by-side with their compañeros de lucha like the ancient mociuaquetzque (valiant women) who, according to scholar Elizabeth Salas, accompanied Mechica warriors into battle, prodding them to victory.

Mo = second person singular; cihua = woman; quetz = upstanding; qui = ending for a person in charge of something–"Your upstanding woman."

Salas writes in Soldaderas in the Mexican Military of the earlier tribal women who defended their people (often facing constant tribal warfare) as they migrated into the Valley of México after 800 A.D. These women were great warriors, and the scarce historical footnotes regarding their existence provide a glint of context to the story of Coyol. Women fought in three ways, writes Salas, "as individuals, together with men, or in separate women's groups led by women."

Las chavas bravas made democracy from daily life, fighting alone, or with the men, just like the women Chichimecas, or con la pura mujerada in women's work parties. They began to own the process of change, and they brought la bola with them. "If we are to negotiate, not just one of us or a few of us, but each from our colonias."

Women who felt old at 30, feel young again in the struggle. Their men told them, "Choose me or the union." And they told the men, "¿Sabes qué? Me gusta la lucha." I like the struggle. And they told the men in the union, "Now we don't want to be the spine. We want to be the brain."

If someone were to make a people's altar, las chavas bravas would ascend as milagritos between la so-called gran puta Malinche and María Insurgente. All the women of the brave class are Adelitas who carry cement bags up rocky hills to build their own homes and pelt a "charra" PRIista for trying to take away their land. Mujeres entradas.

Seven years after "Coyol" was found in the teocalli, las chavas bravas discovered her in their own way from a crescent moon that hovered near the pyramids. The feminist space known as Cuarto Cresciente overlooked the Templo Mayor. Cuarto Cresciente was run by feminist Virginia Sánchez Navarro. She notes that the name meant both "growing room" and crescent moon, "standing as a metaphor for the germinating phase of the feminist movement."

"...it was a way of reminding ourselves and others of a time in history when women were recognized as the creators and the civilizers, when the symbolic representation of divinity was the moon and not the sun," she writes in the article, "Remembering the Goddess."

There, among the herb clinic and mansion rooms with a yawning looking glass, Coyol was "re-membered;" and las mujeres del pueblo were re-membered. They made offerings of copal and conch shells at the Templo Mayor. La concha, Quetzalcoatl's "wind jewel," is a symbol of woman's fertility. On August 16, 1987, "priestesses of the moon Goddess" performed a ritual in front of the Templo Mayor, putting together Coyol's dismembered body with flowers on the ground. And when they took over the Zócalo, la Coyol watched over them.

In 1988, Sánchez Navarro had invited the chavas of the pioneer CONAMUP–which represented 23 of some 50 colonias in the valley of México–to use the space and salvage it from eviction. Women kept 24-hour guard, even with the help of muy macho men–in a space where dances were held and "no men allowed." Then, when the Salinas government came to power, the new city administration of Regent Manuel Camacho Solís promised to negotiate. When the People's guards left believing in good faith deals, goons came and threw the Crescent Moon out the window. So the women put it in the Zócalo. They recreated the kitchen, the room with great mirrors, a cafe filled with herstories. They felt She of the Zócalo, singing at night, playing games, riding bikes through the zócalo. The Abuelitas, founders of the urban movement's women's council, came to stand guard. They fried fish. The women sang with the guitar under the moon and told stories of Coyol. "She is re-membering herself as a symbol of our women who are redefining our worth."

– Yes, the diosa is protecting us, la Coyol.

A little grandmother at the crescent moon: "She was dismembered when the matriarchy ended. With her discovery came the new era of women." And it was. Dicen, "mujeres ya no rotas."

Eventually the women negotiated with the government for a peeling mansion in the historic downtown and created a regional center of "la regional de mujeres" for women to coordinate a people's kitchen and people's school, including sexuality seminars. It was a space for sowing, a place to explore and touch their bodies, to be a woman without walls. A su gusto.

And so, there in Mexico City, the energy of Coyolxauhqui was called forth by these warrior women…. The women of the People made Coyol theirs and reclaimed the ground over the sacred ruins, ruins that are not ruins but living under earth, waiting to break through, like the prophesies said. It was time to feed the spirit. The mystic things of life are not lost because they were always there and what is mystery is only so because our minds eclipse the greater mind.

At that crescent moon, chavas bravas of the grassroots urban women's movement had learned to talk to the classical feminists. In México, a great divide separated the feminist movement from the women's movement. The chavas say these feminists were not like some other feminists who had tried to overrun the mujeres del barrio, with their theory of gender only. The women of combat wanted a "mixed organization" of men and women, a feminism based on the conditions of life, class and gender. The historical feminists called them "mujeristas" and the chavas bravas called them "las chavas del élite." The broncas grew as the combative women became the spine of the women's movement in the early 1980s. The barrio women came out en masse on March 8, International Day of the Woman–5,000, 6,000 women where there had once been only a weak puñada of hundreds. The chavas del elite would try to tell them how and where to march.

There near the stone skirt of Coyol, a mestiza, mujer de rebozo y machete and obsidian tongue, "who wrote a book so that she would not be anonymous," would become the giver of a heart and a face to feminist and chava brava alike. The woman with the white braids would be brought back from the place where people go when they are forgotten.

aunque sea jade se quiebra
aunque sea oro se rompe
aunque sea plumaje de quetzal se desgarra
no para siempre es la tierra
sólo un poco aquí
patriarcado y matriarcado
–Ancient flower-song adapted for la Coyol

Benita

"Oh! How I LOVE life!" The woman in the braids stands in the doorway with her voice of gunsmoke and honey that leaves the trail of a soldadera who does not regret. One minute she was a ribbon of tail wind. Next, pomegranate tears behind a screen door calling to her little pet fox, "la Preciosa…."

I met Benita Galeana when she was 84, or was it 86? It seems her age wobbled. She'd lift up her skirt to show me her legs were still firm. If she didn't have to wear that faja since the car accident that damaged her spine, she'd still be making love. She wore a wooden corset from the blows she received in the struggle. Mujer coqueta facing her own death, discussing the elder Bush–she hated "the assassin Bush." As for Noriega, he sent for her to come to Panama after reading her book; the tamales that she left for him were "bagged" for cocaine in the U.S. invasion. (Then Superbarrio served tamales in front of the

U.S. Embassy in México). She didn't sleep for days after the invasion of Panama. When she did, she dreamed she killed Bush. She'd talk about her romance with a doctor, un joven de sesenta, and revolutionary loves for Roberto of the garment workers union–"Benita is this…the sun"–and Francisco the photographer of the Left. Sometimes 25, 50 people crowded into her house. She was always surrounded by admirers: men, women, students–people who just wanted to be near her, to listen, to talk, to bring her food y apapacharla, to fill their lives with hers. Councils of indígenas who called her mamá, madre, invited her to be la mera doncella at a ceremony, with a carpet of flowers at her feet. "I lost my pistolas in '68," she said. She gave them to some of the students who stopped by the house. When I introduced her to my husband-to-be, she asked Roberto how was el joven Bert Corona. (Then a man in his 80's, he was an elder of the Chicano Movement who had been organizing practically since elementary school.)

She lives on Calle Zutano, Colonia del Periodista, with an old upright typewriter and wandering memories that escape with sighs. Benita in her tehuanas, Benita in pants, "Well, I was the first woman to wear pants…." Benita in bandanas like the Hidalgos of the Independence, Benita in high heels, Spanish Mantillas, Frida Kahloesque. Elena Poinatowska writes that both were women of eyebrows and mustache. Benita was a "soldadera de primera fila." Benita lived what Frida wished she could have. And Benita's walls are crooked windows to another tense: paintings of Benita from Spain, where there are fan clubs and streets named after her; Benita in black and white and sepia, memories the color of dried roses and blood–all next to the famous poster of David Alfaro Siquieros in Lecumberri jail, looking like a flame imprisoned.

– To Prisoner No. 46788: México is with you, prisionero, wrote the pained Pablo Neruda. The walls speak of what they know. Caprichosa, she will only speak of what she wants to and tell you what she doesn't like, con un machetazo through your disrespect, leaving only a dull, sweet wound. Like the Abuelitas say, "The coward wishes while the valiant lives." The machete is useless in the hands of a coward.

In the many suns of Benita Galeana are the girl who longed for shoes and a gold chain,

– the hand that groped at her at night when she was a girl, the hand that returned and found a knife in it, the bandaged hand of her brother-in-law;

– the hand that once grabbed a president's throat;

– the hands that sold El Machete, the communist organ;

– the eyes that can barely read or write, that can barely string words together, that almost went blind from hunger strikes that saw compañeros killed in demonstrations, land takeovers, strikes;

– the feet that marched, that ran from agents during the hard days of early Communism, that were tortured, that migrated from the provinces in search of a better life in Mexico City and escaped men and secret police;

– the body that became victim of sexual "favors," that worked in "El Viejo Jalisco" cabaret, a world of "scratched faces, jackknives and drunken brawls"; and

– the body that longed for love and passion, that stills desires.

Her gut withstood pistols and bore a girl and buried her; her hoarse voice still incites gritos as she did the first time she spoke while standing on a fruit crate May 1, 1921, demanding the release of her husband. I met the heart that I saw grow weak and the mind of a woman with an intellect con un piquete. Benita is the woman who took her clothes off in jail, along with four communist women, to avoid a massacre of comrades planning a rescue attempt. She was a woman who knew what it was to have your man beat you, who stopped fighting out of love for her man and love's illusions. The braids of this mestiza would become a symbol for urban women, middle-class women, and poor women who no longer wore trenzas because that was something "de indios" or "de provincia" but pinned paper and yarn braids to say they, too, were "Benitas."

"The Chinos want to make a doll of me, but all painted up, all fixed up. But my boyfriend says he would leave me just the way I am."

"Benita! Is that why you wanted to paint your hair?" Ay, Benita, carancha. She had a volcanic heart. Her spirit was like a lot of Mexican homes–with Christmas lights strung all year round.

No, she's in love with her canas, trenzas canosas, hair of thousands of years. Some Indian women wear their hair parted crooked, like a snake, like Quetzalcoatl. The braids are what they leave behind when they move to the city and away from tradition, umbilical cords to the past and the backwash of shame. An indigenous woman's circumcision of memory. Their hair weeps for them. I rarely saw the Benitas actually wear braids, other than as paper badges. Though the mestizas were hardly aware, it talked to a place in them, deep where the mind cannot be heard except in serpentine dreams of our conscience, crooked, like a snake part.

In "Aztec México," when warriors died in battle, they accompanied the sun in its descent. When women died at birth with their child, they, too, went to warrior land and accompanied the sun. Once, the anthropologist Eduardo Corona told me this story as we spoke of the coming eclipse in 1991, when the moon would kiss the sun: The men warriors were converted into hummingbirds, and the woman warriors into flowers. The birds would eat from the flowers, and that made love. It seemed Benita was their seed.

– Well, I have little drops of heroism, she'd say, of the Galeanas of the Independence movement. "Our heroes, they lived so others could learn from them. I belong to the heroes. We wait for heroes; but I am not a hero, just an example that is alive. I don't believe I'm a hero because that has to develop from the consequences."

When the Benita Galeana Steering Committee was created to fight for a democracy that honored women, working-class women, union women, middle-class feminists and the women of the Left joined together. In the female candidates' political literature by "the Benitas," they wrote, "Nosotras, un día nos despertamos con rebeldía." We women, one day we woke up with rebellion.

Herstory became a symbol. "A living symbol," said her comadre de combate María Guerra in 1991. Women have always done el que hacer, la frega. How could it not be herstory?

"All heroes are specific moments of time." Like ideas, they find their power at certain moments. Benita was a moral hero not because of her ideology or her party but because she fought for what she believed, because she fought against herself and ignorance. She transformed her fate because of her limitations; she emerged from them. She knew herself.

"She is like a perfume that you smell, like a flower perfume," said Pati Ruiz, the woman who proposed Benita as their icon. Benita wore a sense of participation like a scent. All the agonies and contraries and opposition to what she became, she became because of all that.

When I met a compañera of Benita's, la Yolanda Bernal, she showed me an amber ring Benita had given her that she promised would protect Yolanda. Benita is like that legend of amber. When rubbed, it is said, its aroma protects those who inhale it. The unfolding of her tela lifecloth gathered you around her and you became part of her bolt of living. A tight spirit weave.

The Benitas passed out her books to the women's commissions of neighborhood organizations and the women started reading about her. Her story was read to those who could not read. They reenacted her life in skits. They fought over who would play Benita. They cried as they heard her story because in it they saw their own in that unwritten book of the People. When the women were too shy to speak to her, she broke the silence. "I, too, entered the movement not knowing how to read or write. But we have to learn to say, 'I want to speak now.' We have to develop our minds." (NACLA Report on the Americas, August 1990)

An elementary school was named after her in her native state of Guerrero. Several women's meeting halls also were named in her honor. In the September 19 Garment Workers Union hall, Benita Galeana's face is spray painted on corrogated metal walls, her braids flying in rebellion. When I first met her, she attended meetings with women's groups who did ongoing organizing with "mujeres de base," the mass base of women. She became madrina of the barrios, madrina of San Miguel Teotongo, the warrior barrio of the "lost cities" of México since the 1970s, surrounded by the ruffles y las giggles of 15 girls coming of age at the barrio's quinceañera.

I met Benita the summer of 1991. A 13-year-old girl who had given Benita a legal document died while reading Benita's book. We went to lay a rose on her coffin. A year before, legal reforms increased punishment for rape and closed loopholes that alowed rapists to avoid sentencing by paying a fine. Women were scattered throughout the state working for female candidates. Benita, who fought for women's suffrage in the 1930s, ran as an alternate delegate on PRD. She'd even go out plastering campaign signs, barely able to move with her injured back. "I don't read books," said Benita, who taught herself to read by sounding out letters, "but I seek life." A seeking mind finds meaning in everything.

Benita claims she never wanted to hold an office in the party, preferring to be with the masses, putting up posters, distributing El Machete.

But her memoirs are bitters to her soul. Benita had to teach herself when the men wouldn't. "I have been jailed 58 times for the struggle. I have been hungry, have almost lost my sight, have risked my life for the party. But I am nothing but a politically backward, rank-and-file member, a nobody in the party. The party leadership never attempted to stimulate me to become more aware and capable. They left me alone in my ignorance."–Benita, the 1940 autobiography

"In my years of active struggle, I managed to win sympathy among the people. At rallies people would say–'Let the compañera with the braids speak!' The people trusted me because I spoke in the way that they understood. The party could have made better use of me, by orienting me and helping me to develop myself. But they never did." –Benita, the book

In 1946, she was expelled from the Mexican Communist Party for refusing to support conservative presidential candidate Miguel Alemán. Six years later, Alemán police fired on dissident communists during a May Day march. She dropped out of politics for four decades.

My compañera de lucha Elaine Burns wrote about Benita in 1990 for NACLA's Report on the Americas. Benita told her then: "Courage is an illusion. I always felt fear. I could always feel my soul knot up in my throat. But one day I found out something very important. The other side feels fear, too."

> That was in 1946. We had a number of compañeros in prison, and we had exhausted all legal means of obtaining their release. Our cell decided to organize an assault on Miguel Aleman. There were six of us who said we were willing to risk our lives to do it. We were afraid. All the way I kept saying,–It's not too late for us to turn back, you know. But we kept on going.
>
> As it turned out, all the others backed out and left me hiding there alone in the alley as Aleman's car pulled in. When the door opened and Aleman stepped out, I jumped up and grabbed him. It was one of those moments that last forever. Aleman's Adams apple jumped under my hand as I held his collar. I looked him up and down and even had time to say, 'Our lives are worth nothing.' That's when I realized that we all feel fear, even those who carry the weapons, those who wield power. None of us served time for that action, probably because they felt so humiliated by an unarmed woman.

The warriors sit like old dolls with canes. Benita and Valentín Campa, the people's hero in the railroad strike of the '50s who was freed after the '68 student massacre, attended the inauguration of a park in Campa's honor in fall 1991. A park for your years in jail, Campa. Othón Salazar, who led the teachers' strike in the 1950s, was also there. As I watched these lideres del pueblo arrive, it seemed to me to be a revolutionary honor guard for people of the highest purpose and incorruptibility.

"Where are we?" Benita asks. "I remember the first land invasion. In '46. In la 201. There were deaths. Wounded. Detained. Here…I thought…in la 201. Who here knows of la 201?"

"It's over there by Churubusco Park." On the other side of town.

"It was the first invasion," says Benita. "Each time the colono (squatter) left, they would knock down his jacal."

"No había otra."

"That's when we began to fight with Alemán. Only he could release the prisoners (who were arrested in that struggle). The car was going slowly through a knife slice of people. I jumped through the window and grabbed his tie. That's when I accosted Alemán. 'You are going to give us the prisoners in the morning.'"

"Es la Benita muy peleonera, muy decidida," she says.

She looks at an outdoor exhibit of popular struggles, including the historic "Río Blanco strike-workers' rebellion" in 1906-1907, which raised the curtain on the workers' unrest that helped fuel the revolution and resurgent Mexican anarchism. More than 200 workers were killed and 400 were imprisoned, including numerous women.

"Where is Lucrecia Toris? I don't see her photo. She was the first to do a hunger strike."

"They say Benita is valiant. It is not true that I am valiant. The valiant don't understand what it can lead to. I was always afraid. I don't know anyone who is not afraid. But some use the fear, throw off the fear, to let it not dominate you."

At the inauguration, Campa, who was first jailed in 1927 in the oil workers' union struggle, gets up to speak, slowly. His speech is short. "This should not be a homage to Campa but a homage to democracy. The struggle for democracy is, at the same time, the most important struggle of life and work of our people. It is difficult and prolonged. What is more, I believe, it never ends because we advance and see a few conquests and victory never presents itself completely, and we never seem to be in harvest. This should not be considered an act to Campa but an act that signifies the forces that are in agreement with democratic advances. For that, I salute you and I invite you, exhort you, to continue this struggle, so difficult but so important, for democracy in our country."

The old warriors nodded.

"Puras madres recibe el pueblo," muses Benita. "Democracy is mediocre. We made democracy on our knees; and the bourgeois, they made it theirs. With democracy they made it worse for us and used it against us."

"I suppose Diosito is a little old because he's forgotten his people. But the people continue with a hope, a blind hope. Almost all proletariats don't obtain what God had planned, and they die and don't reach anything. You arrive at what you are destined to arrive at. I leave for my people…I leave a walked road. The struggle comes by herself." When the Zapatistas rebelled, there she was marching, giving oratory that she no longer remembers.

There were many Benitas. La muy luchona Pati Ruiz, who was elected as a PRD assembly woman; and la Gloria Tello, who started Margarita Flores Magon women's center in the 1980s in honor of the mother who inspired one of the great thinkers of the Mexican Revolution. To me, the other Benitas of the heart were the everyday women who know what it means to create revolution from the home without enough money for bus fare; mujeres Marías whose outstretched palms become fists; India Marías with the double-blade wit of el pícaro, who know the beatings as a child, as a wife, to be orphaned and ordered around as maids with bleeding hands from three days of wash, who go to the market wondering what will they cook, with so little money. Frijoles, watery to make them go far, salty to make them last. Mientras haya frijoles, no habra hambre. When the women wearing white marched with doves for peace during the Gulf War, there was Benita, a primera fila, telling la Flor del Tránsito, ánimo mujer, que no te rajes. U.S. marines surrounded the U.S Embassy, armed and at attention. As 3,000 women and children dressed in white passed the "Gringo embassy," the women say guns where pointed at them. She told the women to have courage, that she was right there with them. "How could they gun unarmed women and children. No temen a esos cabrones. Look at those dogs behind us. Why do they fear women so much? We're nothing but women and children. Not with machine guns nor with shotguns should you fear these dogs." Mujeres de fuerza, dice la guerrera Bárbara la brava.

I often spent entire days with Benita, long afternoons made of mole and chocolate, tortillas que bonitas, sacraments of women's rituals. Once, Benita wrapped her hand around her coffee cup, flashing her prized ring with a bust of Lenin and her red-gold bands from Guerrero. I held her hand, looking at this icon; and she began about the Benitas. "They have Benita like an admiration, a symbol, a book that guides them. I continue in their fight," she said.

"My symbol was my party, defending the people. I have had them in my hand, the party, my husband. Now, they and the women, those are my symbols." Life was almost an obsession with her, a passion to the idea itself. She was obsessed with continuing. She worried so if she'd ever get a museum erected–before she died. "Then there will be no more Benita."

Las Abuelitas

"Oh, yes, we know her," said the two little grandmothers of Campamento Francisco Villa–through photographs, through her book. When they finally did meet in August 1991, I took pictures of Benita with her puro and the abuelitas with their gums and tears and filterless cigarettes.

"I couldn't leave without hugging her," recalled Abue Meche.

Benita hugged them both with her thick, handsome arms and told them, "Don't let it come to violence. All with calm and you will see that you will win. You will be women in the movement. You will always be in the fight, and I will always be with you."

"¡Hijole! It was pretty. I felt as if she were my mother. Her history lives on. All that she said was an experience that she left for others, and I do want to learn something. At least if I learn something, even if I don't ever earn a diploma…I want to attend the People's school," said Abue Meche. "We all have a right to be something in our life." She was 71 years old in 1992.

She digs her hands in her duster with torn tulip pockets, the one she always wears. She wears her shawl, the green of life, and her long, white socks that, as usual, are always falling.

The Abuelitas were souls of the urban movement, always together like two halves of a heart. What was it that Henrietta Mann says her Cheyenne people called themselves, "the hearted alike" ones?

– "¿Qúe vamos a la guardia, Abue?" Abuelita Vargas–70 years young–would tell her comadre.

Abuelita Vargas wore the earth in her skin, a raw, honest brown of ollas ondas. A brown that tastes of piloncillo and pinole. Abuelita Meche could read, but the sugar in her blood was blinding her, just as her grandson's drinking. She was getting hard of hearing, so Abuelita Epifania Vargas was her legs. She cannot read at all. Together they were mind and heart. When they talked, they become one abuelita.

– Que la Claudia la PRIista is at it again, invading lands.

– Qúe vámonos, they'd say in voices, sweet like amaranth and viznaga cactus candy.

They'd stand guard over the precious barren land in Campamento Francisco Villa that would become somebody's little piece of tu pobre casa until four or five in the morning, wearing thin soles, and threads and stitches for sweaters in the rain.

Pedro Moctezuma, a pioneer leader in San Miguel Teotongo when it became territorio libre in the 1970s, once explained the souls of movements to me. San Miguel Teotongo is where Campamento Francisco Villa is located.

"Each movement has a soul and it is individualized in each person. When a movement doesn't have this alma, it dies. It is the heroic people of the movement, which in one way is very spiritual, who pull the participation along and are able to propel the masses. They act with personal disinterest. It is active, pure, preoccupied for others. They act as a mirror to return to others their autonomy. There would be no popular movement without this heroism."

"The almas don't become caudillos. They are those who anguish for unity, who don't see the miserable conditions or errors of others. The Abuelitas are those souls. They feed the children, express their feelings from the flower of the skin, which permits pleasure, plains of tears, and sadness."

In my time with these almas, I learned that the Abues believed when no one else did and everyone else had forgotten. It is a heroism that is a process, not short, intense moments of action and lightning. What I found were not two viejitas. They were chavas bravas made young from the spirit to struggle, who embraced the opportunity to fight because it took them beyond everything they knew. I call it la cruzada, the crossing to the part of us that lies in the future, in the unknown, that calls us forth from the possibilities. The battle with life is a battle with how we respond to suffering.

"Every organization has their abuelitas. They are like the Aztec counsel of elders," says Clara Burgada, a 27-year-old leader in San Miguel who entered the struggle when she was 17. Her name means clear, and she is. "They are a moral presence and live in the worst houses, and they are always the first ones there for the fight."

"The struggle came from suffering," said Abuelita Meche. I can hear Benita as a muse overhead, "The revolutionary comes from hunger." There can be no wisdom without suffering.

"We suffered storms, rains, cold, winds, and here we are," Abue Vargas said.

In 1974, thousands of people invaded a rocky stretch of San Miguel Teotongo, one of the first and most combative of the "lost cities" of Mexico City's urban sprawl. Pedro Moctezuma, descendant of the last Aztec ruler, once drew a map showing me how San Miguel had been the domain of the great Mechica warrior Cuitlahuac–the only warrior lord never defeated by the Spaniards–and a region that was a Zapatista stronghold in the Mexican Revolution. The Unión Popular Revolucionario Emiliano Zapata–UPREZ–where the Abuelitas helped found one of the first women's councils, takes its name from that history. Leaders of UPREZ, one branch of the hydra CONAMUP, infiltrated the squatter's movement. A power struggle soon ensued between the charros PRIstas and UPREZ followers. For one month, the paracaidistas, or parachuters, as the squatters are known, began to make the land theirs.

Among them were the Abuelitas.

They came here alone. No one knew of them nor they of the others. Abuelita Meche came with nothing but a little bag she used for a coin purse. She stayed and made a home of rags and timber, spare things from the others. There she met Abuelita Vargas, a Nahuatl Indian from Hidalgo. Rarely have they separated since, climbing that hill of rocks on all fours like old cats with nothing but the light of the moon. Those rock paths that lead to their huts of corn sacks and bricks now have names: La Venceremos, We Shall Overcome; and Pueblo Unido, People United. When they were hungry, they went to the hills and ate herbs and grass. Or they went to the trash dumps, like tirabichis, trash-picking from the refuse of others. They rinsed out the remains of sardine cans. The other people living in the area called them rat eaters. When the rains came, as they do early in June, they slept in a bed of mud and a blanket of rain. They have worn that sarape many times. They ran the people's kitchen and tended to the children. Even then they were known as the Abuelitas, and even then all the children were their grandchildren.

One June 24, 1973, after UPREZ wrested the leadership from the government boot-licking charros of the squatter's movement, the goons came and beat the people with billy clubs, burned their jacalitos and their belongings, and threatened them with bombs. "From here on in, I am going to fight," said Abue Meche. And they did, through rains and dogs. They both still live in jacalitos. Sometimes, still, not even chilitos do they have for a bowl of rice or lentils, a scrap of meat maybe once a week y un atolito de coraje. Later came the fight for water, the fight for electricity, and the fight for drainage. Broncas, siempre, pero bien bonitas, that began with the goons and the march that day in a storm; but I mean a storm, where not even the birds can see they are flying toward death.

But they won Campamento Francisco Villa. "With this name, we won electricity and water. Now, we need pavement, bathrooms." The Abuelitas organized the colonia to get drainage for the families living there. The viejitas dragged bags of cement. Now they are worried about paying for the mortages, which in 1992 amounted to $3,140.

– With money from peeling pecans? $2.60 every third day?

They won it all but with un chingo de sufrir, and some compas have disappeared. They don't return, they don't return, and THEY (the anonymous they of rumors) say they were taken to a cave in the earth and killed. And the compas don't return.

"Cada bronca, pero buena."

The Abuelitas have been in pie de la lucha ever since. Always the first in line, the first to get real bravas with a bag of eggs–"a ver quien tiene mas huevos." Who had more balls? But of course, las

Abues. When they went to negotiate for free breakfasts, the Abuelitas led a human chain. And when they sicced the dogs, Abue Meche just stood there to fight with the goons, 30 dogs in the Zócalo. They unleashed dogs, pero perrotes, grandototes. They asked her to step aside. She kicked off her shoes instead and slowly put them on. When she looked into a dog's eyes, she could see his tail wagging. "These dogs understand more than those," she said.

"Did I tell you I was hit by a woman police officer? She tried to push me down a flight of stairs," Abue Meche says.

Another time, as they were leaving police headquarters after going to protest for the release of a comrade, they spotted a man taking photographs. She lifted up her dress for him to take a picture. When they went to the electric plant to negotiate, they wouldn't let her in. "I got real mad dog with the fat-cat attorney who started pushing me around; and I told him, 'I'll drop my drawers if you don't let me in.' "

When you've survived on chile and water, walked in the rain of bullets, and lost half of your children in childbirth, what's left inside of you that can fear? Her husband beat her enough for a lifetime. "Face up or face down, I will not be humiliated." Mejor vivir sola que con una mano encima.

"Y ay vamos a la bola."

In 1984, at a May Day protest when they were fighting for more subsidies, thousands of women and children stopped traffic for four hours along Avenida Júarez. Police in motorcycles surrounded them. Everyone ran, but the Abuelitas stayed in front. They were livid and rattling like two old snakes. Abuelita Vargas picked up a cement block, threw it on the ground, and broke it into pieces.

"Y ahora sí a contestarles." They started stoning the policemen.

Abue Meche tells me a story she learned at the CONAMUP People's School about the founding of México. "Where the eagle stopped on a nopal that would be their territory–it is the same thing with us. We look for a place to live and give it a name. We fight to have a little piece of land, to eat better."

(They came here alone. No one knew their name.) "We are all the same. Brothers and sisters because we have all the same blood. It is mixed, some with mestizo and Spanish. But it is the same blood. You cut the blood and it is still the same for each. Rich or poor. They say the eagle went to the United States. But they ran it off in the United States, so it landed in Tezcoco."

The Abuelitas came to San Miguel Teotongo when UPREZ had popular control and made this a "free territory." The people imparted justice a la brava. Once, community patrols caught a rapist. They took off his clothes and paraded him to their community center. Tied to his back was a sign, "I'm a rapist. I rape children."

When the women built a milk station with their bare hands and the government put it, instead, in PRI territory, the women set up a plantón. For years they fought for the milk station.

People would ask them, why the plantón?

– But for a milk station? The milk station became more than a fight for the right to distribute milk. It became a symbol. "Que no se va a permitir chingaderas."

"We built this ourselves," said la Clara. Eventually they obtained an alternate site.

The Abuelitas have watched their world become modern. They lived the stonings, the land invasions on their scratches of land. They planted 20 trees with their knotted hands, only to see the youngsters rob the gasping saplings that were to become green spaces in this most un-transparent air.

The Abuelitas saw their ideas appropriated by the government. They saw the tortibonos dry up, the people's store of half-price food. They've been at workshops where women with third-grade-educations (at best) discuss this thing called globalization. What are the new tactics, when pots and pans confront multinationals and corporate nations? The Abues have been accused of robbing money. People forgot how they started the store and arose at 4:00 a.m. every morning, with barely time to eat. Some of the people smirk when they speak up at meetings. What do two viejitas know about the world? And just like the milk, they became a symbol of struggle. "And now we are the Abuelitas of UPREZ."

When I first met them, they were fighting land invasions by Claudia the PRIista. Then it became María Elena, the modernista, which meant she was still a PRIista but a little cleaner.

"Un arbol derecho va chueco de chiquito," says Abue Meche.

San Miguel and the Unión de Colonos, a subgroup of UPREZ that represents Campamento Francisco Villa, was being pummeled by the PRI, retribution for being warrior barrios. In August 1992, right before the senate elections, PRI came in with Solidaridad, the humanitarian program that buys votes through public services. Solidarity. Critics say the government capitalized on the solidarity forged by the earthquake. It was a program implemented by the International Monetary Fund throughout Latin America. The government takes advantage of it. Prior to the elections, the Mexican government put in a metro and brought huge sewage tubes in San Miguel. The barrio residents put in the sweat. Sympathizers of UPREZ were the last to get them. Members were forced to choose allegiance to the urban movement or the PRI. Then when the election was over, the Abuelitas said the tubes just sat there like hair rollers. For adornment.

In June of that year, Antorcha Campesina, a paramilitary campesino group of 300 people, invaded UPREZ green lands set aside for future recreational development. Antorcha was armed and threatened people. UPREZ negotiated with the government, and Antorcha was removed. Then PRIistas, looking to wrest control from UPREZ block captains and delegates, went around threatening people on election day. They went house-to-house, telling the people not to vote, that it would get violent. They stopped traffic and turned over a truck. They marched around the statue of Emiliano Zapata in the People's plaza, shouting:

"We want the head of Clara."

"Die Zapata."

Then they burnt Zapata's statue.

"Ahora sí vamos a contestarles," said UPREZ.

UPREZ mobilized the people and maintained representation as block captains, even picking up a few spots.

The people called it "la venganza de Zapata." Zapata's revenge.

"I do feel a bit of heroism," says Clara. "Shortly before the 1988 elections, our green areas were invaded. The mounted police came. We came to defend our lands. The charros were all over the place, 60 of them. With picks and sticks."

The police were guarding the invaders.

A fight broke out and someone fractured Clara's nose. The children ran and told everyone. Within five minutes they were surrounded by 500 people. The police wanted to take Clara to jail. But the women surrounded them, and rocks started flying.

"People say they will enter when the fights begin, but the hardest is daily life, the daily fights. Las broncotas, that's easier–when you are already a hero. The most difficult is the daily life where you give your life in the process." – Clara.

"Who is going to give her life to generate a movement of gender and class?" asks Clara in a voice stretched raw from too many meetings. "It is a gray work that never enters a newspaper. All the daily actions. Like they say, the silent protagonism."

And to maintain it for a lifetime? Hope?

The constant golpes forced the Unión de Colonos to reconstruct the movement during the summer of 1991.

Leaders posed certain questions. Who is for the union? Do we want an organization of masses or of conscious individuals? They chose to move from being a group of masses, founded on the principles of mass organization by Mao, to one of individuals working and developing in communal structures. They decided they'd rather have a few hundred conscious people, active, who'd suffered through the processes, than thousands who had to be dragged along. Often, they had to mobilize up to 1,500 people 15 times to pressure for a demand. San Miguel was a "lost city"–as the urban sprawl was known–of 80,000 people. But the union had only 400 loyal cells, comprised mostly of women, small business owners and street vendors.

The people get tired. Early on Clara told me, "Consciousness is acquired through practice. It is acquired in the marches. It is acquired in the meetings. It is acquired in the movement itself. The assemblies are the daily lesson. Direct democracy. When you have confidence in yourself, you begin to speak and the leaders learn from the people."

The union decided to win people over–ganar compañeros–looking for ways to influence their neighbors in daily life.

"We're shooting for the total individual," Clara would later say. They looked for strategies so as not to depend on the government, such as developing their green areas and using the ground they possess–through legal acquisition–for recreation and day care.

It seemed that where the union was going, the Abuelitas had already traveled in those explosions of the microcosm that expand the macrocosm. The universe in a drop of water, writes the poet José Emilio Pacheco. A movement can only advance to the extent that the people's lives expand.

To act, to have purpose, gave their lives meaning and even brought out the medicine from inside their bodies. I've been with the Abues when Abue Meche was sick from TB. Abue Vargas bursts into the jacal. "They threatened us! Come on abuelita–to protect the green areas!" Abue Meche rubs her eyes, sitting up in bed. "Cómo qúe no," dice su amigocha. "Ahora sí a chingar a las tareas."

"Sometimes she is sick. Sometimes I'm sick. I get better, she gets better. We go out," explains Abuelita Vargas.

When a caravan was marching to Toluca, the Abues wanted to go. But the others wouldn't let them. They were too old and the walk too long. When the women's regional center offered classes to read and write, there was Abue Vargas, at age 65. When UPREZ members wrote a rock-and-roll song for the Abuelitas and played it for them at a tribute, there they were bobbing in a sea of youth.

"What is better? A lot of land or to learn how to fight?" Abue Meche asks.

"I was born again in the organization," says Abue Meche. The house became the means to self-knowing, not an end in itself. Why do you fight, Abue? And she showed me where strength comes from. "Because we are human beings, because we care about the needs of others. Another's problem we make our own.

"I saw the fight was not only for a house. It was for everything. Why do I live? Why do I exist? Am I not human?"

This day Abue Meche is knitting. "It's like with a wood fire." She gathers the yarn and crosses the needles. "You put some timber, but with one little stick no se puede." She gathers the yarn and crosses the needles. "It won't light. You have to gather more palitos so that a fire grabs," she said. "But that little stick will burn more because it feels protected with the force of the others."

"If one has and the other doesn't, you must help them the same as the other," says Abue Vargas. "This fight has no end. You must struggle until you can no longer." And they do.

Abue Meche loves to be in negotiations. People tell her that they are for young people.

But no one else will do it. "No se aguanta la chinga," says Abue Vargas. "¡Qúe se chingen los pendejos! No les importa ni un comino."

The Mud People

You suffer but you learn, they say. They've been to women's meetings in Torreon, Durango, Zacatecas. Now the children have toys. "Ahora somos las meras chingonas de aquí."–Abue Vargas.

Mujeres grandes know that action evolves from a purpose. They looked for a nopalito and took a hill. They rose "antes que el gallo" and worked until the other side of day. They listened to what the ollas ondas had to say, all so they could find a place to plant their names.

Las ollas ondas say that life is a molcajete, matriz volcánica. It must be cured with lime and salt, but it is nothing without the hand stone (la mano), our heart. Qué se lleva en la molcajete de la vida: miel amarga, vidas partidas, sal de lágrimas, coraje; hierba buenas, te de rosas, lavanda and barbas de maíz for sore backs, nervios and sleeping good; romero for purification baths, warming our insides and remembering; mother roots–osha, yerba manzo–y plantas maestras, la ruda, la gobernadora, estafiate...; ombligos to bury, huevos para limpiar; the three sacraments–chile, maiz and chocolate; rabanitas de aire for food; and don't forget the breath; the shuffle of your mother's feet in yours; the one good dress dominguera; aguas negras and agua bendita for drunken sons, and for husbands, to put in their coffee when they are not looking, ¡Aguas!; the color red, and if you can, the beak of a hummingbird for love medicine; word flints and lengua, espinas because Our Mother made them for a reason; copalli in a coffee can to burn after cleaning the house and to carry our prayers; marigolds so that our dead can find us; cascabeles so that we can make noise.

Mujeres muy luchonas say that when the Abuelitas arrive it's as if The Heart had entered the room. "Abuelitas," I asked one day, "Does la lucha come from the heart?"

"In all things that are done, it is born in the heart," says Abue Meche. "The change has to come from inside. It is because it is born from the heart. We fight so children will no longer suffer. It is for the future warriors."

"The struggle is like un espejismo, a reflection in a mirror. When you look fixed up, it's an image. If you look unkept, you look different. You see in the mirror that you don't look good. That is the way in an organization. If you are not conscious, no tienes ganas. "

All struggle becomes our mirror.

As the Abues prepare to join the earth again, they talk and fret about the young ones, about the fact that people with stronger fists and more time left in this life don't fight. "Que viene la muerte. Orale pues," says Abue Vargas. "Que viene la pelona."

"Youth is passing like a rose that flowers," says Abue Vargas.

"Come to my house. I'll make you a little bed."

"I am alone, alone, sola, sola," she says. "My mother died, my father died. I am alone, just as when you die."

"The earth belongs to no one. We play over her. We live over her. We take our first steps over her," says Abue Vargas.

"On her we learn to walk, we learn to die; and it eats us up. Uno chiquito vuelve a chiquito, que no oye, que no camina. There comes a new era, a near way of work…of marriage, of speaking. La flaca is our path. It destroys us and it eats us."

"The body lies in the ground for three days combating with the earth that does not want to accept it. That is the last struggle."

Herstory

When Coyolxauhqui's mother Coatlique was impregnated by a ball of plumes that fell from the sky, the warrior woman and her 400 brothers and sisters attempted to slay her. But her brother Huitzilopochtli sprang from his mother's belly on Serpent Hill and flung Coyol's brothers into the sky. They became the Milky Way, and the beheaded Coyol became the moon. One legend says she was flung at the feet of Serpent Hill.

People who read carved rocks say she is the moon. Some scholars say she represents the Milky Way. She was the historical leader of a matriarchal clan who was defeated in battle–the feminists. She symbolizes the final conflict between non-warfare society and a militaristic vision and the dominance of men as warriors and chieftains–say others. Salas writes: "Some time after entering the Valley of México, perhaps in 1143 A.D., the Mechicas dethroned a prominent female warrior leader named Coyolxauhqui…." Salas quotes the work of Adela Formoso de Obregón Santacilia that Coyolxauhqui "'ordered the end to warfare and warrior groups' and called for the 'establishment of cities not based on warfare.'"

In the multimedia CD, "Coyolxauhqui An Ancient Myth and Chicanas Today," by Chicanas Ana García, Elba J. Ríos, and Alma E.

Cervantes, Mexican scholars noted that Coyol had been a great leader and had attracted numerous followers (as represented by the 400 brothers and sisters). "She had power." Art historian Carmen Aguilera notes in the CD that she deciphered one of the glyphs on Coyol's monument that held the inscription, "A mi me mató Huitzilopochtli." Huitzilpochtli killed me.

According to one of the post-conquest accounts regarding Coyol, Coatepec was also the name of a place along the Mechica's migration trail. There, Huizilopochtli was challenged by Coyol. Scholar Yolotl González notes in the CD that Coyolxauhqui and her followers no longer wanted to continue on and wanted to stay in Coatepec. She was killed the next day, said González.

She is the universal mother, Our Cosmic Mother, say some danzantes. She is constant movement and the eternal struggle between night and day that in its whole is harmony; she is the eternal "retorno of life," the seasons, "las rondas de la luna"–María Anzures of the Mechica tradition. She does the dance of "reintegration," writes Anzures.

Xicana ceremonial leader Sylvia Ledesma says Coyolxauhqui represents the dismemberment of feminine energy and its re-emergence in everyone. Sylvia, who is writing a book on Xicana spirituality, notes, "We all have Coyoxauhqui inside of us."

The Coyolxauhqui CD notes the scholarship of Beatriz Barba de Piña Chan that connects Coyolxauhqui with ollin: "In the relief, Coyolxauhqui's profile is sculpted with movement…she is moving in a continuous and circular motion."

"While Coyolxauhqui is standing upright, she is running the universe. It is night. During the day, her head is at the bottom. Huitzilopochtli is running the universe. This is the cycle of the day."

Leonor Aída Conha wrote of her symbol in 1988 in La Mata Dando, the newspaper of the "Benita Galeana" Women's Steering Committee: "La Coyolxauhqui symbolizes the defeated; she is the image of the beaten ones. In the Templo Mayor, Coyolxauhqui's stone is situated at the base, at the feet of the god Huitzilopochtli; and it was stepped upon by the prisoners en route to be sacrificed, that is to say, so that the people would not forget the destiny, which, like woman and the transgressors, awaited everyone."

> Just as Coatlique symbolizes the woman-mother, la Coyolxauhqui symbolizes the political woman who struggled for power but was defeated, and with her all the Mexican women were defeated. That society had a vision of life that put the woman in a place that impeded her from changing her condition. There she was, figuratively, by the stone, stepped upon by the condemned, subjugated by man, under rigid laws.... La Coyolxauhqui was placed with a fixed face, always looking toward her victor, and, what is more, in eternal movement, in a circle from which she could not leave.... Finally, we want to imagine that because of her rebel movement, her cold eye, her strong hands, her experience can bring her to break the circle, to run to encounter other women, so that together they will leave the eternal repetition of tradition in which others have nailed her in, break the circle of her eternal submission, find another life, leaving behind what her name signifies: la Coyolxauhqui.

Mexicanas, Xicanas, and lesbianas began to re-member ourselves with la Coyol, put ourselves back together. Some Mexicanas took her as a spiritual muse of political battle. Lesbians found truth and spirit in her. For Xicanas and women in the "danza Azteca," Coyol brought a deep, spiritual knowing. She has spawned the Coyoxauhqui CD, which unfolds like a multimedia codex. She is the muse of art, modern dance, and storytelling by women artists in the community. The Coyol CD records the story of a L.A. mural of Coyolxauhqui that was ripped and clawed. Teen males had not liked the image. One male said the mural had been "Coyolxauhquied."

Perhaps we did not re-member her, but she re-membered us. She called us into her circle dance. "She is speaking through us," Chicana muralist Yreina Cervantes notes in the CD. Citing our ancestral legacy of women with "spiritual power and public power," Chicana writer Naomi Quiñonez notes in the Coyolxauhqui CD that while Coyol's monumental stone marks the transition of female power toward a more patriarchal society, she should be remembered as whole–she remains "intact in the circle." Coyolxauhqui does not represent a loss of power, notes Quiñonez, but rather, because of her historical conditions, there evolved "a multiplicity of power." As many of the grandmas have shown us, there are many ways to assert power. There are many paths of power and influence–the powers found in mother energy, in quilting and beading, sewing and cooking, in nuestras yerbas, and grounding a family and community in our spiritual earth.

Coyolxauhqui, Madre Cosmica, is not dismembered. Her separated body, which floats free of gravity, reflects the natural lunar and solar cycles. From her celestial chaos the world is born; the world and matter manifest, writes Anzures in Coyolxauhqui, Nuestra Madre Cosmica.

"Coyolxauhqui is the chaos of the initial act of 'separation.' She emerges like the universe, a mythic being that is pieced apart, with the world being born from this sacred division. She gives rise to an organized world."

As Anzures notes, Coyolxauhqui emerges transformed from having given birth to creation. "As every woman knows after giving birth, 'one feels descoyuntada' (pulled apart)."

Consejo from Anzures: Coyolxauhqui is the DANZANTE COSMICA, the cosmic danzante, the danzante of reintegration. The "Mother of Manifestations" brings equilibrium to creation; and as taught by Anzures, she reflects in all of us.

While all change is a deeply spiritual process, it is not always recognized as such by the Left. In México, even the word spiritual does not translate as meaning something in addition to the construction of "God." The urban women's movement was one of the few to invoke a female energy as part of their movement. As Xicanas helping to build a spiritual nation, we seek to understand Coyolxauhqui's message. We are piecing our people back together with la palabra (the wisdom, the words) of women. While initially we sought to change the structures, eventually we began to also follow the lesson of curanderas, looking for remedios to heal ourselves, our families, and then our community. Some remedios came from the medicine of justice. And we began to return to our grandmother's ways, to experiment with las yerbitas, los tés, los remedios, las limpias, el apapacho (para nosotras y nuestra familia social). We have sought to bring the medicine out of our bodies, our communities, and our histories. As la comadrita Sylvia says, "Healing is part of self-governance."

We are entering the new sun, a new age of feminine energies in the world. I call these times the eve of the millennium of the feminine. In our indigenous teachings, it is better said as a new sun or a new moon. In this new time returns the eternal truth that Creation is fundamentally feminine. Creation energy expresses a feminine aspect that humans can understand. But the masculine energy is needed, as well, for life. And so in this rebalancing of life, the feminine will rebalance in all things, men, women, land. And the masculine as well. Just as there is male rain and female rain, just as we, as human beings are an electro-magnetic field of positive and negative energy,

alkaline and acid,
cold and hot,
wet and dry,

so must our human relations come into balance with the feminine and masculine. The Mayan medicine man Apolinario says our hearts have a female valve and a male valve. As males and females, and human being to human being, we must learn to treat each other differently. If humankind does not come into balance, the Earth will not survive. Because we are part of Creation, we cannot maintain imbalance and not affect the rest of nature. La comadrita Sylvia gives this definition of the meaning of Coyolxauhqui's name, "a heart adorned in the old way that is moving in a certain direction."

Speaking of the time of the Sixth Sun, "a new sun of justice," Sylvia says our hearts should be moving in an appropriate direction for the new sun.

These are the moons of "Grandmother Time," the wisest of all feminine energy in women. This is the time of the circle, las enaguas, our wide skirts. Just as Coyol may have marked the defeat of matriarchal leadership, her re-memory calls for us to return to matriarchal societies and traditions to preserve all of life and for the return of men and women societies that strengthen communities.

I remember when Chicana artist/sculptor Gloria Osuna Pérez was creating her massive installation of la Coyol. She would fire her clay, and it kept exploding. Then she worked by the light of the moon, y la Coyol emerged into beauty. Later, I learned there are 400 billion stars in the Milky Way. I realized our ancestors knew something about those 400 brothers and sisters.

La Trenza

"Have you seen my movie? Tonight, I am going to play all my pictures. Tonight…is…Saturday. Tonight I'm going to spend it all night seeing all my movies." Benita's earrings bob about like Victorian parasols.

My friendship with Benita would witness her momentary decline. For a time, I saw her heart grow weak, the power of her mind wander to confusion when she spoke in public. My ideas came from the moment. Like that, she'd say and snap her fingers. Then she would ask me what she had told the crowd. "I don't understand. Sometimes when I speak, I don't know what I am saying."

Sometimes I helped her dress in her satin huipiles for an event, her heart thumping like a baby in the womb when she lifted her arms to pull over her blouse.

"The struggles of the people make me live," she'd say. Then I saw her cry and sigh at the doorway. Homage had kept Benita alive. She lived on their adulation, the march down the aisle, the applause of the intellectual and proletariat. It was as if she hoped they could keep her alive forever, really alive. The streets named after her, the spray-painted images of her at the costurera local, the awards, could not change the fact that she would die.

"They keep telling me to prepare myself, to prepare myself…I walk with the orders of nature. Entonces ya no va haber Benita." She trails off, inside of herself.

"I must accept it. I have to accept that I must walk that road. It is coming."

Friends and admirers would always stop by unannounced for coffee. They brought her food. When she was sick, they took turns nursing her. But often at night she was alone, left with her video memories. She constantly solicited help in editing her book in progress on yellowed typing paper, a poetry in phonetic passion. She was determined to finish the book of "palabras sangrientas" before she died. It was for her as necessary as breathing, and she would get so frustrated that she could barely string together letters. She was still desperate to have her home turned into a museum.

"Miguel, document this," she'd say. "Benita seguida por vender el filete." That's what they called El Machete.

"Pati, read me this…"

I read the phonetic letters, at times not able to make out the words.

"Nor I," says Benita.

"When I was poor and it was said que muchachita hermosa, between the play of la niña pobre y la Benita, the play of this character, and I knew what they said of me, from that moment I began to prepare this enormous castle of fireworks, full of tenderness…I began to take pieces of tenderness, and in this way passed many years, but many years, and I continued to care for it and continued to gather these pieces of firewood, of words. And the years went by and I built this enormous castle of fireworks for the man who was coming."

The dream did come, in 1928, by the name of Mario Gil, journalist and writer. He helped her edit her first book, and they later fell in love. Benita writes, "He had the fortune to receive this enormous castle of fireworks full of tenderness. And just as I give this to you, I want you to treat me with this tenderness. And I put it into your hands. But death came, and, in the confusion, I don't remember if he took it or if he left it because I cannot find it anywhere."

It was a great love, with freedom. Me, my way; you, your way. "I was free to go to jail, to go my way to the struggle, to post propaganda, to look out for police. And he would get me out."

Benita loved to talk about love.

"At the end after all, al fin y al cabo, I left much, so that the woman can free herself, an honest liberation so that she can free herself, honestly. La mujer cries and errs when she cries, when she feels secure, loved, and wanted. Then each makes their castle of fireworks. This one is mine that no one can take from my soul and say this is borrowed. I will enjoy a few days, and then it ends. We need man to go out, to pass time. We can't enjoy a walk alone. Life forces you to have something, to enjoy it with someone. We need someone to accompany us, even when we have a family. Life clarifies woman and man; and when strong times come, we blame the man. We don't say, 'You made me spend a happy night.' I suppose these are things we should value. Lo hacemos mios instead of asking how long will you be here. If there were a law that said he is not yours, if they made a law that said he is borrowed? Love is important. Love makes me live; love is more than physiology. We need it, you and I. All this combines that is life. We want love, all or nothing. But we want it all.

"Then you suffer the hungers, the ones that are most interesting for a home."

"Que chifladura," she says of today's relationships between men and women. "¿Qúe libertad tienen?"

– My boyfriend called on me again. He wants to marry me.

Benita Galeana

She even went to the doctor to see if she could have sex again. She lived in a melodrama, sleeping with the passions of a woman with thorn roses on her breasts. Benita, old, became a girl en tiempos de señorita con su pretendiente.

Elliptical charlas: "…and I wore my skirt from India…and I remember a pair of shoes in the window (in 1930), and he loves me like a viejita. I am his idol. He likes to say, 'I am the one who loves Benita.' 'Don't get wet. You are an institution, and you are getting wet. And if you die and the people are left without their Benita? ¿Sin su Benita?' "

She finally received a government commitment to establish the museum. On September 10, 1994, on her ninetieth birthday, she danced all night at a celebration for her life. And when she went to bed, she was a girl as she slumbered on a bed of new memories. "Ay, Pati, you should see how they love Benita…."

"You've given me life," she says to some young friends who have come to lunch with her. "I have everything–my house, my pension, your esteem. What martyrdom to live like old women who only lived for their families, now mute in their four walls."

"She was ready, Benita, when she died," says la Benita.

"Even though I'm a revolutionary and I've seen blood run, I've become more sentimental."

– Even if you are a communist, you still feel pain.

"Now I have fears, fear of being alone." She often changed her mind about death. Yolanda Bernal told me how Benita was rediscovered in 1980 by the women's movement. She was near death and opened like a flower. Yolanda said it was because Benita lived by giving her life to others.

Later, Benita would say, "My life is complete. I have everything.

– In the end, I say death is bonita. It is a liberation.

Once as we spoke of la muerte, I read her words to her, "Mi pueblo me necesita allá, there where they died of hunger. Al fin de la jornada, I reached the moon…."

We laughed. And then she told me, "I'll go and organize the people in heaven."

"I carry the revolution inside," she said. "I just want the people to be happy, but I live in them. I will always live in them."

The Mud People

When people die, their spirits remain, las ánimas. In their death, they are more alive. If they are in our hearts, they are here. They live in our actions. We choose whether we will be remembered as builders or destroyers, or as accomplices by our silence.

There are times when we carry the ánimas in our bones, and times when they enter our guts and burn. They course through our blood until we do something that we are supposed to do. At times we feel them in our hands when we make Good. Sometimes they water the struggle as tears offered to the road. There are times when I feel them in my braids, when I have uncovered new meaning to my memories, and I hear the warble of long afternoons at an old woman's kitchen table as if she wrapped my heart in her shawl and pinned the rebel braid of three women to my life. "Time martyrs your steps with lived acts. Al fin y al cabo dejo mucho. In the end there was one woman who made her castle of fireworks that is mine."

Benita pauses, soplando el pasado and the attendant spirits of her life, "El mundo es mio." The world is mine. At the end of the campaign, at the end, after all.

Chavas Bravas

Inside the local, to be inaugurated Women in Struggle Benita Galeana, las chavas bravas sit in student desks made for six-year-olds.

These are women who no longer speak with their hands over their mouths. Mujeres que solo sabían de la cocina, de la cocina sólo sabían.

The women chant:
pioneers-to-transform-society-transform-yourself
mujeres-que-se-organizan
no-planchan-mas-camisas
More chants.
La-mujer-luchando-y-el-mundo-transformando
when-a-woman-advances-no-one-can-stop-her

Clara speaks. "I want us to remember some compañeras. The Abuelitas were founders of the women's council."

The Abuelitas stand with fists and tears in the air. "I'm very sentimental. I always cry–from happiness–with every little thing I cry. I always cry. Whatever happens, tears always come out of my eyes. We first started fighting for our young, and we'll continue to fight. It doesn't matter if they sicced the dogs on us. We dream for our children. Because of this, it doesn't matter that they sent dogs on us. For this we fought."

Another Abuelita from another colonia stands and speaks: "I have fought and I have suffered. And I feel proud that you have asked me to speak even though I can't read or write. They put dogs on us, but we stayed to fight."

Again, las porras:

mujer-educa-a-tus niños-en-la-lucha

Clara addresses las compañeras: "We had not one idea of how to form a women's group. We knew we were part of the urban movement. We only knew that we women had to give our own fight, and we didn't know how or from where to take examples. We did not know a thing. We didn't know how to build a movement. We just wanted to be a part of the women, to do our own fight. Yet we began to realize our power as women.

"So we began the fight where all fights like ours begin, from the gut."

"During those times, eight or nine years ago, we didn't know the magnitude of what we were about to build. Anyhow, we began tenaciously to have this fight everyday, making demands of the government. The fight is responsible for our food for the children, and then we began to recognize the force we had as women."

"We told our organization we didn't want to be the base that made the bola in the meetings, the marches. We wanted to play an important role and command the protagonism of the urban women. And in those negotiation meetings, we went with all the fear, all the responsibility of all the women."

– And the compañeras who were always quiet, las calladitas, they began to scream, to infect their families, and to tell them, que saben que sí me gusta la lucha.

"Our organizations didn't take us seriously. Now the women's commission is the space that is always working, strengthening the organizations. The men accused us of dividing it; now instead, we've made it strong."

"At the same time, too, we changed. We always think we fight to change our family, the very society in which we live. But along the way I believe what we've changed is ourselves. None of us are the same women. We have changed. In this decade, we have shown the new face of México. We women, you. It is the face of women who fight, que no se deja, the face of a woman who is changing herself, her family, and all of society. We are showing a different face, another face of the Mexican woman, that we are not submissive, that we are not subjugated. It is the face of struggle."

"This local is not a gain of the organization. All women of the urban movement are united earth, for all of humanity is united. All our work, no matter how small, is part of a new current among the popular movements of México, of the mixed groups of men and women, who both have to change to obtain something. Now we have to see that our companions fight and develop. The fight is going to come sometime, who knows when, and we want to gain something."

Tears are streaming now.

Again las porras.

¡Benita-vive-la-lucha-sigue-Benita-vive-la-lucha-sigue!

Benita stands up slowly, steadying herself on her cane. She stood still in her pink shawl and gazed at the faces of woman.

"This fight of yours, I want to tell you that I admire it, that I am always with you." Her voice cracks, the tears come, she leans on her cane for strength. From her voice comes a procession of dead. "We in our time, we were fighting for demands we had at that time. Then the army came. We suffered all the vicissitudes of the time so that you wouldn't have to suffer the death of a son, of a mother, of a father. You don't know the suffering of mourning in your house, bloody fights, the struggle of those women of that time, who gave their lives, dedicated women, pregnant women whose guts were spilled on the street. (I remember her telling me, "They used caballos on us. Horses are beautiful…very intelligent, caballos preciosos. It wasn't their fault.") Let us offer a moment of silence, and may you take with you a grand embrace, for now I give to you the struggle!

"It is not the struggle of Benita, but all the women, of many great women. I MAKE IT YOURS!"

Mud Woman's Ombligo

When my grandmother was born, my great grandmother

buried her ombligo in the earth just as my tatarabuela had done for her daughter, just as my grandmother did for her daughter, just as her daughter did when I was born and just as I will do for my children–because that is what you do when a child is born, to marry it to the earth that feeds us. I have had many grandmothers of blood and of community. I had a grandmother who the winds carried like a withered plume and a grandmother who dressed in the snakes of Coyolxauhqui; a grandmother who made me Jesus and Holy Mary crosses of tissue paper and sticks and one who drank whiskey under the ramada of dried saguaro, passing me fire. Another taught me about las velas milagrosas, the miracles in candles, and the message of the rooster's crow. They have all been my great mothers.

When I met the Abuelitas of Campamento Francisco Villa, I remember both my great blood mothers. Abue Vargas, with her Indian face the brown of wet earth, always gave me dried tortillas and government milk. And if I had asked for a pair of shoes from her mountain of chanclas, zapatos y tacones, she'd have given me that, too. She could have been the twin of my grandmother Chenta, whom they called "regalitos"–little gift. My abuelita was called this because she always gave people gifts–quarters, trapos and stale food folded away among her panties in her choni drawer. She cried when she was happy, and she cried when she was sad. My grandmothers were mujeres indigenas, yet lived seemingly mestiza lives. My grandmother Carmen, "the daughter of el brujo," was a lot like Abue Meche, corajuda, yerbera. She loved to dance but never let me kiss her until she was old and I was learned. Later I took care of her when she was old like a baby and she loved my frasco de chile. Once when the pecans turned green, she promised to come back and take care of me when I was old. Like Benita, era una mujer de rifle y trenza. Several times she almost died, pero "Diosito" kept throwing her back. But my grandfather came for her on his birthday with a loud knock. She knocked on my tía Nene's door to say goodbye, and Aunt Jerry's cat cried. We dressed her in gold slippers and my tío said they danced all night, chanclando in heaven. And now I walk in her shoes. And not long ago, I dreamt I had become her, her face revolving on top of my neck.

When I remember the Abuelas, I see wisdom. I see 200, 300, thousands of years of living memory. Tienen la palabra of all those years. The memory of their abuelos resides within them and I am stirred to preserve it. Perhaps I have always searched to honor our grandmothers of the earth. The earth I speak of is a spiritual land. It has spiderholes to wisdom for us to climb out of. In this earth of life, the contraries create meaning. Because we have problems, we seek freedom; because we have limitations, we find movement, we expand. In the earth of our sufferings, we sift for our meaning, our root in "el retorno a la tierra." It is a life not free of suffering but forged strong because of it. Then the wisdom submerged in the future makes itself clear to us–if we fight to make it appear and demand that it teach us something. We create meaning from our suffering when we ask, "What am I supposed to learn here?"

People of the land call winter el tiempo muerto. Even in the Dead Time, life is waiting for its time to appear…en el retoño, when life returns and flowers again. I often say woman is the desert because it is fecund with tenacious life. Woman is saguaro because saguaro survives hundreds of years, watching over the desert. Woman is nopal because, even if it is cut from its family and falls to the ground, it will root by itself. As long as it touches the earth.

I often tell the little grandmothers and little grandfathers–the youth–we all are Mud People, always becoming from our earth. "Somos gente de barro," the old ones say. Long ago, in one of the first worlds, the people were made of mud until it was time for transformation. Many ancient cultures often speak of emerging from the earth. I have heard stories of how we came from inside earth's belly. The Haudenosaunee were born in the mud of Grandmother Turtle. The Aztecs and Mayans emerged from the caves, ombligos de la tierra, earth mother's wombs; and the ancients believed their bellies corresponded to the place of seven caves. Buddhists say that bodhisattvas postpone their enlightenment to stay in the "mud-stained" world to lead others to happiness. The beautiful lotus blooms in a muddy pond.

In that zoquete espiritual, people who suffer have the greatest right to happiness. That is what gives me hope for México. With so much suffering, in the depths of so much pain, run profound veins of wisdom, precious turquoise, and eagle feathers.

When you understand your suffering, you can make it your freedom. It is a freedom of strength. It allows you to walk into your heart and see your face. Only with that struggle will you see yourself, will you know what you are made of. "You will meet yourself," says la luchadora Lillie. It is that very struggle that gives our life movement.

There, among the shacks of earth floors and beds on bricks, mounds of clothes and tiny mountains of shoes, next to the altar of broken-prayer mirrors and quinceañera fans and lights and shadows that slip through curtains made of corn sack, there I met the stone mothers. There, where girls pick through lice and are scolded for losing a precious school pencil, y los vientos make old women's bones rattle like shells as their turkeys cry near their beds, there I saw lives en la lucha por la luz that were prayers to the earth when they are one with the place in life that is not void, but just waiting to be moved and made into something. Like clay waiting for the hand, as a flower waits for the seed, as the barro waits for the earth.

When the moon kissed the sun, los gallos looked for a place to sleep, the lamb looked for where to sleep, and the birds stuck close to the fence. El beso celestial, an eclipse, brought an unearthly light. And even if I grow old as a saguaro tree, I will always remember the Abuelitas like the smell of tierra mojada, two hearts walking up the hill, emerging from their earth. Mud People Abuelitas, wherever the earth holds them, elders of the ground.

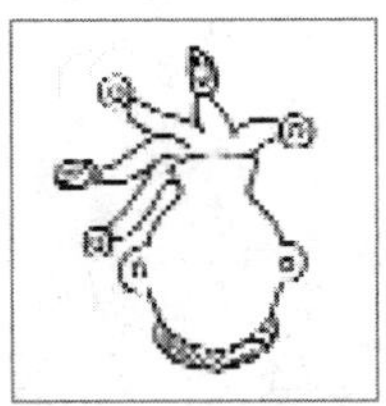

Las Abuelitas have retired. The Regional de Mujeres is now largely inactive, but la cocina popular continues to feed the people. The elder women pioneras continue to defend their kitchen as their last vibrant public space.

Benita died April 17, 1995, on the 300th anniversary of the death of Sor Juana Ines de la Cruz. She carried a part of me to the other side.

She left me gifts, feminine energy, fighting energy, y trenzas espirituales. I still wear my huipiles, and other grandmas have entered my life. Benita's still scolding me from the spirit world as my grandmother did: "No andes greñuda." Keep your hair tidy and braided. Huipil y enaguas, an Indian skirt and blouse, are honorable clothes.

– Grandma Emma: A huipil is cut square so that when the woman puts her head through it she is the center of the four directions. "When we come through it, we are the center of the universe. We are the ones who bring life to the earth."

– Martha, la joven abuela: A tortilla is round like the sun and the moon and a woman's skirt. The creative beings gave us the comal and the fire, and together they remind us of the sacred act of cooking, feeding, and eating. The comal represents the earth; the fire the sun; and the tortilla humanity.

– Another elder: when a woman makes tortillas by hand, she puts her energy into the masa as she pats it. This is how the woman's energy is spread throughout the community.

And when I follow the moon's face, I think of Coyolxauhqui quartered and growing powerful in phases…the parts greater than the whole. I imagine Benita's organizing the people in heaven, throwing pots so that all the spirits will have food. And speaking from a crate to the Great One about that arc of the universe that bends toward justice. The spirits are shouting: "Let the woman with the braids speak!"

Tlazohteotl–The feminine energy that generates everything
with love.
Tlazolteotl–The feminine energy that regenerates all that has
completed its normal cycle.

– from Calendario Mexicano by Arturo Meza Gutiérrez

The Women of the Unwoven

Beat your bellies, beat your buttocks, spray milk from your breasts
on the Invaders
Throw your spindles, your weavings, your battens, your brooms
Dirt, excrement, tortillas masticadas
los instrumentos de tlazoteotl
the chile is hot, the cook is mad
la escoba is both spiritual and physical
bring my broom

– Inspired by the defense of Tlatelolca women against the 1473
battle with the Tenochcas.

Té para susto

Before you read this chapter, prepare this tea. One part toronjil, one pasiflora, one part estafiate. One tablespoon steeped in one cup boiling water. Tea to calm your heart, mind, liver and nerves. Say a prayer and drink.

Hermila Guerra

Juchitán is a place of winds, dust, and female potencias on the hot isthmus of Oaxaca. It is the birthplace of the historic coalition of Zapotec campesinos, workers and students known as COCEI, which in the 1980s became the first leftist group–and most likely the first indigenous people–to officially run a municipality in contemporary México. This movement for autonomy by the descendants of the binnigula'sa', the Zapotec ancestors, is rooted in indigenous culture.

Chapter 6: Tlazoteotl–Guerra florida de Juchitán

"Hermila Guerra, viuda de Carrasco."

She extends her hand as she introduces herself to me. Hermila Guerra stands near an altar as tall as the room that is a salon, a bedroom, and a back room to the tiendita. A sign overhead: "Coca Cola es mucho mejor." Their wedding ring pillow sits on the altar.

The flowers are changed every day for the man she loved who became one of the early martyrs of COCEI, Rodrigo Carrasco. Today the flowers are flamboyanes.

San Vicente, the patron saint of Juchitán, es el guardian. "They say that when the Spanish arrived that he liked Juchitán and stayed. He seems más teco (Juchiteco) than español."

Today, we are in the Colonia Rodrigo Carrasco, taken with many hands, made with the bodies of old people who were run over in the violent response of la toma. Hermila's home was made with their many hands, made with all the hands of the people of the colonia, as are all the homes there.

This is the woman in the postcards of Juchitán of the flowers of the warriors. In the photos of Graciela Iturbide, she is always in luto, in a black mourning shawl. I remember carrying a postcard of her image for years. When I went to meet her, I did not know it was the same mourning woman. There is not grief in her eyes. Her eyes are obsidian arrowheads. Iturbide made her image famous in the photographs of the Istmo women with iguanas on their heads, the fish-market women who call out to anyone passing by, "topopos güera." Topopos are a flat, crispy tortilla of the isthmus, "rotund like the perimeter of a skirt over the earth," writes Poniatowska. Calling someone blondy is a sales trick.

The women of Juchitán are as "fat" as the moon. They are so fat they are beautiful. Gorda like a woman grows with a man's semilla.

Son señoras gordas con la lucha. When they dance, they look like bouncing moons. Luna mamasota. With their gold ropes, twine and ribbons, they are the gold teeth of the Istmo. They are the dooyoo, Zapotec placenta of their people. Here to be fat is wealth; folds and mounds are sensuous and political. But Hermila is not fat, despite five children. Llenita está.

Hermila is calm. Hermila's voice is the sweet of chocolate, flower petals, and sugar, like the ancient drink. Aguadulce, sweet river waters. You can't even hear the torture, the toques, the electrical shocks. But the aftertaste of loneliness is there. Agua ardiente.

Many people have written about Juchitán de las mujeres grandes who weft threads of a matriarchal society, where women spread sex openly, control the economy, and give their husband a "penis" (an allowance). This is the Juchitán of the "velas" or fiestas to santos, the dead, and for marriage and ceremonias of living, where women danced together long before it was a political statement, or considered natural. And they'll shame you for not being able to down bottles of beer as they can. Those tecas exist, just as market women may show you a penis that pops out of a coin purse. Like the widow de Carrasco, some wear a loneliness, always dancing with their shadow while the husband works the land and, sometimes, other women. It's not unheard of to hear how fulana pulled the greñas out of la de la casa chica.

The Juchitán de Guerra florida is the one of fierce flowers. They are red at the front of the battle. Legend has it that even Porfirio Díaz hid in the skirts of a Zapoteca. For a man to hide in the skirts is not unreasonable. It is said PRIists hid in other Zapotec women's skirts to flee COCEI. When President Salinas de Gortari avoided COCEI territory, the women said it was because only people with huevos arrive there.

Hermila says she is strong because she comes from a family of fighters. Her great-grandfather fought against the French in the 1800s, and she grew up hearing the oratory of General Heliodoro Charis, a Zapotec hero of the Revolution who became a cacique in the 1960s. COCEI says all the women are las resistencias encarnadas, descendants of a people where men and women each had their own lineage and were given the honor reserved for priests. As one teco told me, they come from the lineage of foremothers who beget "dioses" and sacred energies in their culture.

Son las herederas de la India Teresa, who is said to have killed a Spaniard in one of their rebellions. Following the Spanish invasion, the Zapotecs led the now historical Tehuantepec rebellion in the 1600s in which the Spaniards were kicked out and a Zapotec government ruled for more than a year, writes Howard Campbell in Zapotec Renaissance, Ethnic Politics, Cultural Revivalism in Southern México. He notes that many women were especially remembered for the throwing of many stones. When the Spanish returned to power, one Magdalena María, "la minera," was punished for sitting on the corpse of the Spanish alcalde and pummeling it with stones and other maldiciones. She was flogged 100 times and her hair and one of her hands were cut off and displayed near where the incident occurred. (Campbell writes that the women were especially angry at the priest, who had forced them to produce numerous religious mantles.) The rebellion was sparked when the Zapotecos, already riled by having to pay a lot for Spanish goods and receiving little payment for native products, became enraged after the alcalde had a native man flogged to death for delivering inferior mantles and ordered the whipping of another, writes Campbell.

During a key battle against the French on September 5, 1866, women rang church bells that alerted the people to the attack on San Blas. Tona Taati also is said to have egged the men on, threatening that the women would do it. As the story goes, a woman "'aware of the psychology of the men of her race'" rang the church bells and shouted to the men, "'If you cannot get them (the French) out of the center of town, speak up!, and give us, the women, your weapons and you will see if we get them out or not.'" – Zapotec Renaissance, Ethnic Politics, Cultural Revivalism in Southern México.

Tona Taati is mentioned in "El corrido de 5 de septiembre."

"Tona Taati, mujer con enagua de enredo, gritaba entren de frente, no vaya palpitar el corazón de ustedes. De esta manera se mata a los extranjeros."

"Recuerdos de Anastasia Martínez" – from Guchachi' Reza 23 (a Zapotec journal of arts and culture): Anastasia Martínez told writer Macario Matus that her mother, Margarita Jiménez, buried rebel leader Che Gómez and his men. For that, she was pursued. She escaped detection by hiding in a large trunk and later fleeing out a window. "When we were with Charis, there also were other women. There was

Checha Ngoola, Cata Tama, Nisia Vidal, Linda Bail, Cata Vivi, and, well, a variety of women. There were mi tia Juana, Paula y Valeria." They were las Juanas, or soldaderas, who followed Charis.

Anastasia's grandmother, Na Marga Binu Gada, was among the women who sounded the bells when the French entered Juchitán. When Carranza's forces arrived in Juchitán, they left Margarita and the bugle player in charge of pacifying the men. She made everyone carry "banderas blancas." Had the people not obeyed, when more forces arrived, they had orders to burn down Juchitán. Margarita often prepared for battle by pounding a box that hung from her body.

"Memorias de Ana Ruiz" as told to Macario Matus–from Guchachi' Reza 23: "We were soldaderas because our husbands got mixed up in the revolution.... When our soldiers were right in front of the line of fire, each soldadera would look for her husband at the moment of his arrival and in the middle of combat." The dead would be wrapped and buried in a petate, piled one atop the other "like leña." The women had babies in "el pleno camino."

– When a child was born, we only had to put the baby in a rebozo y listo, hacia adelante. Nos importaba seguir a nuestros esposos.

Whether banging a drum to alert the people to battle in the Revolution or passing messages in their enaguas and topopos, storming the embassies of India and Guatemala, or attacking the governor of Oaxaca who had fought against the guerrilla of Lucio Cabañas, tecas have always been in battle, and at the front. Eran 200 mujeres who protested the ban on the use of the colors red and green (representing opposing groups–ricos contra revolucionarios) in 1912. It was a woman who demanded that the government open electoral urns in 1966 to check for fraud. When they refused, a group of women tore up their ballots and destroyed the amphora. – Juchitán, Lucha y Poesía

"In the strike of '58, Demetrio Vallejo, the labor leader, related that las tecas of large skirts and huipil de cadena would extend themselves across the tracks to prevent the trains from passing and they filled their skirts with rocks," writes Elena Poniatowska. "...On May 5, 1920, Gen. Charis entered Juchitán and the green women fought against the red ones."

She writes in Juchitan de las Mujeres that when women fight they dare to lift up the skirt of their opponent. "Tener poblado el pubis es una garantia poltitica; en su frondosidad reside su fiereza.... Decirle a una mujer, 'Tienes el sexo pelon' es condenarla a la derecha: 'Hasta en eso, eres reaccionaria.'"

Then there's the mosquito battalion of children. Youth as young as 13 have been tortured. Children and pregnant women have been killed, such as Lorenza Santiago in 1974. "She was the one who died that year," recalls Hermila.

Coraje

Two women talk in a room, a long salon with beds, cartons of eggs, an altar of pain in purple and red.

The women look at each other. One was tortured. One was raped. The wounds know each other. This is the "altar of our protests." The action still lives under our skin.

There are things I will not ask, cannot ask. My wounds won't allow me to intrude and walk on your scars. I am not a journalist in these moments. I'd rather be a civilian today, a sister, a friend. I don't need to know, and yet I know torture. Rape is a form of torture to violate the memory and to control us long after the act. It inseminates our minds with poison. As pyschologist Judith Herman writes, the rapist's intent is to take away our autonomy. When I heard that Cecilia Rodriguez, then the U.S. representative to the Zapatistas, was raped in 1996, I thought of all our foremothers who ate deadly herbs or threw themselves off cliffs, rather than "know" the Spaniards, or carry their seeds. Or the woman who was thrown to the dogs for resisting the advances of a Spaniard. Our bodies become the violated fields of war, where battles over memory and control are fought; whole villages of women in Chiapas bear the memoria of violating men. With each rape of our sisters, the invasion occurs again. Scholar Teresa Córdova writes, "The memory of violence is the memory of invasion." And yet, most of the media chose not to tell Cecilia's story. Because she was an activist, her word was suspect. In Zaire, the women call the seeds of genocidal rape "children of bad memories."

– And what happens when the bad memories become your cells, asks my comadre Raquel.

Sometimes I draw a picture and wonder what part of my life was wounded. Can I pin a milagro there, and everything will be healed? Or wear a rosary with big beads, the bigger for more protection, like my uncle Sammy. Put a Virgen on my back so they won't stab me there, like the pintos do, especially to guard against anal rape. What saint is good for healing this? Light a vela milagrosa? A tincture, un te. Pomadas. Hang hinojo in the house for protection, osha and ruda; rub my body with sage and chile like a warrior in Tierra Amarilla, New México, once did. During the land struggle there in the 1960s, he escaped police dogs by doing this and hiding in a tree trunk for days. Remedios for rape and torture: Bury your memory and flesh in the earth. Let it compost inside Our Mother; go inside her womb and sweat; leave flowers, candles and fruits at the place of bad memories to recover myself from the past; chant until my whole body vibrates with a sound that spirals in the universe. Sometimes the trees have taken care of the rest. A curandera told me I had a strong defensive layer of energy right under my skin. As such, it was once hard to penetrate for healing.

"Are you afraid?" Hermila asks me. I pause and think of my rape and how many women fear it will happen again. I do not fear this. No, for me, the trauma of my rape is sometimes like having aire in the back or reumas. At first, I feared the night, open windows, and houses with wide open spaces.

She asks because I keep asking her what it means to have no fear. How does one arrive at this? Do some people have courage or not? I wanted to feel as she did, to have no skin of fear left.

The Juchitecos tell stories of how their ancestors were born from rocks, emerged from boulders and roots of trees and animals that makes them "invincible," tenacious. Hermila speaks the words of so many people in struggle: they cannot take away what is gladly given up for their people. When people decide to struggle and live in dignity, they accept danger. And people willing to die are a most defiant force.

I've tried to understand fear from los grandes, the old ones who say fear makes you creative, that fear is not something that goes away but that is conquered as you act through it. All people live with fears, the fear of unemployment, sickness, death, the loss of a loved one, uncertainty, or the fear of ourselves. But in the United States, most people from dominant culture do not contemplate whether they are willing to die for an idea, to take their beliefs to the last possible sacrifice. Most do not know what it is like to fear your own government, to fear being gunned down by the army, or disappeared by police. That is, unless your are from a community of color. For many of us, the police is the state, and we may fear even calling them to respond to a prowler in our house.

I think of myself when I became four legged, long ago, just days before my 25th birthday. Aware of my breathing. Even as I write this more than a decade later, my nostrils become as they were that night, smelling my own scent as the hunted. Praying to anything out there, to whatever God was, the skies, the stars–to live, to survive my attack. I knew then what it feels like to be an animal, the instinct, the primal will to survive. I will always remember my breathing that night, my jaguar breathing. The terror of seeing in the dark. And I had thought that if it happened, it would be in Guatemala. I had prepared myself for going into the war zone when I was assigned to write about the war and social change there. These months of seeing dangerously would change my life–seeing dying children, dead soldiers, scalps split open like the skin of an old baseball. Soldiers, alive one day, crossing swinging bridges over cold, rushing rivers, dead the next day on the roads we had traveled. Most of all, I remember the people struggling in clandestinity, preachers and Mayans who knew they most likely would not live long enough for the next encounter. Some were guerrillas, others dangerous because they spoke truth; they saw truth; and they sought it out among their people. I remember watching Rigoberta Menchú cry in a Mexican Sanborns and thinking that my life was so easy and of little risk compared to theirs. She and I were close in age, and I felt so insignificant and superficial. While I was in Guate, I was not afraid because it was a useless emotion in this green and frightful land. But when I returned, I had nightmares of when I was questioned by police. Only in dreamtime, I was tortured, many times. And so was my mother.

Months later, I would be raped in my house by an intruder in a ski mask. I would fight to stay alive, just to breathe. I did not cry. When he escaped out a window, I calmly called the police and the credit card companies to report my stolen cards. When I was taken to the hospital, a funny short man with a Micky Mouse stethoscope came to examine me. His hands looked big and shadow-long like death claws and I started to shake and scream and cry. Then, I returned to my violated space called my home, unable to feel anything. I came to realize the value of my life over the long struggle that the rape presented. Did they hurt you? Did you fight back? Everyday, forever after. I put the memories in a jelly jar, left many toxins in brown eggs and breath that turned a sacred wheel of life. Much later, I battled with an immune disorder while writing this book. Some of it was caused from environmental pollution; some of it was from toxins in the soul. Or was it because my mother went hungry when I was inside her belly, or because I drank the susto of her womb? Or because she almost died a couple of times while I was in her arms or because we hid in closets to avoid my papá?

A decade ago, I made a prayer to have happy cells, and all the suffering and susto began to move inside my body. All that I had kept hidden, even from myself, all that I had refused to hear from my life poured forth. My body had become el susto, my liver the rage, my kidneys the fear, my central nervous system, my ovaries.

Vino en chorros. One day, I could no longer get out of bed. My body could not bear the suffering any longer. My cells began to attack themselves.

I could not walk. I could not think. I could not remember. I could not dance. Forced bed rest for years. My muscles atrophied from inactivity and a chronic virus. I lost my life as I had known it. My illness stripped me of all transient identities: Patrisia, the daughter of Martha y Rosendo; indigenous woman; xicana; wife; columnist; worker. I could no longer separate myself from my pain or detach myself from the environment my mind created. Psychologists call it disassociation. It was as if I had lived an out-of-body experience. Despite a life of great joys and triumphs, there was a silent, suffering current inside of me. Like a second pulse for grieving and spirit pain. Part of me fue desaparecida, disappeared. We men, women and children who left our bodies to survive the violence are the other disappeared. Violence disappeared our being, our memory, our feeling. For many of us that have been violated, not feeling and not remembering is how we survived. For so long, I lived outside of my body, watching myself from the ceiling. El susto. I became numb so I wouldn't have to feel the fear. I have mourned the decades I did not know my spirit's whereabouts.

My life was forcing a limpia, a spiritual cleansing. Get el huevo, las flores, la yerba. And so, like Coyolxauhqui, I began to piece myself together again, to re-balance my four directions: the mental, the emotional, the physical and the spiritual. But first, I raged and mourned from my pores, like a sweatlodge cleansing. For seven years, I prayed to bring the medicine out of my body. I prayed to the Creator inside of me. And I began the most revolutionary act. I began to love myself. This is the daily fight against oppression. For while we love our communities, we often don't love ourselves. This enigma called spirituality is, in great part, a love story.

I prayed to see my face, for I had become an old woman. I saw the face of the girl at seven, the girl unable to defend herself or her mother. I felt useless and worthless because all that was left of me was Patrisia, the human being, an ordinary woman. And because I was simply this, I was most deserving of happiness. I was a human being and alive. But my cells struggled to become happy. More so than from the rape, my ability to trust and to feel whole had been taken from me at age seven by a boy who thrust his fingers into my vagina at a school named after all the saints. He threatened to tell the sisters that I had written on the building blocks. For fear of getting in trouble, for fear of authority, for fear of the sisters, I became a victim to a sick boy. I was spiritually mutilated. My reality had become traumatized, secret and hidden. I lost faith in those things that were supposed to organize meaning and life in my evolution from girl to woman. My life became ordered and structured by violence. Yet somehow I still believed in justice, even if it was not meant for me. When I began to look at my legacy, I saw that my antepasados had lived through inter-generational alcoholism, sexual abuse, Indian Wars, hanging trees. One of my great grandmothers was stolen from her people and forced to marry a man she never loved. She bore 16 children. Which perpetrator was there to confront for the rape of oppressions?

Later, feminists clarified for me how women live in a rape culture, a culture that accepts as normal that women might be sexually violated, just as I had braced myself in covering the war. Except you don't need a war for women to be tortured by rape.

Scholar Jane Caputi concludes that sexual violence is a sick initiation ritual to condition little girls, as I was. I did not feel shame when I was raped. That is his shame. Perhaps it was because I was still seven and ashamed. My soul was already disfigured.

When I wrote about Subcomandante Ramona, I admired the truth that Zapatista women and children had declared themselves a liberated free zone, though they were surrounded by army. Ramona dared the government and entered Mexico City. She, like the villagers, had become contested space. Her mind was contested space, a liberated free zone, just as the village contested the values that gave guns and the army legitimacy. This is why after the Acteal massacre of mostly women and children, the villages were threatened by their enemies that the women would be raped first, then the girls. Fragment the autonomy of women to wound the autonomy of a people. This is why Native wisdom holds that a people are not defeated until the hearts of its women are on the ground. Everytime I fight my attackers, my violator, my abuser, my lack of confidence in my words, my mind, my tongue, I contest the space they tried to take from me. I do not place myself in the pain but in the power of my own medicine. Only I can stop my mutilation.

Medicine: We have medicine–our breath, our words, the medicine of our heart. The ancestors said the heart is our house. It is where our soul lives. In ixtli, in yollotl. The wise, the healed, they have a heart and face, the ancestors said. The heart is our medicine. Yollo patli. A person healed is a person in movement. Ollin.

One day, I watched Freddie II with Hermila's grandchildren. I found it ironic because, as a result of the rape, I could no longer stand violence in the media or most "chase scenes." It is the most obvious sign of my trauma. I relive all the violence of everyone over and over again, though it has lessened over the years. And no one hears the screams, again. I will always remember my animal, the breathing of knowing you are prey. In writing this, I burn sage; receive blessings in an abalone shell, an eagle bone whistle, a bell rung three, five, seven times; bury tobacco and ashes to curar what I conjure up. The jaguar is dancing again and I must let it go out the door.

I have always been public about being a rape survivor. When I became ill, I began to publicly name what happened to me as a child to put language to my experience, to create a narrative to what had happened to me so that I could be one with my life again. It is said that trauma takes away language. The pain takes away our ability to name what happened. The denial of that pain can scatter you across the universe. So much energy spent into making pieces of the truth. As Gloria Anzaldúa writes in Making Face, Making Soul: "For silence to transform into speech, sounds and words, it must first traverse through our female bodies…. Because our bodies have been stolen, brutalized or numbed, it is difficult to speak from/through them."

I have spoken and written these words for them to course through my body and heal it. As they have coursed my breath, they have been healed by the air. Sacred Breath that breathes through me, "aliento de la Vida." "The private pain is transformed into political or spiritual dignity," write I. Agger and S.B. Jenson in the Journal of Traumatic Stress.

You have borne witness.

Mar Viva, Ola loca

I go to a virgin beach and they tell me not to wear red to the sea. It makes the ocean mad, mar furiosa, fury red. Red is the color of a warrior. Con rojo, el mar se enfurece. Mar y cielo. The women of COCEI wear red when they fight, red flower coronas in their hair. Red huipiles, enaguas. They dress for ceremony. Protests are like processions. They throw red confetti. They walk with the drums, turtle shells, bamboo flutes, and oxen carts decorated with flamboyanes, banana leaves and paper flowers. They are the sound of red. My friend, anthropologist Marinella Maino, calls it the "festivization of the struggle." It becomes the festival of life.

They wear coraje like the protection medicine of other warriors. Coraje swallows the fear.

Coraje, pure coraje, justified rage, it is a quality of courage that comes alive when we face injustice. "On the contrary, it made me want to fight more," Hermila often told me in recounting her travails.

Coraje. It's a word that is untranslatable in English. It's a feeling that rips from the heart, a stubborn courage that makes you "see red." It makes your heart hot. Even a small cup of it makes you strong.

"Blood always runs in the struggle."

"Siempre nos comprendemos," says Na Hermila. Na is an honorific Zapotec term similar to doña. "If my husband could not go, he would tell me to go. 'I can't go, but my wife can,' he would tell the leaders. 'Apúntate a mi esposa.'" Sign up my wife.

"Since I liked the struggle, he would tend to the children." Or ask his father to baby-sit, so that Hermila could fulfill her duties.

Together they walked with COCEI, from the 70s, when Juchitán lived in a state of siege and the army occupied the region.

In 1975, Hermila started to hear men shouting about the poor from bullhorns. They were leaders of the Coalición Obrera Campesina Estudiantil del Istmo (Coalition of Workers, Peasants and Students of the Isthmus) COCEI. She liked what she heard. She started going to meetings, secretly. Then one day her husband asked her if she thought they should attend a meeting. He, too, had been attending secretly. Here she was, waiting to get approval from him. The meetings would be on street corners, a calvario (cemetary), or someone's patio. This is how they entered the struggle, in takeovers of communal farmlands, marches on the Pan American freeway, the pedrazos against the PRI. Many times, COCEI leaders were protected by the pescadoras, or fish-market women, where they escaped into the defenses de la mujer.

"Apúrate. No, this way."

– Nos haciamos tontas, or we would pelt the police with tomatoes and fish en el momento da coraje. Or the police would try to get la mamá del lider, Leopoldo "Polo" de Gyves Pineda, una senora grande. Qué feo. Qué feo.

In 1978, Víctor Pineda Henestrosa (Víctor Yodo) was disappeared. Na Hermila and numerous women held a hunger strike for 400 hours in Oaxaca and then took their hunger strike to the United Nation's office in Mexico City. The whereabouts of Víctor Yodo are still unknown; but Polo, who had been arrested, was eventually freed. Some women say that is when the women's movement began because the men could not leave their jobs to pressure the government to release Yodo.

The women always fight with the men leading, Hermila said. She said the women tried to organize a separate women's group, but it did not work out. The women could not get away. They had too many chores or did not take it seriously–neither they–nor their husbands. "Here, there is no woman who the people would call a leader."

She adds, "Sin la mujer, el hombre no es nada." Without woman, man is nothing.

The police would beat up the women and say it was because "éramos necias." They even shaved the hair off some of the women. Or they pulled them by the greñas when they would jail them. They fought with palos, as in the fight against the French. "It is our custom," Hermila says.

When COCEI saw it could not break the PRI's political monopoly by electing its own, it decided not to wait for autonomy to be granted. It created it, instead, by forming a parallel government known as the "People's Government" or Ayuntamiento Popular. Much of the foundation for the government was composed of neighborhood committees in which mediators negotiated politics and conflicts within the barrios, a Zapotec tradition. As Julio Moguel writes in Juchitan, Lucha y Poesia, "El Pueblo hecho gobierno es imaginativo y audaz." The People made Government is imaginative and audacious.

When Polín de Gyves de la Cruz, Polo's son, ran for mayor of Juchitán in 1980, the PRI was accused of votos rellenos, ballot stuffing.

The army occupied the township after 10,000 protestors took City Hall on November 20, 1980.

"I told my husband not to go inside. It was dangerous. The police were on top, and the people were downstairs.

"No te vayas a subir," he told Hermila in turn.

As it turned out, she went up one set of stairs; and he went up the other. They met at the top.

"It was a movement of coraje. Spontaneous."

COCEI refused to leave City Hall and took it over for more than a month.

The women went about organizing the tequio, an indigenous practice of collective work, for frijol, tortilla, dinerito to sustain the rebels in City Hall. "So that the people would remain firme in the struggle."

"Many people say we made the struggle with actions, not words," Hermila said.

This time, COCEI mobilized international support and the government was forced to install an interim coalition government of PRIistas and COCEIstas.

In 1981, Polín was elected mayor. But during the next two years, as COCEI battled for increased government finances, City Hall was refurbished with the indigenous tequia/tequio system of collective work for communal good; and schools and libraries were built. In 1983, the COCEI government was impeached, following a melee between coalition members and PRIistas in which two people died.

Once again, COCEI refused to cede City Hall. A reported

25,000 people, dressed in the rojo y negro of COCEI, protested in front of City Hall. Leaders held the building until after the November 1984 elections in which the PRI claimed victory (as did COCEI). Many women helped guard the building. Cambell writes in Zapotec Renaissance, "The Coalition also set up an extensive network, composed primarily of women, to provision the occupants in City Hall, passing messages, maintaining the movement's activities during this time of crisis."

Eventually, the army stormed the building and 90 leaders were taken, most of them beaten and tortured. But 3,000 people, with women at the front, broke the military cordon, only to be pushed back. Street fighting continued into the following week. COCEI members tried to retake City Hall numerous times with rocks and palos.

With the ongoing army occupation–when a man could be arrested because he was on the streets–it was the women who dared to defy the state of siege in which many of their programs and buildings were destroyed. La mujer tomó las calles.

Rodrigo would die and Hermila would be tortured–for the first time–in the repression and revancha that would follow their movement. "I thought I would die in the movement," says Hermila.

"A woman gives herself up to the movement; she also gives herself up to the home."

On October 9, 1981, Rodrigo and Hermila walked together for the last time, he to work at the Ayuntamiento and she to sell downtown. She never saw him again. "That day I felt depressed, but I didn't know what was happening. Night came, and he did not come home. He would come home at 7:00 p.m. I waited for him to eat. All night, I couldn't sleep."

The next day, she went to look for him at City Hall. "Someone said they saw him, but they must have been mistaken. By that afternoon, I started to cry. I felt a bad omen. At 6:00 p.m., there was a crowd of people at the City Hall. My father-in-law said, "Hija lets go see what's going on. Vamos." A corpse had been found on the road. "Vamos. But I'm sure it is not my husband."

– I was the one who found him. We found him, and he was dead. Esto fue el primer golpe and the last time I cried.

After the death of Rodrigo, Hermila cried all the time for six months.

– How I cried. I cried so much that I ran out of tears. Llore, llore, llore. That was when I stopped knowing how to cry, that I could no longer cry.

According to COCEI, el compañero Rodrigo was kidnaped October 9 by the Brigada Blanca. The next day his body was found on a road that leads to the Air Force base. His body showed signs of torture and four bullets in his face. Hermila says the brigada was after Polo but killed her husband, instead.

– Ya no supe nada de mi, como que me quedé loca. Cuando me di cuenta, it was the next day in the morning and a compa of the First Section neighborhood was talking on a speaker, announcing the death of my compañero. He died at 29, joven todavía. They had been married almost 13 years.

After Rodrigo's death, "It was another life."

Hermila washed clothes, hacía tamales. "No sé si por lástima, todo lo que iba a vender, todo lo compraba la gente." Even a taquito.

Así fueron las cosas. Changes come, as do the vientos of Juchitán.

The coalition asked her to run the municipal kiosk. She moved in with her parents. Often, journalists would come to interview her, but many were really spying for the PRI.

On the first anniversary of Rodrigo's death, compañeros of the COCEI convinced Hermila to speak.

"You must speak as a woman, as a wife, as a widow," they told her.

She did her vela for him. Prendió veladora, los santos vinieron. She offered fruits and bread.

–Valío la pena por muchas cosas que se han dado.

"I poured myself into the movement. It made me mad. It gave me ánimo to confront the PRI. Today, my word is respected, even now. When I speak, my children respect me."

"At least, I have the respect of my children."

It was a solemn refrain. I heard her say it often.

Her mother did not want her to be a militant. Instead, her father took care of the children. Or he would tell his wife, "Stay with the children so that mi'ja can go. And he would go with me."

After she was tortured, her mother gave her the I-told-yous.

"Ya ves, hija. No entiendes. What if they had killed you?"

Hermila's father said nothing, and she can boast that she's even been to Buenos Aires.

– To do an action, you need much valor, she said. "Es el deber del pueblo. The duty of the people." Because before COCEI's movement, the poor were bien pisoteados.

On January 1, 1984, they kidnaped her.

– It was an awful night.

"COCEI had just won the elections, but the PRI did not want to let go of the power. We forced our way into City Hall. They shot at us. There were many wounded. One was left crippled." At least he did not become crazy, as one youth did from earlier persecutions. The next day, Hermila was asked to check on the wounded. She was with six women who were helping the wounded. The police recognized her and they grabbed her–like an assassin–and chained her.

– Híjole. Ahora sí me chingaron.

"I thought of nothing else than that I would die that day." They took her and another man, David Velázquez, and stood him at a door so that she could see him. And they tortured him with electric shocks until he fainted. They tortured her, too. They made her take off her clothes. Entonces, electrical shocks everywhere. "I would tire and they would tire of me. Then once again el muchacho." They asked no questions. At 3:00 a.m., 11 compas of COCEI were brought in. "Ahora ala muerte de seguro vamos."

– It was really cold. I was very cold because I was thinking of my death. If they killed my husband, for sure they would kill me.

They kept asking her where was Polo de Gyves. They accused her of burning down the Banco Serfín. She says the PRIistas did it.

She looked her torturers straight in the eyes and said: I am innocent.

Her torturer, replied, "Te voy a matar."

Hermila: Cuando quieras. I am ready to die. ¿Tienes hijos?

– ¿Porqúe?

– Because the day that it is your turn, you will remember them.

Hermila was disappeared for three days and detained for fifteen. The police denied knowing her whereabouts, though she was in a post of the state police.

They fed her rotting orange rinds and banana peels with excrement. "On the third day, they forced us to put the spoon to our mouths." They took a picture to have proof that she "was taken care of."

When they transferred her to jail, her sister saw her. Hermila signaled to her not to let on that she knew Hermila. "Tell my parents that I am fine and that they have me."

An international condemnation of the Mexican government gained their release. "On the contrary, it gave me more courage. On the contrary, we continued even stronger."

"When I was a girl, I was delicate. Something would happen, and I would cry. But with all of this, I changed."

"I never thought about fear. We all had coraje. No one was afraid. El coraje daba fuerza."

COCEI participated in a coalition government with the PRI from 1986 to 1993, when it won complete control.

"If the people had not fought fiercely, there would be no COCEI. La gente es COCEI. And without the leaders, the people would not have had the courage to confront the PRI."

Hermila grew up poor. The family lived on camarón, frijol. Sopa, pescado, huevo de tortuga–food of the rich today. Her mother sold chocolate. Hermila's prized inheritance is the metate her mother used to grind the chocolate.

– When we wanted a pair of shoes or pretty clothes, my mother could not buy them. Today, her mother even has a telephone.

Rodrigo fell in love with Hermila from a photograph. "She will be my wife," he told her brother. Rodrigo started calling at the house after her brother "robbed" his wife, as is the custom among Zapotec Indians. He always watched Hermila. "Híjole, there's something here and I like it," she thought. Finally, he began courting her and told her "cositas bonitas." In 1968, la robó because that was the only way her father would accept that she would marry.

– Que salió virgen. Her mother sent three women. When they saw her virginity, they told the neighborhood and set off firecrackers. The next day everyone came to see her virginity. And with flowers, they adorned her virginity of precious red on white bed sheets and made a feast.

All the vecinos, relatives, and family brought a big bowl of flowers for the corona to make crowns of flowers for the girl's relatives. Tulips, carnations, gardenias, bougenvilleas, hibiscus, geraniums, red flowers–the red of virginity–were brought for the headdress. The madrina's is made of flowers, de puro rojo.

A list in preparation for a wedding and vela:

50 pollos

12 pollos a la casa del novio

12 pollos a la madrina

6 vivos, 6 cooked in mole

2 jars of chile

mezcal, cerveza, cigarros

tortilla, pan

dos velas (one to be lit to the saint de la madrina and the other to el santo of the mother)

incienso; coal to burn the incense

a broom, a pail, a jícara to make the coronas, about 20, to give away to the bride's family

Three nights before the vela and wedding, the novio Rodrigo serenaded the houses of la madre de la novia and la madrina.

He sends a live chicken to the madrina, huevos, un kilo of sugar, and flowers for the crown.

Around 2:00 p.m. on the wedding day, the wind band arrives and goes to fetch the bride, relatives and close friends.

La Flor de la Mujer

The mother sees the parents of her son's girlfriend.

"Please come inside," she tells them.

The parents confer. "I knew he was with the girl," the mother says. The girl was still in her school uniform.

"¿Ya la tocaste?" Have you touched her?

"Pues apurate." Well, hurry up.

The woman calls her cuñada Juana, her cuñada María, and the neighbor Petrona. "Ven, porque este chamaco robó mujer." They check the white sheet for her proof. "Go tell the girl's people. Call the neighbors."

Everyone brought flowers for the bowl. The girl's virginity was also placed inside, with the rest of the picked flowers. Hermila prepared for her son's wedding.

And she thought of love and death and where she would get the money for a beautiful enagua, but the cuñados or friends came through with money. She will not marry again, she told me, "But still I have the respect of my children." Was it that she could not divorce the memory of Rodrigo?

"I can never love another man as I loved him." Perhaps she had loved, secretly, longed secretly. Her partner in the loneliness was her children's love and respect, and the struggle.

There she remains for me in the corridors of memory with a fearlessness that disturbs power, and I am honored to say I know women who know no fear, women such as Hermila Guerra, viuda de Carrasco.

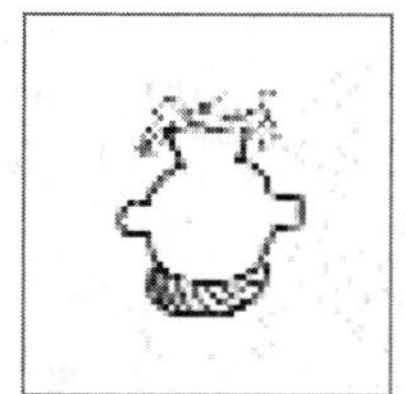
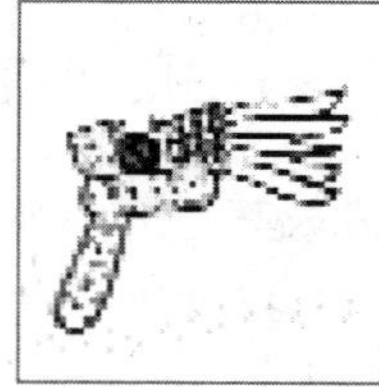

When I was a girl in braids, I could never find my face in society. Nor that of my mother's, nor my grandmothers'. Consequently, I never saw myself in any mirror. When I would look into one, I never saw anything that society said was the beauty way. Cara de indita con nopal en la frente y elote entre los dientes. Indian faced-girl, so Indian I wore a cactus on my forehead and corn between my teeth. As Indian as nopal cactus was not beautiful. When I read the history books, I did not see myself again, for I rarely read about being native, much less about being an indigenous woman, other than fifth grade lessons on Pocahantas and Sacagawea. But I did not look like the Indian princesses; I did not sell baking soda, tobacco, or "snake medicine."

I wore guaraches and had a big nose, and, eventually, big hips. The only reference to my many blood lines was of Kickapoo Joy Juice–whiskey–in the comics or phrases I'd overhear the grownups say when they got mad–"me sale lo comanche, lo indio." My Comanche, my Indian fury comes out. The only thing I heard about my abuelos of the south, my Nahuatl-speaking foremothers and forefathers, was that they ate hearts. But my abuelitas told me que somos Indios, Kikapu, Comanche, indios mexicanos. One was beautiful with a belly round like the earth and hips made wide and beautiful from bearing 11 children. She was born near a sacred pyramid known as Chicomoztoc. Both my grandmothers were indígenas and had the healing traditions and somehow their braids and tobacco were my medicine, even when I couldn't see myself.

Eran mujeres de rebozo, mujeres de trenza y rifle, mujeres de tobacco. Cachetonas. (Women with big cheeks–big butts.)

In her book of essays, Yellow Woman and a Beauty of the Spirit, Leslie Marmon Silko writes: "…the beauty that Yellow Woman possesses is the beauty of her passion, her daring, and her sheer strength to act when catastrophe is imminent."

She writes of the Laguna Pueblo belief that Thought Woman is Creator and she thought up her three sisters. They came into being and together they are Mother Creators. And they work through many women. But it would take a long time for Thought Women to create my ability to see myself.

It wasn't until college that my face began to present itself to me, slowly in seasons of years as moon shows her face to us in fours. The refracted knowledge of the mothers and sisters who went before me has reached me at different points of my self-liberation. At different times, I have seen myself in the foremothers who spat in the invaders' faces and slung stones against them, banged pots and pans in the rain of bullets during revolutions, and pummeled the corpse of colonizers with stones and curses. My mothers and sisters were most revolutionary in growing the three sisters–squash, beans and corn–and just trying to live long enough, plant long enough, sing long enough so that we would appear. It has been through these women that Thought Woman has been my teacher. For me, all the women in these pages are Thought Women, thinking into existence a new way of living and treating each other into existence.

So much as has been debated as to whether Juchitán is matriarchial. Perhaps it has threads and circles of matriarchy. So often matriarchy is judged and debated as if it has only one form or expression of women deciding, determining, and completing the now and the future. Despite all that is still male-centered there, the women have one important freedom. They are strong. They spit in Fear's face.

Zapata said that people don't need strong leaders; people need strong people. Strong women are the roots of matriarchy. Only then can we form the women's councils to pick the leaders, to determine war, life and death; to create women's societies for the coming of age ceremonies for girls; and for wise women ways.

One summer, I walked outside and saw the feminine energy in the grass, in our abuela pine tree. The beautiful copalli sap sweating gold, shimmering in the sun. I saw it as the wind blew seeds on the ground. I felt it on my skin, on the pelitos on my arm. Life glistened with female creation. I knew I had healed and that my own feminine energy, so wounded in life, was healing, for only then would I be able to understand this energy with my life. Some long-standing problems began to resolve themselves.

"That was Tlazoteotl," said la comadre Sylvia. She spoke of the energetic function of Tlazoteotl. The Mexica female healing energy that absorbs ills and recycles and purifies life had taken what was no longer useful. I had learned of this energy where so much healing occurs, at the kitchen table.

Sylvia had made a tincture, "Tonica Tlazoteotl," for women going through the Change. Sylvia spoke of her as a feminine healing energy. I am forever indebted to Sylvia for how Tlazolteotl began to show itself in my life and became part of my healing. Then, I began to hear her name again and again, evoked in women-ways ceremonies. Long ago, I had read of Tlazolteotl. Tlazolteotl or Tlazohteotl has been translated as "the filth eater" and a "diosa" of sex and sin, depending on how the word is spelled, with tlazolteotl having the root of tlazolli or waste, or the root of tlazohtla, love. Teotl = sacred energy.

According to oral tradition, many elders say that there was no such thing as filth or sin among our ancestors, that those are European constructs. Even biological waste was looked at in a different way. My friend and Nahuatl teacher, Mapitzmitl Paz, says even this controversy as to her various faces shows a teaching of dualities and complexity. She is a complete woman, a healing and sexual being. Many Xicanas have written of her sexual nature as one face of Tonantzin. But that never called me as did her healing nature, her entity as guardian of the temazkalli (medicine sweat bath) and energetic function of parteras, or midwives.

After Sylvia told me of her healing function, I began to invoke and meditate about Tlazolteotl and to make offerings. I began to understand her broom, her weaving cotton, her rebozo, her plumas. It was through these experiences that I began to see her weave my life. When I felt all of feminine nature in my body and how I was transformed, I reflected on how I have sought to move energies within my life and thought of the mothers of the disappeared. I came to feel in my very body that Tlazoteotl had indeed worked to help move democracy forward in México through the women, moving through the energies of grief, loss and terror.

Arturo Meza Gutiérrez writes in Calendario Mexicano that Tlazohteotl is actually "la madre tierra como generadora de la vida, dadora de cariño y protección." My teacher and friend, Martha Ramirez, a founder and cihuacoatl or administrator of Nahuatl University, has taught me and many others about Tlazolteotl. "The feminine force of rejuvenation," she calls her.

As the warrior Sophia says, Tlazolteotl is the great recycler. "Women don't waste anything." As part of my asking permiso to write about and honor Tlazoteotl, I asked Martha if I was understanding this energy and its function in social change. "Women are always transforming," she said. They transform matter, and so often with love. Martha calls Tlazolteotl la fuerza creativa de lo no tejido. The creative force of the unwoven. Spiderwoman. "Her spider web is the DNA, Tlazolteotl," Martha said. She is ever present when there is purification and rebalancing.

Now I think of Tlazolteotl, her colors of green, amber and turqoise, whether the earth is fecund or fallow, la luna llena como un vientre. I know she is with us now, sweeping up and absorbing things that are no longer useful.

Thank you, Mother Creator, mother energy. Toci, Our Grandmother. Tlazocamati Tlazohteotl, thank you Thought Woman. I offer you my salt, mi viento, my vientre, my luz, mi flor, mi tejido.

Part 3

Morning Star and the Moon

The Guide, the Announcer
The Moon Wanes When the Morning
Star Appears.

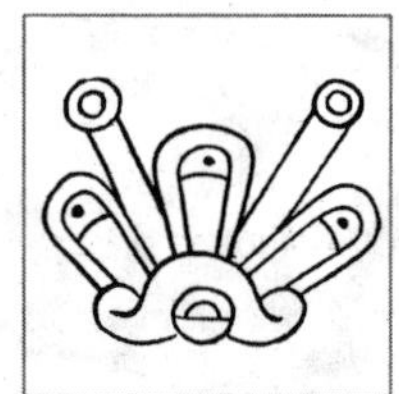

Ch. 7 Mónico: El Hue Guerrero–A teacher of the Left whose life is entwined with other men of struggle from Morelos

Ch. 8 Quetzalcoatl y el Relámpago–The meaning of this life force today and how it is interwined in times of change with Zapata

Ch. 9 Jaramillo–The inheritor of Zapata's land struggle in Morelos

Once, I camped out alone in the Rockies with nothing but a sleeping bag and a plastic sheet and string for a tent. As I lay upon the cold earth, I went to sleep gazing at the Evening Star. When I awoke in the dark before dawn, Venus was the first light to greet my eyes. I had slept in the same way of my ancestors who left stories of Quetzalcoatl and the journey he makes as human being, ant, dog, wind and planet. I had slept and awaken to that same celestial being that had called me to México so long ago.

Mixe Legend:

A woman, a man, they call the mountains,
the plains, in mythic poem:
we have been born
we have blossomed
there is no darkness
there is no evil
there is no fear…
mixes mixes look be alert…mixes mixes alto, mixes medio,
mixes bajo…the sun will soon be born
it sees everyone…it sees everything
soon the sun will be born
with its splendid dawn song
llanos, montes
the sun, the sun
the moon, the moon
they have been born…
now there is a guide
los mixes!
…we have been born
we are blossomed
now we will live
we always want to live in the always
look, be alert
now you, king
raise your hand
take out your shield
take out your wrath, ire
call the llanos
call the mountains
llanos
montes
twenty peaks
twenty divinities
open your ventranos, to begin us, to initiate us…
cloak us
you will win, you will win
they will win

We followed relámpagos to the House of Colors. Wherever we went we'd see twins. Twin dolls, twin strollers, twin babies. I'd hold my breath because twins run in Roberto's family. There were signs everywhere. Finally, in Chiconcuac, we saw triplets. We wound up loving each other at the stones of Xochicalco, near a candle at the piedras de Quetzalcoatl. Relámpagos y truenos....

I told Raúl Álvarez Garín: There is a candle without a name at Xochicalco, the Place of the House of Flowers. "It was for Rubén," he tells me.

We walk around Tlatelolco and speak of agua quemada and plumed serpents that fly in clouds. "There is a type of fleecy cloud, and it comes from the northeast. These winds–trade winds–produce a certain type of cloudiness. The winds from the Pacific are counter trade winds and they are high winds that produce clouds, very torn and tall. When they come together, you will see the serpent entering with the clouds. This is the plumed serpent, and another thing about burnt water that people do not understand: Quetzalcoatl, which is aquatic, roars. ¡Ahhgrúa! The thunder comes, and the water falls that gives life."

"The night they held the wake for Rubén Jaramillo, Tlaquitenango was filled with light. Some attributed it to the thousands of candles that were lit for him that night. Popular voice sings now that this light was the soul of Jaramillo." – La Jornada 1992

Chapter 7: El Hue Guerrero–Mónico Rodríguez

There in the workshop of el hue guerrero, Zapata lives on canvas, "painted with coraje." The fantasma of Ricardo Flores Magón floats inside the silhouette of a moustache or overhead, breathing the winds of anarchism that would give Zapata the famous line, "Land and Liberty!" Zapata flies over dead campesinos representing the death of the ejido with the constitutional change known as Article 127. Zapata's gaze speaks. "Bueno, hijos de su tal por cual que han hecho, porque me dieron en la madre." This is his house of colors.

During my many visits to one who knows something, I came here to the ritual mountains of Xochicalco, what was once in the ninth century a great center of wisdom and trade for the peoples of Mesoamerica. Here is where the priest Ce Acatl Topiltzin Quetzalcoatl was schooled, where the ceremonial teachings and rituals to the sacred energy Quetzalcoatl flourished and evolved among the old ones.

Here, on the skirts of speaking rocks, a hero of the campesinos was sacrificed in 1962. Some people call Xochicalco Tamoanchan, the place where human beings reside, "the house of rest," or the place of origins and destination.

I have followed lights in Morelos, the fecund land of Zapata, Quetzalcoatl, and Rubén Jaramillo, lights of dusty roads and chalk, maíz, nopaleras, and candles. Light that slithers through hills of pyramids and white mantas that old men still wear…the white of revolution and butterflies in a patio of cane reed, where I saw the sun and tears of an old warrior who is a knower of things, of caves and plumes and revolutions born in straw mats.

Not far from where Moctezuma bathed in hot springs, almost daily there are revolutionary pilgrimages to see el güey guerrero, Don Mónico Rodríguez, master of hands and wars, 74, robust, a machinist, a painter. El hue guerrero, the grand warrior, he paints the colors of all

Don Mónico Rodríguez

the flowers as if he were a Toltec. He fills his days with good work, making mills for the Indians; carving plumed serpents on guitars; painting Zapata in purple, dayglo fiesta greens, happy colores, draped with flags in the red, the black of ancient wisdom, of el pícaro, of anarchism. He meets with people who are in movement, students, indígenas, intellectuals. They are what the Nahuatl Zapatista manifesto (translated by Miguel León-Portilla) termed: "lo que viene dando golpes con piedras." What comes hitting with stones–the revolutionaries.

– To do a job libertona (liberating work), you need only three cabrónes…señores del pueblo, not three wise men, but three people from the masses. I came from the masses. I lived with them. They discovered me.

Mónico retells the stories of the strikes; the railroad workers; the communists; Rivera, Siqueiros, Revueltas (hay que revueltas Revueltas); of his compadre Jaramillo; of overthrowing caciques with guaraches and creole corn; piecing together the history people make from the tepalcate shards of an old man's memories, as old and worn yet clearly marked as the remains of broken pots at the pyramids of Teotihuacan.

– A mí me tocó. It fell to me.

"I am very pleased, it pleases me you have come," he starts to cry, "because I feel…I thank you very much…because I feel that the work will not be thrown away. Everything I have done, I have done with all the warmth, with all my love, even though it did not work out because we were pendejos. At least there's someone who is interested in the pendejadas that I did."

His voice shakes out tears and you can hear the boy who would talk to the moon now facing his night, de petate a petate. In a straw mat you are born, in a straw mat you die.

– "El Mónico," Mónico the old jaramillista, how he stands it, the old man, we have not made justice of him, says his neighbor Ricardo.

"I get pissed off when an idea doesn't grab."

For many in the Left, Mónico was a huehue, un abuelo, un hombre grande, a knower of things who guarded a codex of movements within his heart…to the clash of shields between eagles and jaguars…and Mónico had spent his life looking for heirs to pass on the knowledge, to give movement to hearts firmes as stone. His ideas have floated like a "knife in a river," coming and going, waiting for taking hands. As the Zapatista manifestos in Nahuatl said, "to hit with stones"–that with which the struggle is made, the action of struggle.

"The work of emotions makes us born again to put into the hands of others to multiply the task, everyday." All one has to do is ask and listen, and he will "pass the book" in his voice of gunsmoke and honey, his pistol in his morral. "...to make the face turn against the no-good governor [to rebel against tyranny]...for that which turns you around or changes you–[revolution]..." say the old Zapatista manifestos.

– Come to my cave.

"Life is reduced to a bunch of paragraphs, although there are many revolutions," Mónico said as we walked the Street of the Workshop, past old ladies with lasso braids and ribbons that have been washed too many times. At his house of painting, there's a swimming pool he built next to an airplane hull. He shows a cane mill he built for the Cubans, the house where he painted his life and love for Georgina Adalberta (Beta), festooned like a squat pyramid, a plumed serpent wrapped around the front door. The grapefruit trees grow fat and tall outside his art workshop, where old Zapatista rifles and small guitars with winged serpents hang from the ceilings like bat spirits and a seven-headed serpent floats on seashells and water. (Chiconcauc, where he lives, means place of the seven snakes or seven springs. Mónico designed a hydraulic fountain for the city, but it never made it off the drawing board.)

On some shelves in his workshop are stacks of newspaper articles about the old warrior. In them, Mónico is portrayed with a volute floating from his mouth, the ancient symbol of the flowered word, poetry, what is beautiful, the pretty word. Lo bello, lo precioso, lo bonito, lo florido. Flowers that last in your hands.

"First of all, what is precious in life. First of all, it is to speak and it has to be good speech of wise words. In addition, it has to be flowered words. That is the trunk of beautiful things, to be able to talk wisely, to be able to make the people understand, to know their history, to make the people understand what this is." Mónico used his palabras floridas for dialogues with the spirit, dialogues with the workers for the "triumph of unity, which implied a spiritual and moral control."

The Making of a Communist

Mónico's great grandfather was a gypsy who walked from California to Zacatecas and danced the flamenco. His father Samuel, studious, "muy a todo tren," finished his second year of law school and became a tornero and an anarchist who hung out with the Magonistas and rode with the bravo del norte, Pancho Villa. He wore white, silk Chinese shirts and introduced himself with verse and flourish. "Soy Samuel Rodriguez, alias el Húngaro o El Chimuelo, matador de toros y teniente coronel de la División del Norte. Por ay va la rata. Quien la pisa, quien la mata. Torreon, Coahuila. Yo estoy impuesto a brincar los muertos de dado balado y velarlos con cabeza de cerillo. Arrancame para dos. ¿Porqué tantos brincos si está el suelo tan parejo?"

After the revolution, Samuel worked for oil companies with some of his old Villistas along México's coast. Mónico learned from the "borrachos de Tampico." Mónico grew up listening to their stories of the Revolution, of Villa "en cuchillo a parar." Mónico studied the stars and the planets and listened to the workers speak of women; assassinations; so and so got so and so; what the Revolution was like, historias bonitas, such as how Villa was seated under a tree. The battlefront was near. He changed seats. A bit later, a shot hit where he had been seated.

Mónico remembers a story from his youth, "I was next to a sack of corn. Next to me was un pelado, a campesino, with a machete, todo aquello, lying down drinking a beer when two arrived to do him in. I see the atropello of the horses, and this guy puts down his beer and takes out his machete. They began to machete each other."

As it turned out, it was a fight between campesinos who had the tradition of trading pasture land for dry land. The oil companies were buying out the dry lands, and the Indians were fighting over the property. "They began to machete each other. They cut him here, and they cut him there. He was wounded big time, and they escaped in a boat on a beautiful wave. All the kids ran to see where they went down the river. That stayed with me. I didn't understand it."

As a boy, Mónico attended the workers' discussions about national themes, the price of a barrel of oil, "prolitariate vigils" for Nicola Sacco and Bartolomeo Vanzetti, two anarchists who were executed in 1927 for two murders in a trial inflamed by "anti-alien" and anti-radical sentiments in the United States. The repercussions of those times had reached México.

"The boy Mónico, Samuel's boy, has something to say about Sacco and Vanzetti." Mónico read a text written by his father.

"I met the bravos of Guerrero, Zapatistas with big, old mustaches and tejanos (a style of straw hat). They always dressed in white guaraches and they always had a machete." He grew up hearing Zapatistas were "bandidos, atilos." His father always told him, "If you're going to be a bandido, be a good one. Bandidos take from the rich but not the poor. To be a bandido was an honor."

Mónico hung out at the philharmonic musicians union, and there he'd hear "the winds of the liberation of the prolitariate." He would listen to the musicians practice with the "workers chorus." They performed acts to the masses without saying much about communism.

"Go with Juan Chanclas and buy one of those newspapers, El Machete," his father would say. Slowly, by tasks here and there, he became caught up in socialism. José Revueltas, the writer and communist pioneer, and Mónico secluded themselves in a room (filled with Siqueiros paintings) for six days to convince Mónico to help fortify the Mexican Communist Party.

During World War II, he worked as a railroad bracero for North Pacific Railroad in New York, Illinois, Montana and California. He says it was his part in the fight against fascism. The Mexican government made him a lieutenant in the Mexican army in recognition of an invention that altered a cannon, adding an automatic triggering mechanism in 1938.

Then he met a small, pretty, dark girl, la Beta. Beta's family tried to save her from the-no-good-for-nothing and took her away from Veracruz to Morelos. He went looking for her in Cuernavaca. For five weeks he looked for her, carrying a bag of gifts, bottles of honey. He spotted her in the plaza in Cuernavaca and a relative took him to where she was staying. She was sick in bed and they allowed him to visit her. He later tried to "rob" her, but she slammed the door on him and his kidnaping attempt. They were married good and proper, and she followed him and his dream to change the world. He believed that within three years México would be a socialist country. He wrote on the back of a photograph of a five-year-old niece of Beta's, "Your daughter will grow up in a socialist country, where there is no misery."

Mónico lived trailed by the law. He organized the cane workers and helped lead an uprising in the thorny lands of Atencingo, Puebla, where 8,000 hectares of cane land were wrested from William Jenkins, a former U.S. consul. There, he and others organized a cane mill union and helped create a cooperative of cane growers. For Mónico and Beta, there were days and days of not seeing each other because it was too dangerous. The judicial police, guards disguised in plain clothes, spied on Mónico and Beta's house. Yet he would dare come home at two or three in the morning, longing for his family. "Fright would overcome me every time he arrived," said Beta. She taught the children to notice who was on the street corner. Neighbors would help Mónico leave. Beta gave free injections and showed the women how to sew, so they protected them. Beta's mother read The Arabian Nights: Tales From a Thousand and One Nights to her as a girl, so Beta would retell the tales to 15 kids in the front room, telling them of love, embroidered with her imagination. Once a woman and child were interrogated for three days about Mónico's whereabouts, but they said nothing. All the señoras knew what to do.

She wanted a "beautiful spider web just like in the movies, with music in the air." He, just a mat so that they could sleep anywhere. He said he became Beta's "paño de lagrimas."

"I'm a cabrón and I've taken a little dove and caged her here, por corajudo, my going on strikes, uprisings and other things," he often thought. So one day he leaves her some money to buy cheese and butter and food for a few weeks. He tells her "if you want to leave, go."

"There goes 50 years."

"All that valaje of honor and faithfulness returns."

– Let's go to the park, says Beta.

– No. There's no money.

– It doesn't matter. With a basket and a bunch of tacos, I'll get a rock and make a fire and we'll go. Don't make any more commitments.

But he does. "You carry something inside" he says–and cries.

"Hay que jugarle a estos." Mónico had to keep fighting.

"You have been dragging me and my velices, cardboard boxes and an old stove," complains Beta.

And Beta carried those memories for a long way, too.

La Mística de las Cosas

The Mixes heard of an old warrior. They came to him to ask for help. They invited him to their house. He told them their wealth was in the wind and the strings and the children whose feet do not touch the floor when they sit in a chair. When he came to the house of Mixes far inside Oaxaca, the priest Florenzo gathered the people and told them Mónico had "an ideological infection." The warrior responded, "You're looking for a way out of hunger and misery and to have freedom and rights. If Luther or the devil, or however you know him, came down and he said this is the way and proved it, you would follow him. Well, that devil is me."

The Mixes lived in a community of 8,000 residents. Among them were eight bands of 40 musicians each and two bands with children who rehearsed after school and the fields. "The Mixes did what México couldn't," said Mónico, run a music school for the people.

– Vamos a soñar, chingado. We are going to dream, chingado.

Imagine workers who are going to make instruments and at the same will learn to make machines from discarded railroad material. From that a workshop will be mounted. "We'll play las mañanitas and take a wind band instead of a protest march. We'll serenade the president's grandmother and he'll invite us in for coffee. We'll tell him we want machinery to create workers in the hills, in the mountains."

"The free trade agreement is going to come and the problem will be that there are no workshops. We want it so that the people will not be tied by technology." The mística, Monico said, is to connect the indigena with technology, to open their creativity and to start industries in their own communities. "It will sound like a machine gun."

"People are always throwing a bunch of rhetoric, chingado, instead of practice." (The struggle erroneously becomes 80 percent theory, 20 percent practice, says Mónico. Then people only complete 15 percent of their potential role, and 80 percent is wasted.)

"Practice is sublimated for theory," he said. "Practice equals action."

Mixes were sent to spend time with Mónico. They went to México for five days and 14 concerts. Now they tour around the world. But at the hour of having the president's ear, the Mixes said nothing of the workshops, the mechanics shop.

"They settled for a bunch of hard tortillas."

Mónico always said we must discover what kind of justice we want, and for that we need to know in what way we are exploited. "What is the alternative? For that we need to know laws and history."

"What's the immediate need of the people?" asks Mónico. "You must speak with complete truth. Either it jives or they kick you out on your butt."

"We have great wisdom that has not been touched, my daughter."

In the 1970s, Mónico organized support for the guerrilla Lucio Cabañas from the warrior state of Guerrero. The Zapotec indigenas heard of the güey guerrero who knew Che and Fidel. They came to him from Yalalag, Oaxaca, 2,000 meters high to the skirt of the moon. There the fog is so low women look like they are floating on clouds as they walk up the mountain, where you walk among the wings of clouds and fantasmas. You can't even see your feet, only the heads sticking out of the clouds, carrying jugs on top. There, they make tortillas as wide as a man's chest. There lived 600 guaracheros. They had good corn. Another "improved" corn was introduced that yielded more but tasted bad. When Mónico met with the Zapotecs in 1973, they had 20 caciques they wanted to get rid of. "We want you to burn the caciques," they told him. This was at the same time of Juchitán, where Zapotecs of the Istmo were organizing a now famous movement.

"It turns out they wanted me to kill them."

– y que ¡ay chihuáhua!

"So we closed ourselves up in a meeting room and we discussed the motives and causes of why the caciques had the power over them through the means of production because the Indian machinery is old.

"I cannot enter like a plumed serpent," he said, his hands slithering through the air. "You try to get the people convinced of what they want to do. A percentage of consciousness emerges from the necessity of the masses." He spent one month meeting with them daily. They discussed how to plant corn, how to pick corn, how to alter the mazorka to reform the seed. The government sent engineers to kick them out. The caciques controlled the mills. They had control of the stores; they sold the corn seed.

"I will make a mill for you," he told them. "I made a mill. And with that we went to overthrow the caciques."

Out of 20 families who approached him, 10 remained. "Bueno."

They wrote a document telling what the caciques had done for 20 years. Within three years, they were self-sufficient. Other families started to join the fight, forcing a showdown. In 1980, the people took over the municipal palace for 15 days, surrounding it in a spiral of people. The town was closed off. The food finished in five to six days.

The caciques wanted to use arms. "We want peace. We don't want blood," the guaracheros said.

The caciques called in the army. It turned out the colonel of the outpost was friends with one of the leaders fighting the caciques.

– Compadre, whose side is right? The compadre spoke, and the caciques lost. Every year, they honor their liberation in those mountains.

– "Ese tiene mística."

"Mística," I asked, "what does it mean to have mística?"

– Mística is dignity; it is respect, veinte pelados en la chinga, el saber de veinte matamaces. For me, mística became inherent knowledge that comes from deep within, a knowledge that builds and gathers force.

– Everything that I have done with the wood, the machines, has been with the idea of directly, or indirectly at times, la bronca de levantar las luchas. We, as communists, because I cannot deny what I am, we can't go with only rollos verbales. Mónico always returned his stories back to the dialectical materialism of Marx.

Mónico said activists can't appeal to the people out of charity, like "carmelitas descalzas," barefoot Carmelite nuns. "We had to rescue the instruments of production that were used to subjugate the people. The worker is concentrated knowledge of technology; es el crisol. To me, the most important thing is to resolve the problems with the force of the people."

Consejo: "Conscience is the amount of knowledge one accumilates for action. From the masses, you will get human material, people. Just as you studied from the masses, you return to the masses what you know. Heroes come from the masses."

And who are they? "The masses are the totality of people

where you live and work."

"Yo soy soplador," says Mónico, like the winds that sweep the floor for the rain. "The question is," he said, "how to adapt knowledge and how to transmit it. Our struggle has to be over consciousness."

Chapter 8: Quetzalcoatl y el Relámpago—-Zapata, Quetzalcoatl

A song from the Spanish civil war scratches on the stereo.... "Andrés, to war don't you go, for without fighting you win more...." Mónico talks of cosas fregonas of history...the mathematical measurements of pyramids, el gorra prieta Francisco Ruiz, who organized the first cane union and was an old guardian of the Partido Comunista Mexicano, and other names of the first union leaders.... How Alma Reed, sister of John Reed, fell in love with Felipe Carrillo Puerto, the revolutionary governor of Yucatán (their romance was the subject of the famous song "Peregrina").... How a bruja poisoned a foe of the people with a polvito in one of the land movements and Diego Rivera in gatherings of communist cadre said the Mayans populated the East, not the other way around.

Mónico: Morelos was volcanoes turned into manantiales. Zapata's family fought in the independence and Zapata was born where the cane grows eight metros high in Anenecuilco, "the land where rivers stir." Cortés made mills along the way after the conquest of Tenochtitlan. The Spanish called cane green gold; and the macehuales, the common people, became beasts of burden for the sugar mills, finally revolting in the Mexican Revolution. (Mazehualtin=los que merecen, as in those who deserve to be born because of the sacrifice of the creative beings.) These are párrafos of the minutiae and anonymous of history.

"Ya viene la cosa grande"–the revolution–and when it came dicen los díceres, the rumors say...Zapata's error was when he acted alone and had Otilio Montaño, the "professor ideologue" of the Zapatistas, killed (he was framed). And in the heavy deeds, las cosas gordas, pesadas, Zapata usually called a council of "natural leaders;" but not that time. Otilio Montaño had connected Zapata with Flores Magón to study the land laws. Flores Magón told Zapata that there was no way that corrupt judges would recognize the ancient Spanish documents granting Indians communal land rights in Zapata's community. He told Zapata: "Para estas leyes, Emiliano, sólo hay una solución, los muelles...las pistolas, armas revolucionarias."– For these laws, Emiliano, there is only one solution, guns, revolutionary arms, goes Mónico's account.

Montaño was framed as a traitor. Zapata, blinded by anger that his best friend had betrayed him ("I don't accept betrayal"), told his men to mete out justice. Montaño was killed without a council of leaders being conferred. Dicen los díceres, "Zapata's movement is weakened the moment he starts to act individually."

"There is a ball of paragraphs."

Que dicen los díceres, after chevis and cigars, the mother of Beta said she went to visit Zapata in a cave in the 1930s–more than a decade after Zapata was assassinated. Que dicen los díceres, it was not Zapata; it was his compadre who was killed, the Arab tailor who made Zapata's shirts. It was an Arab from Jojutla.

In another verse of the story, in 1936 or 1937 there were secret meetings with a tailor who would gather the people and they would go to a cave, a cave where they saw him. He said he would come back. Zapata recommended that they continue united, that he was going to come back. But for now, he was going to Arabia with his compadre. "They say he died in 1986, that he died in Arabia."

Sometimes on the anniversary of his death, a man on a white horse rides the hero path through the town of Chinameca, where Zapata was murdered. Beds of corn still dry in the hacienda Zapata took over. And old men with white clothes, machetes and a younger man's chest will tell you what they saw when they saw him die, if you ask. Or show the way to the hills that cloaked him. Some say it was not Zapata who was killed.

On his birthday, the government appropriates Zapata with crowns of flowers that smell of the PRI. Mónico and his compas often make an anti-act. When there was talk of transporting Zapata's bones from Morelos, Mónico and others kept an armed, revolutionary vigil. They still guard the bones on occasion.

"...in cachi huei tequitl tlen ticchihuazque ixpan to tlalticpacnantzi, mihtoa Patria." These are words from Zapata's manifestos in Nahuatl, as translated by León-Portilla. (...de alguna manera el gran trabajo que haremos ante nuestra madrecita la tierra, [lo que] se dice Patria.) When I read these words "of the great work we do before our mother the earth that is called motherland" from Zapata's manifestos in Nahuatl, when I saw the references to "la palabra" of his army's council, it underscored for me that Zapata helped lead an indigenous movement, as well as a land movement, to return the earth to the grandparents of México. He showed us how to live as Indians, even one whose Indian-ness has been defined away as mestizo.

Today there are those of us who call ourselves mestizo, indigenous, or Xicana who acknowledge our spiritual connection to the land, the mountains that breathe like pyramids, sacred, because like the thunderbolt, that is where heaven and earth meet. Zapata lived what we have done since. For many years, I thought he was a mestizo who did not deny his indigenous blood. Yet, he showed us the Indian within. Elders kept pointing me to the indigenous Zapata. In 1992, an old Zapatista said that people had yet to understand Zapata through the eyes of indigenous peoples of Morelos. He said the indigenas made a revolution that told Europeans, "Your world is false." The tatas of Morelos have taught me their Zapata. History has determined he was mestizo, though he spoke Nahuatl and organized around indigenous principles. Over the years, as I have contemplated "Indian-ness," I have been taught that there are certain key elements that help to define what is an "Indian." They include a definable land base and connection to place and Mother Earth, a common language, communal structures for decision making, cultural traditions and cultural affiliation. One day, I created an ollin for Zapata, to identify how these elements were in movement in his life and moved or ordered his world and decisions.

Land base, indigenous knowledge: Zapata fought for a land base founded on indigenous codices or documents that identified the people's territorial lands. He used indigenous documents and knowledge that were entrusted to him by his elders.

Communal structures and indigenous decision making: A council of Nahua elders bestowed upon Zapata the Mocehual title of calpuleque (leader). Even today, monuments in his hometown refer to him as el Calpuleque de Morelos. Calpullis are a form of organization for communities, trades or families.

Lucio Leyvud told me long ago that the Revolution in Morelos was strengthened by the fact that those indigenous structures and organizing principles remained in place. Zapata made many of his decisions based on the council of elders. He was also given a bastón, or indigeous ceremonial staff, representing his authority among the people. Today, a Nahua from Milpa Alta carries that sacred bastón. Some native peoples still refer to Zapata as "tecutli," a Mocehual title for someone who governs.

Language: Many of his manifestos were written in Nahuatl and the language shows an indigenous understanding of la madre tierra and social change as a responsibility to Mother Earth. The Nahua curandero Don Aurelio once recounted to me the story of a Milpa Alta grandmother who questioned Zapata about why he was fighting. He responded to her at length in her native Nahuatl.

Cultural affiliation: Zapata's roots are primarily indigenous. While some consider him mestizado or a "mixed-blood," he is undeniably a native son of the Nahua people of Morelos. He was allowed to retreat into secret and sacred sites for refuge. In their movement for autonomy, the Zapatistas took his name and spirit as their name. Not long ago, I learned an old Nahuatl lullaby still popular today. That lullaby was sung to Zapata.

In Zapata's hometown, residents still sing him "las Mañanitas" on his birthday. At midnight, vienen con antorchas, atole, tamales y le cantan las mañanitas. Until she died, Doña Fortunata Salazar López "dresssed the altar" with his cigarros y su sombrero y sacaba sus pistolas. When they created a play of his life in the 1930's, the elders discussed at length who should play him. They wanted a man of upright character. They selected Silvino Cortés, a man who looked like him. He was a good charro and excellent with las pistolas. When he walked on stage that night, recounts native story keeper Lucino Luna, the people gasped. He looked just like el Calpuleque. "¡Es Zapata!" some cried out. "¡Que es él!" Y lo tocan. Cuando voltea, luce su lunar. His compadre sees the mole and exclaims, "My compadre has returned!"

"Yo soy campesino formado por los ancianos," says Lucino as he explains la mano de Zapata. Zapata's hand is associated with the ancient symbol for water. "Los abuelos hablan en Nahuatl sagrado que (Zapata) era una luz."

"La historia lo ha mestizado," said Don Aurelio. "Zapata was indigenous."

In reality, most of the world is "mixed-blood," but that doesn't make a black person white or a white person black because they carry the other in their blood. Their spirit, historical conditions, and their elders determine where they belong. Because of how "Indian-ness" has been constructed by the State in the southern hemisphere, the idea of the mestizo has defined away the original peoples. As Thaayrohyadi Bermudez, an Otomi leader, notes, "the ideology of the mestizo" was created to diminish the power and presence of indigenous peoples and to divide us. "The mestizo was created to negate the Indian," he told me. This is why many who interpret history have had trouble finding the Indian inside. Even after Chiapas.

> ...man ti mo palehuica to zepamiampa ihuan ihcan tic tlanizque neca huey tlanahuatile ipehualoni tlale, libertad ihuan justicia; man ti cumpliroca to tequi de nete-huiloanime-huiztique yhuan quimati tlen quichihuazque; nan, tlen huei ihuan tlen tlalticpac-tlazohnantzi.... [León-Portilla's translation:] "...ayudemos hacia nuestra unión y así lograremos ese gran mandato, los principios de tierra, libertad y justicia: que cumplamos nuestro trabajo de revolucionarios decididos, y sepamos qué habremos de hacer; allí, eso grande y eso (para) nuestra querida madrecita la tierra...."

This is how the old Zapatistas told the people that they would create unity and obtain their mandate of land, liberty and justice as part of their work as committed revolutionaries, for they knew what to do, this grand work for their beloved mother, the earth.

La gente Chicana grew up with portraits of the Revolution, of Zapata and his lieutenants, of his army of the south, sepia rememberances of our viejitos. Many barrios had their guardian Zapatatista, Villista, even a Carrancista. Raza donned their memory as an ancestral eyeglass. When I heard Mónico's stories of the Revolution, I could only imagine how my grandparents' times were woven with the intrigue of Mexicanos who fled to San Anto, El Paso, Los Angeles, and the borders. Los Magonistas and their radical newspapers fomenting change from North of the border, Madero's flight to San Antonio and his seige of Ciudad Juárez–where the bullets crossed international boundaries and killed norteamericanos on the othe side.

The legendary Emma Tenayuca remembered those Mexicanos' heated charlas in plazas and parks. Imagine how those stories formed her as an organic leader, organizer and intellectual. In fact, many Mexicano natural leaders would be deported in the 1930s to cleanse our community of any legacy for change.

"In addition to deporting strike leaders and labor organizers, ferreting out and deporting alleged subversives became a favorite tactic of INS agents. Dissidents and social reformers were labled communists and radicals," writes Francisco E. Balderrama and Raymond Rodríguez in Decade of Betrayal, Mexican Repatriation in the 1930s. It took the Mexican community 10 years to recover from this decade of trauma, and, the scholars suggest, that may be why the Chicano movement did not rise up until 25 years later.

Our greatest legacies have been the stories and strength of la gente humilde, men and women who maintained their dignity against brutal power. Ours is a history of a communal people, el compadrazgo kinship; las comadres and their informal women societies; the mutualista collective aid. Our hard work ethic we inherited from our original indigenous instructions not to be lazy, to be self-sufficient, to take care of one and another, to share corn and chile and slaughter a cow for the winter so that all could eat, to believe that our homes would be the sacred places and the fathers and mothers our teachers.

You still find these legacies in villages in New México. Where my family lives on Comanche Territory, otherwise known as part of Tejano farmland, we still survive because of a communal culture. Several of mis tíos and tías live next to us or within a mile. We still fix each others' roofs, help out with cars and air conditioners and adding rooms. Hacemos un tequio, the indigenous practice of communal work and sharing resources. Tequitl=trabajo (Mocehual). The original tekios or tekias evolved from farmers helping to clean each others' fields.

My folks have given a hand to Mexicanos who have migrated here, and they, in turn, bring us tree saplings and tamales and help lay gravel. When the earth is on fire and the grasses dry, everyone runs to help when there's a wild fire, even the man with a Lonestar flag painted on his barn. We watch each other's animals when the coyotes come and worry about peacock.

Though we have become an urban people, many of us have not forgotten that we were formed by la madre tierra. As Luis Rodríguez says, we have a "communal cosmology" that is contrary to the U.S. cult to the individual. In our movement as a people, the Xicantlaca returned to México Profundo, to seek inheritors of the continuing indigenous knowledge. There, we sought to find "the heart and the face"of our people, ourselves.

In the 1960s, the poeta Alurista evoked Aztlan, or the bronze continent (others interpreted Aztlan as the homeland in the Southwest from which some of our ancestors migrated), as part of "the spiritual plan" of our people–"el Plan Espiritual de Aztlan." This was our ombligo, our root, center and ground. Some Chicanos sought power and to change political structures; others sought to bring out the medicine of history with the original teachings, the spiritual power of a people, and the "social energies" put into movement through prayer and collective action. Elders such as capitan general el maestro Andrés Segura of the conchero tradition, que en paz descanse, became an abuelo of the movement. He was sent to the United States in the 1970s by his own elders to teach us. As detribalized people, we have had to recreate the structures that were lost as a result of colonization, especially our connection to our elders. Other elders from our relatives would become teachers, Diné, Lakota, Onondaga, Hopi, waiting for us to know ourselves again, to return to our ombligos indigenas. "They had been waiting for us," recalled one Xicano elder.

As people considered either mestizos or indigenous, Chicanos have lived a legacy for mestizos of Our America, of how to re-member our ancestors again. Recently, I met an indigenous man from Peru who said our movement as a people has helped other detribalized peoples in the South to reconnect to their original teachings. "We have been watching you," he said. It is a lesson México has barely engaged in as a result of the Zapatistas.

Mónico was like the elders we sought, a warrior and a spiritual man who bridged time and knowledges. He was a man who dialogued with his own heart, as the ancestors said a wise one would, hombre de alma, de energías sociales. He was a huehue, a grandfather, de las luchas. "We want elders, not olders," the youth often tell our generation. I believe many of us among my people will grow to be like him as we walk toward the elders' road. He would tell me intricate details about social movements and then speak of Tamoanchan, the spiritual house of human beings or the place where some say people come from.

Once, when Mónico was very ill, I went to see him. I sat in that room of Zapata and recited a Buddhist prayer. "What was that?" asked Mónico.

"Prayer."

"Was that you?"

"Yes."

"It sounded like many voices."

We spoke of Buddhism and how Buddhists believe that all great change is preceded by changes from within our lives. We call it "human revolution," the revolution within our being. He asked me to record the prayer, and he would listen to it when he was sick. "Yes," he said, "we've got to change our behavior."

Mónico put his own light to the world, like many of the old pionero communists who had stayed ideologically pure and honorable. In the United States, many people don't take communists seriously anymore; but in México, los viejos, the old ones, Mónico, Valentín Campa and Miguel Angel Velasco, who were jailed for decades, were treated with reverence for having continued uncompromised in their beliefs. I wondered why Mónico, who gave his life to the masses, who appalled individualism, only painted the silent caudillo, never his army.

"Zapata should be an instrument of struggle, a weapon, and it is in the hands of the government." Instead, the presidential plane is named after him.

I remember Rivera's painting of the Alameda and the gendarme who kept the unwashed masses away from the decent folk.

"I paint Zapata con garra, con punto rojo y negro," Mónico said one night. Black was wisdom, red was el picaro of the black and red ink. Black…as coffee from Veracruz, red…like a very fine Veracruz chile in oil, a red hotter than habaneros, hotter than fresh chile de arbol. "…because some people have taken possession of him, two or three gendarmes of the system who placate people with a bag of beans, a little box of something and a cow, and they tell you you are doing wrong." It reminded me of a PRI local I often passed on the way to

Mónico's, not much more than a wooden table and sacks of beans.

"Don't lose faith in the good life," says the Zapata manifesto in Nahuatl, the ideal to live in freedom.

I slept deeply many times in Mónico and Beta's home. To awaken inside a white gauze mosquitera, surrounded by diaphanous Zapatas and guns and women making love to jaguars in a purple sea from the Zapotec stories of a matriarchy long ago. Zapata illuminated, as if struck by rayos y relámpagos, lightening and thunderbolts of books sacred.

This is the house of raw thunderbolts and bougainvilea, brick walls and good woodwork, machetes, morral, dream lassos on the wall. When it rains, you can find the place of the navel when Quetzalcoatl was the life-giving spirit of the water to the Olmecs, when Quetzalcoatl life-giving forces resided in the waters, life-giving water snake spirit, companion of the jaguar, writes Román Piña Chan in Quetzalcóatl. Fertile water–fecund earth. With time, asserts Piña Chan, it became the serpent-rain cloud associated with celestial waters and the rayo-trueno-relámpago celestial fire. This thunderbolt energy evolved over time into two forces: Tlaloc, the sacred energy of rain; and Quetzalcoatl, the rain cloud and wind (as Ehecatl) that sweeps the floor for rain–and the creator force whose history and powers would be personified and married with priests of the same name.

The elders say Quetzalcoatl is the primordial energy, the first gases of the Universe. I have heard Quetzalcoatl described as the creative energy of life. I have heard some say Quetzalcoatl is not viento, wind, but aliento, life itself. The first energy of life.

The maestro Andres Segura told me in 1992 that the next 500 years would be "the cycle of Quetzalcoatl." Not the cycle of the mythic personality, "but of what is inside of us, the rebirth of the spirit."

And the white bird of Morelos called Primavera sings between 5:00 and 8:00 a.m. When spring time is born, it begins to sing half sad with nostalgia and lots of melody.

La Cueva

"I know of a cave of mi general," Rubén told Mónico on occasions.

The cave? I have heard legends of caves, where the moon was

born, where she turns in to herself, sheltering, conceiving greatness. Quetzalcoatl was born in a cave in Amatlan, Morelos, reportedly on May 4, 843 A.D, say the people of Amatlan. He was conceived in another. And people prayed to him in the surrounding caves.

The people of Amatlan say Zapata would retreat to Quetzalcoatl's caves to meditate, near the hill of time, near the hill of offering, near the hill of eagle.

A tin sign in Amatlan, Morelos, marks the place of sacred men and sacred springs. "Passerby reflect an instant. You walk now in the birthland of Ce Acatl Topiltzin Quetzalcoatl of the senorio tolteca years 843-895. Here, he took his first steps with his sandals of gold." Roberto and I walked with reverence to this place, where those sandalias still echo inside the land.

"The cultural hero of México and all of Mesoamerica, here he was born," writes Nahua elder Don Felipe Alvarado Peralta, the keeper of memory, in Ce Acatl, an indigenous magazine. Don Felipe's Indian name is Nican Mo Pohua Poa (aqui se cuenta). When we visited him, he told us, "He prepared himself in Xochicalco. There he prepared himself for 20 years. He was adopted by a priest of Quetzalcoatl. The old people knew him as the one God...."

Here, in "Amatlan de Quetzalcoatl," grow plums, guayaba, lime, naranja, aguacate, mango and coffee. Here fly wild doves, eagles–now there are few–and wild galleros that look like peacocks. The old ones said they announce the rain.

In Amatlan, where the first people lived in caves, Quetzalcoatl was also known as the guardian of the caves. According to the memoria of Amatlan, he was born near a magical well, or miraculous spring, in the canyon of fish, from where "mana el agua de las tinieblas, que brotan de las profundas entrañas de la tierra." From the fathoms of the belly of the earth stir these sacred waters. Agua de nahual, hidden water, mystic waters of great secrets where people came to have their destiny revealed.

The Toltecs revered Topiltzin Quetzalcoatl as the great cultural hero. Ce Acatl Topiltzin was a wise man of the Quetzalcoatl cult. He arrived to become "high priest" and to his name was added Quetzalcoatl. With time his life was enshrouded in the celestial and mythical, or allegorical, robes of Quetzalcoatl's sacred energy and its various avatars. Plumed Serpent, Erect Serpent, Serpiente Hermosa are various translations of this energy. Topiltzin Quetzalcoatl was known for his rule in Tollan, where he banned human sacrifice, instead sacrificing butterflies, snakes and quails. He fell from grace after drinking pulque from the cup of Smoking Mirror. Some say it was a symbolic fall, representing humanity's wresting with its own conscience. "La cruda moral," says Mónico.

In prayers to Quetzalcoatl, the people made offerings to the rain; flowers, fruit and incense for the spirits to come out. They left figurines for the niño Quetzalcoatl, so they could be cured during the first rays of the sun or the dusk's first vespers. They would leave offerings in the caves, the canyons, the ant hills.

The people of Amatlan still speak of Zapata's connection to Quetzalcoatl. "It is understood that the people of Morelos spoke of the los güey tlamatines, great wise men. Their spirits assist certain señores, like Zapata, who had on his side the great wisemen who assisted him in his defense. To the old people, the illustrious men were like saints who evoked the one God," said Don Felipe.

"That is taken from the idea that Zapata lived in those caves. The caves were places of the Zapatista camps, his lieutenants. The caves were used, not just by the revolucionarios, but also by the common people." (He notes that Zapata se casó por el civil in Amatlan to a woman from here.)

"I know. I learned from the old ones," said Don Felipe, son of an elder and Zapatista colonel who recorded the stories of the old ones. He sits with bottle-cap glasses, so thick there are clouds inside, like the kind sold at the metro stops. He is surrounded by white gladiolus, ollas, and two bottles of whiskey.

Every fourth Sunday in May, danzantes burn incense and move energies through dance prayers with torches before the first rays of dawn and people leave little dolls to the boy Quetzalcoatl. Don Felipe says the old people still associate Zapata with Light, with the spirit of the people, Quetzalcoatl. "Todos los hombres sabios tienen la misma finalidad. El lugar rojo y negro, donde se termina la noche y empieza la luz." All wise men have the same end. The red and black place, where the night ends and the light begins.

Quetzalcoatl Tiene Garra

"Quetzalcoatl was not one, but many Quetzalcoatls."

What does a Quetzalcoatl need? I asked Mónico one afternoon.

"Quetzalcoatls have been reproducing the Mónico's, the natural leaders."

"A Quetzalcoatl has to discover other Quetzalcoatls. Right now people look at Quetzalcoatl as almost venerated. They don't see the connection with nature and with reality. That reality can be astronomical, agricultural, mathematical, or magical."

"Quetzalcoatl is to know and to give rosal, hay que sembrar the cane blood of everyone."

"Quetzalcoatl dominates many practical things. If we put rollos y rollos of words without practice, then we are contradicting Quetzalcoatl's meaning. Quetzalcoatl was someone who applied ideas, techniques that were practical. You must cut on a certain day of the moon because the light exerts pressure on the precious body."

His explanation was the first common sense application of Quetzalcoatl that I had been exposed to at any depth.

"Quetzalcoatl participated in concrete wisdom because of his love. Quetzalcoatl, all Quetzalcoatls, represent love of self."

We discuss the role the spirit plays in struggles. The spirit of struggle had called me for years, even to México. "The spirit is not enigmatic, but concrete. You need cerilla, rama and ceniza. Match, branch and ash. Thesis, synthesis, and the physical. The conclusion is ceniza (ash). You need a cerillo (match). When you strike it, it's a flame."

"We are covered by a cosmic material all over the universe. From one planet to another, there is a cosmic material, an intangible thing when two luminous bodies reflect their light. It puts pressure at a luminous center. It will gather from the volume of cosmic matter, which will make it gather at that moment. It will make matter join matter, one molecule with another and another with another. The chispa with that makes the fire greater; and the fire gets bigger and the bola greater, bigger and bigger, and more and more. It will be constant until it makes a ball of fire, and that cosmic matter will continue in different phases of the universe. There comes a moment when it explodes, and it produces another chemical phenomenon. That is how a star is born."

And revolution? I ask.

"Claro."

"Cosmic material topples with one another and something happens–gases, sparks. Translated to society, it is the same chemical phenomenon, physical and qualitative. We are positive and negative currents of energy."

And does the struggle lie in our minds or our hearts?

"Our conscience is the eyes, which pick up and pass to the mind. The mind judges whether it's just or not. The face draws what is in the heart. The heart is what rules the brain. Everything is controlled by emotion."

"The spirit for revolution is the group of things correct and honorable. Your spirit in action is noble, honorable, just. If you want to implant your own spirit, it is through action that your spirit is transported to others."

"Lo moral is to create responsibility in the subject. Quetzalcoatl transmitted it; he did not guard it. Your mission is not to betray yourself; to be master of your mind comes from the heart."

"Quetzalcoatl is wisdom. It exists in all of us."

Agua Quemada

I asked Don Felipe what was the connection between Quetzalcoatl and the rain, the thunderbolts, and wind. "Los vientos, las nubes, relampágos…. You need wind, clouds and thunderbolts, the three elements that awaken the rain so that everything will become fecund. Without rain, there is no life." Zapata, Jaramillo y Monico, they were relámpagos, the rainmakers of movements. The announcers, the guides. They gave their viento to the people.

In el hue guerrero's backyard, the cane of Morelos grows tall, creole cane, la de sangre de toro, la cristalina, la rayada. Mónico sits on his lilac hammock as wash water runs through the patio. Beta is washing and, as usual, she has one eye vigilant on Mónico's penchant for everything that he loves but is not so kind to him.

"How do I get meaning from life without wine, without cigarettes, without love?"

What do you mean without love? asks Beta from the wash area behind the house.

"I mean to be able to make love. It's an attitude of civil death," he mumbles, feeling limited by his wife. Mónico speaks of the Aztec's three plains of death: the physical, the moral, and the spiritual.

We preoccupied ourselves with how to "make beauty for the spirit."

"It has been my life to drag the people along. People come looking for chevis and a matamas, gente dolidas." People still come to him to fix their problems. They don't value their own force. "Gente sufrida ogando en su propio chocolate." Suffering people drowning in their own chocolate.

"People are sieve."

– You want clean frijoles. Hay que rajar el pulmón.

"There will be a period of neutrality. This generation must end. People don't fight anymore, and people stay because they are responsible. That is the percentage of la bola that stay with dignity. As you start getting into traps to resolve your problems, you start to lose the little percentage of dignity that you have."

On another occasion, Fernando, el Cuervo, came for Mónico's social wisdom on whether to advise the PRD. "Yo vengo de mamar de tu saber social no no mas tu saber individual." (I've come to suckle from your social wisdom, not just your individual wisdom.) They also discussed the meaning of productivity and how the origins of the phrase "to testify" came from when men would display the testicles as a sign of their virility and honor. Mónico likes to say that we must not gilguerdar–to make things pretty but with no substance. Mónico builds his stories, saying, "Hay otro cuete…hay otro pelo."

Chapter 9: Jaramillo

Un borrachito, bohemian, but serious told Mónico after a union organizing meeting in 1934, "You've got to try the food of Morelos, papas with frijoles, frijoles with papas, huevos with chorizo." So one day they went to Morelos and landed in a cantina.

Mónico got into a fight. And there came Rubén Jaramillo with his chaleco, his watch, his camisa de Holanda that Zapatistas favored, roomy enough to stash tomatoes and peanuts.

"Chachos, Chachos, calm down." He threw a verse from the Bible. "Don't fight boys. The kingdom is with you."

Words of concordia from the man who continued Zapata's Revolution in Morelos, forever caught amid the waters of legality, non-violence, and the clandestine guerrilla life.

Four years later, Mónico worked with Rubén in organizing the cane workers in the sugar mill named after Emiliano Zapata in Zacatepec. His job was to develop labor, and he helped create a "cell laboratory." (He conducted discussions between the cooperative and the union among the cells "and then to the masses.") He fled to hills with Rubén's guerrilla, once narrowly escaping arrest by dressing as a woman.

"Oh, here comes a very important paragraph. I become conscious of what I am, of what I like, of my role in Zacatepec.

"You do fight for your life," recalled Mónico. "You have to think that this is going to kill you and you walk with this thread. The fear gives you illumination."

One night after a heated meeting at the union, Mónico was followed to the home of a friend. But the federales didn't have a search warrant, so the friends of Mónico asked the lieutenant: Can the women leave while the lieutenant goes to get the search warrant? The women were granted permission to leave.

"I crawl on all fours and put on something. A woman went to get more women. It was around 11:00 p.m. There were some women, tall and gordotas, and he left among them. He told the women to clear the way. He ran off shooting, wearing a dress. Many of the women were known to throw tomatoes and rotten eggs at union enemies.

Mónico drinks the Indian way, three chorritos to the earth y ahora si. Mónico plays songs from the Revolution and handles a Zapatista rifle as the afternoon drifts with the chevis. He shows the pistol he used with Rubén–a Colt .38 special, real smooth, in a hand-embroidered holster made with so much artistry that it seemed painted.

– Everyday you have to fire a little shot.

"Está cabrón, como se dice, como el camarón."

Where is your pistol? Machete? Knife? Hmmm. He rubs his beard.

On the wall are pictures of Jaramillo and a portrait of Jaramillo and Zapata engraved with names that are now silent history: Antonio, Rubén, Porfirio, Reyes, Roberto, Sarita....

And other names of revolution...Pablo Torres Burgos, Emiliano Zapata, Rafael Merino, Proculo Capistrano, Manuel Rojas, Juan Sánchez...among them...Refugio Torres, Jesus Becerra, Viviano Cortez, Celestino Benitez, Catalino Perdomo."

"A list of the first to raise their hands," says Mónico. "Con los muelles, desbarata las leyes. With them the Zapatista Revolution began."

The painting is signed. "This frame was ordered and financed by Rubén Jaramillo, Epifania Zúñiga, Enrique, Filemon..."

Rubén was killed before he finished the portrait. "After he was assassinated, I included Rubén's family."

At age 14, Rubén Jaramillo rode with Emiliano Zapata and his Ejercito Liberador. Three years later, he was made first captain in charge of 75 soldiers. When the army began to disintegrate and soldiers pillaged and turned sides shortly before the caudillo of the South was assassinated by Carranza's forces in 1919, Jaramillo called together his compatriot Zapatistas. He told them, "Facing the current conditions of fatal Revolutionary decadence, we should in no way submit ourselves to the hands of the enemies who, based on strong compromises with the North Americans and national plutocrats, have fortified themselves by recruiting people paid to fight us. But in this case, it is not many the men who triumph but the ideas based in justice and the social good...."

The words come out shaky. Mónico, the güey guerrero, cries as he reads Ruben's words from his son-in-law's anonymous recollections of the Jaramillistas.

"...from now on the revolution, more than with arms, should be with just ideas and great social liberation. The people, and more, the future generation, cannot live as slaves; and it will be then when, once again, we will put ourselves in march and although we are far from one another, we will not lose sight of each other and, come the moment, we will return to reunite. Save your rifles, each one of you, where you can return to it...." – Los Jaramillistas by Renato Ravelo Lecuona

After Zapata is killed, the land he and the campesinos fought for is redistributed from hacendado lands in the 1920s. Rubén, son of a soldadera of the Revolution who died from a scorpion bite, great-great grandson of a Jaramillo who fought with Benito Juarez, returns to his birthplace, Tlaquiltenango, Morelos. He fights for land redistribution there, sells rice and follows the Word as an evangelical minister.

From the 1920s until his death in 1962, Rubén gave his life for his people, starting a rice cooperative so that campesinos could control the production and the commercialization of rice. The cooperative doubles the price of rice but confronts corrupt bank officials and caciques who are the heirs of the hacendados and part of the cacicazgo that evolved after the revolution, new enemies that for five years tear the cooperative apart. Thus begins the long fight jaramillista. Jaramillo already had his cabal of revolutionary people, and among them was Mónico.

In 1938, Jaramillo organized a cooperative of campesinos and workers at the "Emiliano Zapata" cane factory he lobbied for from Lázaro Cárdenas during his presidential campaign. Soon the corruption sets in. Pro-government officials try to bribe Jaramillo, telling him, "De aquí depende los frijoles." – Rubén Jaramillo, Autobiografía y Asesinato.

He is ousted as president of the council and stages a strike. He writes in his autobiography that police and judicial police surrounded and ransacked his home several times (even taking the chicken eggs), but he escaped.

Eventually he is forced to flee to the hills with 100 mounted and armed campesinos, starting a guerrilla movement and the tenuous balance with legality that would define his life. For 18 months, he led uprisings all over Morelos and Puebla, where 26 years earlier he had fought as a Zapatista, engaging in skirmishes with the army and government forces. Caciques would be done in; his soldiers would be killed, tortured, disappeared. People died for Rubén to protect him from the enemies' bullets. At one point, 30 to 40 people enlisted in the popular army every two weeks in Oaxaca alone, only to be killed and replaced. Eventually Jaramillo would ride to the death the horse, "El Agrarista," given to him by President Cardenas.

Finally, Rubén realizes people are no longer as prone to go "a la bola." To stay close to his people, he chooses the open, legal road. President Manuel Avila Camacho offers to send him to cultivate San Quintín Valley in Baja California, but he refuses. He receives amnesty in 1944, works to expand ejido lands, forms the party Partido Agrario Obrero Morelense (PAOM), and twice runs for governor in 1946 and 1951. He loses as a result of fraud and each time is sent back into clandestine life in the hills due to government retribution.

Rubén would help people resolve their problems. He would neglect his crops and the people would give him a manota–a big handful–of beans or a chicken. But when he became angry, he turned to grey, very grey.

Rubén had two wives, both named Epifania. The first was inseparable from him, but she didn't follow him to the mountains. "The first died of sadness. She turned into an old woman," says Beta. The second "raffled her life away with Rubén, carrying a pistola in her rebozo," writes journalist Froylán Manjarrez in Mantanza de Xochicalco. She taught Rubén how to read and write, once saved his life, and outlasted other men who sometimes passed out from traversing so much terrain.

Then, in the teachers' strike of the late 1950s, Mónico–as a parent–helped lead a national strike and takeover of the secretary of education for one month and ten days. He had done so without following orders from the communist party. A tribunal was held, and he was charged by Hector Revueltas with acting without orders, dividing the party and being a cacique. Mónico was already in trouble for having associated with Valentín Campa in the railroad workers' movement in the early 50s. Campa had been expelled from the party as a Trotskyite because he refused to kill Trotsky, recalled Mónico.

One of Mónico's daughters was born in the party's local headquarters. Another was born during a strike. The family was evicted from the home by the federal police. So Mónico eventually left the party to earn a stable salary–he had two girls with TB and a son with a bad leg. With the winds of a U.S. invasion in Cuba seeming imminent in 1959, Mónico said, members of the party asked him to go to the one man who had experience in preparing a counter invasion, his compadre Rubén. Though Rubén was at odds with the party, "They had me visit Rubén Saturday and Sunday." Eventually, Mónico just stayed there from June to November. Though Rubén was never a member of the party, his long ties with Mónico eventually made him willing to reorganize his political party into a "party of masses," said Mónico.

"I told Rubén: What do you think? I have una bola de cuates, politically prepared, that if I tell them, look, we're trying to form a new organization of workers and campesinos, they'll go for it...the idea was to generate an organization, let us say, really revolutionary...knowing that you can't decree a revolution...." – Mónico in Los Jaramillistas

Rubén was to sell his house, given to him by President Cárdenas, for 70,000 pesos. He and Mónico would go to villages, picking five people to prepare them, telling them, "Well, compañeros, you know all the history of jaramillismo here. This cannot just stay here the day Rubén is gone. We want to prepare you, that you become as capable or more capable than ourselves...for this reason all the history of our struggle will be collected and it will be discussed...we have to learn how to face the enemy."

The plan was to create a secret cadre in the PAOM to be prepared for armed struggle. Rubén would disappear and only a few confidants, at the given moment, would know where to find him. "The plan was to look for a cave in the mountains...."

"I know of a cave of mi general," Rubén told Mónico on occasions.

"Jaramillo went to a cave.... That is another paragraph."

"Well, I have a cave that was my general's," Rubén told Mónico.

"We were going to sell the house and we would go to the cave.

Perhaps it was near Los Hornos, rancherias like Villa's cave with little holes that you can't even tell." – Mónico in Los Jaramillistas. Campesinos were going to plant around the cave for camouflage.

Rubén was afraid to endanger or dissolve the PAOM. Over time, with discussion, "he saw it as the seedling, el alma, where we would nurture the organization, more prepared in secret. From this would come seedlings that we would take to many parts."

"It was to form many Rubén's."

Epifania vetoed the idea. She was negotiating with President Adolfo López Mateo's wife to start a garment workshop for the campesinas. Rubén, now almost 70, wanted to live a life as a "good campesino," Mónico said. He launched his last peaceful land movement.

La Bendición

In 1961, government agricultural officials approved his plans of possessing vacant land for 6,000 campesino families without knowing that the uncultable land was slaited for irrigation, making it highly profitable. The government renegged and accused Jaramillo of an uprising after the campesinos took over the land in Michapan and el Gaurín. It was to be named after Otilio Montaño. Twice evicted by armed forces, 1,000 people were unarmed at Jaramillo's behest. The people wanted to fight, but Jaramillo forbid armed defense–"not even with a rock." The press accused him of taking up arms. Again, he is forced to the hills to protect himself from the army. The jaramillistas say that the government evicted and jailed them because they were united.

The publication Protesta writes: "Jaramillo knew he was in danger of death. Before occupying the llanos for the first time, he, his wife and the principal leaders of the group made a will and the mother of Epifania gave her blessing and said, 'Go tranquilly. Go as if you had no mother and fight. Win the land for the campesinos.'"

Journalist Froylán Manjarrez interviewed Jaramillo while he was guarded by the hills. He asked him if he was tired of the struggle. "Pancho Villa used to say, and he was right, that a man should only rest when he is in the tomb, my friend," Jaramillo told him.

Eventually, Jaramillo agreed to an amnesty in late 1961. People tried to tell Jaramillo that the government would kill him and give him a hymn. The President gave him "el abrazo de Judas."

In the memoirs of Paula Batalla, the jaramillista recalls Rubén telling her, "As long as I am on this earth, I have to walk fighting in defense of my people–and what is more I am fighting with the law in my hands.

"Then, I answered him, the law is what will kill you, compañero. He replies: 'I know I am going to die, but behind me will be others who will lift my banner. I have people who know my history, what I have fought and what I have suffered, and we have suffered together. This struggle will not end. It will have to continue generation-to-generation.'" – Paula Batalla, Donde Quiera Que me Para, Soy Yo (Autobiografía de una Jaramillista)

Paula Batalla, a loyal soldadera, passed on a letter from a stranger warning Rubén that his life was in danger. Rubén would not listen.

"We walked a bit more and he stopped and said, 'Look,' pointing to the ground, 'they are going to sow me [put me under], they are going to bury me. But there will bloom from this earth another who will help you all as I am helping you.'" – Paula Batalla, Donde Quiera Que me Para, Soy Yo (Autobiografía de una Jaramillista)

Manjarrez gives this account of Jaramillo's assassination:

It was a Wednesday when Rubén was given a "box and a crown," as a popular poem said of those times. The great railroad leader Demetrio Vallejo was in jail. So, too, was the muralist David Siqueiros, who had been jailed for criticizing the government's imprisonment of political prisoners, such as Vallejo and Campa. They were jailed in '59 as part of generalized government repression after a railroad workers' strike.

On May 23, 1962, Rubén's home was surrounded about 2:00 p.m. by police, plain clothes officers and state military, their machine guns pointed at the house. They reportedly said, "¡Rindese, agrarista!" Rubén tried to show them his amnesty, but they insisted that he go with them to Cuernavaca. The family was forced into a plain, grey car. Two hours later, Rubén, Epifania, and his sons Ricardo, Enrique and Filemón were shot at the steps of Xochicalco. Another account in Raúl Macín's biography, Jaramillo: Un profeta olvidado, alleges that Rubén reportedly pleaded for the lives of his family and faced his death with the cry, "¡Viva Zapata!" A guard, who heard the shots west of the ruins, saw a grey car, filled with military types, leaving the scene.

Part of Rubén's head was blown off. Pifa's bloated body showed "the double homicide." She was six month's pregnant with Rubén's first child. "Oh, Rubén should be very mad, very mad," said Beta. Mónico and Beta's son Javier was with Rubén hours before he was killed.

"There were always campesinos in his house but that day, no one, no one. I thought I would never stop crying," said Beta.

After Jaramillo and his seed were given the coup de gras, their bodies were dragged on the brush and stained the stones that seem to grow out of the land like ancient teeth. Later journalists found the spent shells–a .45 caliber with markings from the National Munitions factory, years '53 and '54, solely manufactured munitions for the army, according to a report in Protesta. Manjarrez writes that the newspapers bought the official versions, claiming Rubén was planning to attack vacationers on the main road. Some denounced the mass killings as "the sacrifice at xochicalco." An official investigation was never completed. Manjarrez called it the third death of Zapata. The second was the betrayal of his sons, who became PRIistas, writes Manjarrez. Two of the men believed to be the main assassins of the Jaramillos, Captain José Sánchez Martínez and Heriberto Espinoza, known as "El Pintor" and who burst into Jaramillo's home to apprehend him, were later killed. "Los campesinos cobró vida por vida," writes Manjarrez.

– Les dieron chicharón, says Mónico.

According to Francisco Guerrero Garro in La Jornada:

The campesinos put the corpses of Rubén and Pifa's on a table and they brought a Mexican flag used by Rubén during all of his military and political actions, which he called a "flag of combat." They put it over his body. The house was surrounded by military. A lieutenant got wind and entered Rubén's home. He tried to take the flag, yelling, "The flag only is for heroes."

"Rubén Jaramillo is a hero," retorted a voice in the back and the room became tense. The lieutenant put his hand to his waist and threatened to go for his holster; 12 jaramillistas did the same. He realized he was with people "forged" with Jaramillo and ready to die there. He backed off, and eventually the army left.

At the burial surrounded by the army, a campesino concluded, "Se murio el jefe, ahora todos somos jaramillo." Our leader has died, now we all are Jaramillo, writes Carlos Monsiváis in his book, Días de guardar.

"We will not relate more, because we no longer want to speak more of those times. But yes, as long as we live, morelense por morelense, campesino to campesino, mexicano to mexicano, we will remember that the agrarian campesino leader Rubén Jaramillo murio por la raya, like the best men who know how to die for a revolutionary cause." – Los Jaramillistas

People have asked me how big a hero was Jaramillo. Did he deserve to be mentioned in the same breadth as Zapata? He did not start a revolution. Some say he continued it. He did not fundamentally change a nation, but some say he was a symbol of hope and resistance. He was like many people of struggle, lost in the "imperceptible changes" of history.

He, like Zapata, changed the possibilities. He, like Zapata, was no different than his soldiers or than us today. He was an ordinary man who listened to the muses of justice, whose whispers are heard louder by some hearts more than others. And I think of Jesús Sotelo Inclán, who wrote the famous Zapata biography Raíz y razón de Zapata.

Sotelo Inclán: "Zapata is not one, nor does being the one matter. Zapata is many behind him and not of that moment because I am not referring to only men of his struggle. I am referring to centuries before and far from the Republic of México."

"…For all of that, the life of these people comes to be a heroism sustained over more than six centuries of history; Zapata is only one of its moments. The People is the true hero, the man a simple expression of that heroism."

Both Zapata and Jaramillo tried at first to live in legality. Both were forced to armed struggle. In this virulent country like México, almost certainly, peaceful struggles feed the ground para huertas de muertos.

Still, writes Revalo, people come to the jaramillistas and ask: "Que señalemos la cueva de los bandidos." And they refuse to show the cave of the bandidos.

And the hue guerrero waits for someone to pick up his knife

and continue.

– To begin this paragraph…

> House of painting, House of Colors
> spirit land, land of flowers
> radiant flutters
> birds, spirit of slain warriors
> jaguar flowers, shield flowers
> calling the warriors to resurrect the battlefield
>
> – Cantares Mexicanos

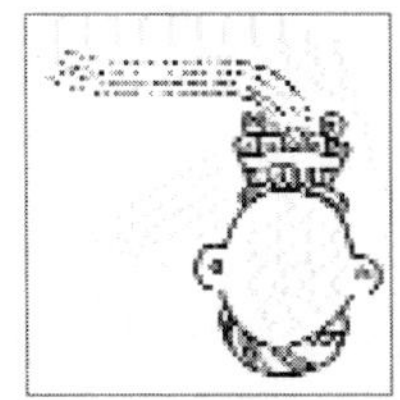

As I prepared this "pot script," I began to look at the old symbols of Quetzalcoatl. One was a hand that symbolized Venus. That night, I dreamed of a jeweled concha, a concha that I actually bought from a fisherman in Isla Mujeres years ago. The concha was covered in black, water-smoothed stones from the South Pacific that fell off, giving way to jewels, jade fish and obsidian symbols, diamonds, pink quartz. One was an obsidian hand, like the ancient Mesoamerican relics for Venus. Creation symbols. I was shown how to use that concha for my healing. Since then, Don Aurelio Ramirez of Amatlan has shared with me the knowledge of those caves where Zapata and Jaramillo found refuge.

Mónico died of stomach cancer December 4, 1998. He died without our seeing each other again. We spoke briefly on the phone in 1995. I made a slight reference to the Zapatistas, but we couldn't say much on the phone about those matters. Because of my illness, I would not return to México for many years; the toll was great on my body and marriage. When he died, I felt his loss rip from my heart to my stomach. Even now, I grieve for him. Mónico was familia. I was part of his family. They helped me plan my wedding. Mónico designed a pattern of the old Zapatista shirts for my husband's wedding attire. They gently scolded me for not keeping better contact with them.

When I returned in 2002, we all cried at the steps of Nahuatl University. I read them this entire chapter, translating it as I went along. As we parted, his daughter Marina, my sister in the Indian way, told me, "Don't forget. Mi papá carried an ollin in his pocket."

Although el hue guerrero has passed on, I pray that his spirit and teachings live on in these pages. I have passed what I could of his book. To pass the book, in the old ways, is to pass the knowledge. I will always honor him as mi abuelo de lucha. Que en revolución descanse.

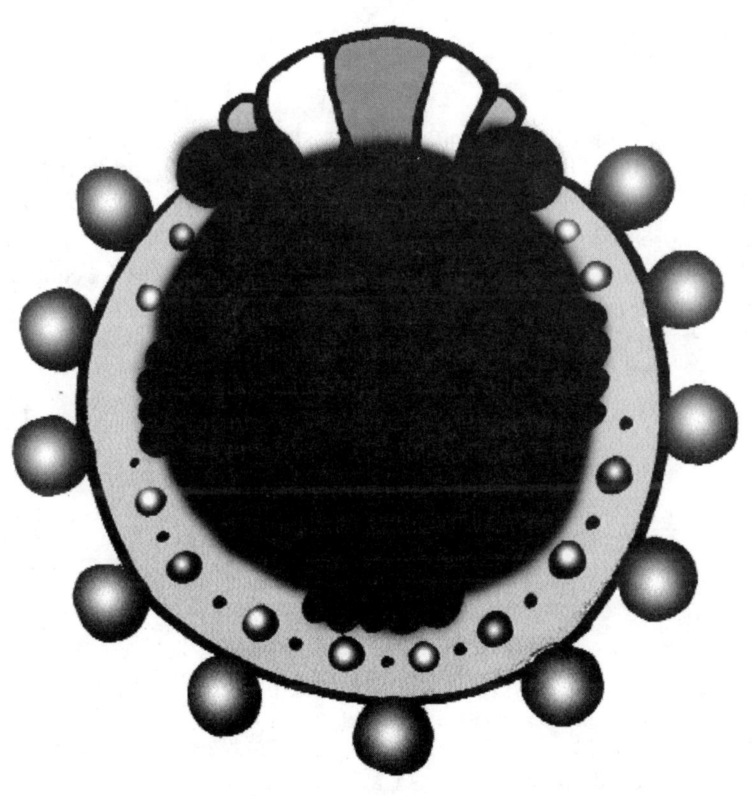

Part 4
Dark Moon

A Time of Consciousness, Healing

Spirit Plate

The spirits have come to the kitchen table. A long, yellow wooden table. They all gather at the table, ancestors from North and South. They have come here, to the house of earth. They come again, as in a procession, to my book. Another obsidian moon. They walk to the mud place. They know which mud to use for healing. La comadre Josie warns me, "You'd better start taking your book seriously."

At the kitchen table, the ancestors tell me, "Don't worry."

"We'll take care of your book."

They are ready to eat. Time for tobacco.

Chapter 10: Memoria de los Agravios, Becoming Time, Retoño

I have spent many hours in the re-membering of the past. Where do I graft myself in the re-memory? Where do I re-member? There are songs inside the earth.

And I ask, where does memory reside? Inside an ant? In a seed? A cell? A memory as deep and old as the seven caves, womb of our mother? They say that caves are her ombligos. Or do we reside in memory? And I remember where my mother buried my ombligo, with ash, romero y resos. Y yo se donde está mi ombligo.

Sometimes I feel we live inside of our memory, walking with our emotions all around us. It veils us as we try to find the truth in the llovizna of time, shifting, passing, stirring the fault lines. Or is it we who pass through memory?

Our memory dances inside the speaking rocks, stones like teeth, stones the elders say are the "bones of our spirituality." A public memory remains in the pyramids and sacred cities, built upon each other–to preserve memory for the stone clan. But how we read the public memory differs.

Still, what is our memory built on? Stones of official history that created memory to justify authority? Books written by the conquerors when all of México was an inquisition? The bearded ones and the ones bearing crosses came and tried to destroy our past, our books. Then they burned our knowledge, the books, and the makers of the books. They recreated what they wanted us to remember.

Enrique Florescano writes that our ancestors became informants and objects of history, never actors, at least not for the white eyes of conquering time.

Reducción. Settlement of Indians. "Reduced," as in no longer being hostile. Indians being Christian or in the process of being Christianized. – Glossary entry from Raramurí, Thomas E. Sheridan, and Thomas H. Naylor, editors

Reducciones served to reduce indigenas, both in spirit and on the land, into missions and nearby villages. Reduce their Indian spirit to make room for a Christian.

With reducciones, the church could spiritually kill the Indian. Missionaries did this by settling indigenas into compact villages where they could be Christianized, and, therefore, contained and controlled. Reduce the Indians' soul. That process taught indigenous people to hate themselves and to see all things indigenous as things of the devil. To hate the Indian, to hate ourselves, this is how they controlled us. The story of mestizaje is clay fashioned by their hands. This is the susto or trauma of history. Our faces, our skin color, tell us we are Indian. But it is the not knowing–of our tribes, of our native tongues–that is our historical trauma. Es el susto de lo que fue desaparecido.

Still an oppositional memory exists. You won't find our oppositional memory in books. It struggles in those fires that burned our books. It fills our veins, nos da coraje. But en las escondidas, our grandmothers and grandfathers passed the book, the knowledge. In the stories. Andrés Segura once told me of the memory that resides in the cocol, or "smallpox cookies," still sold at some Mexican bakeries. Cocoliztli is the Nahuatl word for illness. In the first mazorca of the harvest. In the matitas. Our resistance is the remembering. Our memory is medicine. Now it is creation time.

Our memory resides in the land. Our memory resides in our ancestors. The conquerors took their names, their lives, their land, their place. But still we know, our faceless, nameless memories walked here. So it is painted–tiny footprints across the earth. Their flesh and bones are here. Though grass and flowers grow strong and high above the ground, their spirit remains in the earth. The abuelos are our ombligos.

The Europeans reinvented America, says Latin American writer Eduardo Galeano. But the guardians of the land will rebuild America with ancestral sovereignty–a moral authority over this land because our ancestors are of this land and in this earth; buried, they became her. American cowboys look at the land and may see rugged individualism. We look at the land and see our ancestors. They breathe inside her. We share the same breath.

As I write these words in 1993, I am recovering from a serious illness that has sequestered my memory and pierced my spine with 30 syringes. I cannot walk. Every strike of a key fills my arms with hurt. I have become pain. I cannot remember if a certain politician was elected or re-elected, if I took my medicine, or what Roberto said to me moments before. Or when the land greened this year. Or when the cranes like to perch on the backs of cows, like the magpie on the buffalo. But I still remember the color of butterflies that cry yellow for me.

In my efforts to bring out the healing medicine in my body, I have realized people who are battered by life often choose to forget. It becomes a social amnesia. Illness, however, is the pain of memory. It has made me wonder, what are we without conscious memory? Is not time a series of memories and does not memory–an even non-memory–lead us to act?

Henry Kissinger once said history is "the memory of nations." However, there is little space for the sovereignty of people in official memory. I prefer another interpretation I once heard–that history should be the conscience of the past. Some say we are merely red-brown vessels whose souls were claimed. Others say our Indian spirits live beneath the imposed European culture.

The great Chicano scholar Tomás Rivera once wrote that the struggle to know who we are is the struggle to remember. I know it is time to heal the memory. This is our healing time, the time of ombligo people. Y yo se donde esta mi ombligo.

Naming the Santos

When I was living in México, I went to a conference regarding the border and human rights. There, I heard David Lujan, of Tonantzin Land Institute, introduce himself as an indigenous man and a Chicano. How strong it made me feel to hear him say that. I had spent more than a year there, where many Mexicanos mocked me for saying this. I remember once at a party a Mexican intellectual was talking about los chicanos. She did not know I was Xicana. "Oh no," she said, "Chicanos have no culture." I went livid. "Yo soy Xicana, y si yo existo, tengo cultura. Un ser humano no puede existir sin cultura," I told her. Later, I thought, people like her think we have no culture because we allow lo indígena to break through the lies we've been told about ourselves.

Renato Rosaldo says that when we cross the border we become Indians again. If we sought out the European, then we would be like them and, therefore, with culture. Earlier, an anglo art collector with an impressive collection of Mexican and Chicano art said he was more Chicano than most because he knew pop culture and could name all the saints and their days. I responded, "To be Xicano means your ancestors live through your veins. It's to look at the land and know they died for you, that they prayed you into being. It's not naming all the santos."

Rememory

"Tell me your dream."

"…A man and a woman are walking along the water. It is cold. They are looking at the water. There are lots of foaming, crashing waves. They are saying goodbye. They wear buffalo robes."

"Tell me your dream," Rusita tells me.

"…A man and woman are walking along a big body of water, an ocean, perhaps a big lake. They are very cold. They wear buffalo robes and draw the hides around them. My father and mother stand closer together looking at the water. It is grey. They are sad. He points west. They are saying goodbye to the motherland."

"Tell me your dream again."

"…We are walking along the water. We are cold and gather ourselves inside our buffalo skins. We draw near to each other. We are barefoot. We are standing on jagged rocks or cliffs, kind of like hard lava. Our feet are wet and cold. My husband points to the left, to the west. We are sad. We are saying goodbye."

It is our migration story.

My memory reveals itself in an indigenous liberation gathering. Marcie Rendon, an Ojibwe woman and leader in the Re-evaluation Counseling Communities, spoke of how we, as indigenous people, had been "targeted for destruction." Our ancestors "did what they had to do to survive," she said. Yes, we were not supposed to be here.

We had been asked to name ourselves as indigenous people. Naming can bring up so much fear, Xicana Kikapu, Opata Chicana…

which comes first? What of my other peoples, the ones known or not known, the ones with no stories? So often we become fearful. Will they accept me? Can you hear the doubt that flattens my name? Can I? For me, it is not the naming I struggle with as much as the fact that I can remember so little. All my life, I can remember little, especially my childhood. I've walked with that dream all my life and can see it in my mind's eye. I realize I don't remember the time I found out we were indios, but I remember this dream I had when I was very young. In my adult years, I realized it was a vision of our migration story. It was as if the Great Mystery had gifted me some sight of hope to hold on to as I lived painful years as a little girl. You won't remember anything to survive, but I'll give you a dream.

Our Migation Story

My great grandparents were native, their children considered Mexican. My mother was Mexican American (though she lists Mexican and Native American on the census) and I grew up Chicana.

My great-great grandma Mama Mencha was born during the migration of the Kickapoo as they came south from Illinois. They went to "Old México" for refuge from the wars against Indians. "Old México" back in 1822 was what is now Texas. She eventually migrated to Nacimiento, México. When she returned to the United States as a sheepherder, her grandchildren were considered Mexican, though she and my great-grandpa prayed in the traditional way. My tío Chema remembers she'd pray under a tree when there was no rain and told stories about "el Geronimo." Her granddaughter, my abuelita Vicenta, was born in a wagon yard in Lytle while the family was herding. She would later live in a cave outside El Paso, working mines, "just like an Indian," my aunty would say.

I can only imagine how we became Mexican in the migration trail. Though for a long time, being Mexican was just another kind of Indian. At the turn of the century, it was not safe to say you were Indian. You'd be forced into "Indian Country" in Oklahoma, and you couldn't own land.

On my maternal side, my grandma and grandpa crossed the border when it was just wind in the sand. Their ancestors were Northern peoples who went to México for refuge and ancient Mexican

Indian people who came from the North. When they migrated back to the United States, they were Mexicans. My grandpa would have to buy his papers, though he was Comanche. He told my uncle Chuy that the Comanche were great horsemen and that they ended up in Guanajuato. He'd tell my uncle Chuy he'd better behave, "You're mama is Kikapu."

My grandpa saved all the names of our ancestors and their Native American lineage on a papelito for us, but my uncle lost it. When I was little, I remember my elders saying que somos indios, but I never asked what kind. Somewhere along the way, from listening to my abuelos, I knew we were Kickapoo and Comanche.

I grew up Chicana, raised by Indian people but in the Mexican-Chicano community. When I did ask one of my grandmas again when I was grown up, then she was so old that she could only remember she was una india. "And what is the name of our people?" I asked. My grandma looked off into the distance as she searched her memory. "I don't remember."

My Naming

For a long time, I did not name my tribes…well, my grandparents are Indian…. "All my grandmothers are Indian," I would say. It was not out of shame that I did not name myself, it was out of wanting to be honest, out of respect for my indigenous ombligo. I had no feathers, I did not have the language. Only a few words to pray with. But then in Philadelphia as I would go to pow wows with light-skinned native folks, I would wonder why am I not American Indian and they are. I began to feel called to name my ancestors by naming myself Kikapua, Mexican Indian, Comanche. Eventually Xicana was not enough for me anymore. I was missing part of my name.

At an indigenous gathering in Temoaya, México, el abuelo Gustavo Gutiérrez helped me name my ancestors. I asked him for guidance. As an indigenous woman, how do I name myself? Chicana Kikapu, Kikapua, Kikapua-Xicana, Chicana Kickapoo, daughter of… "You are Kickapoo," Gustavo told me. Later, the Kickapoo elder Picajana would acknowledge, "You are Kickapoo. You are my relative."

Vistin' and doins'

In 1992, my ancestors started to visit. First an elder and a warrior came to me in my dreams. "The Kikapu people will always be strong," they said. Then the grandmas started to visit. My aunties would speak to me in Indian, Kikapua, Nahuatl. "It's ok," they told me.

"They're calling you home," the Kickapoo elder Marvin told me.

Barefoot Indian

"When you go to see the ancestors, you must go barefoot," the elders told me.

And I offered a bit of my flesh on those stickers in the dry prairie. I sacrificed with stickers from thorny, black locust trees the Europeans introduced. I walked in the earthen bowls of the buffalo wallow, the land still rutted with the weight of bygone days. The land still remembered them. I saw maple trees my relatives planted. Here, on a farm in Le Roy, Illinois, I gathered blue jay feathers and the stories of my people. This is the land of the Kikapua, known today as the Kickapoo Nation.

Kikapua: People who keep moving about, moving here, moving there, making the land sacred where they go. I am a descendant of the thousands now buried under cornfields here in what was once our Grand Village. The heart of the old ones remains alive in this land. Buried here, our ancestors made this earth sacred ground. Dying, they became the earth.

The village was the capitol of the Kickapoo Nation, when 10 million acres of Illinois became home after the Kickapoo migrated from the Great Lakes region. "They thought they'd be safe in the village forever," says water clan leader John Kaskaske. Then came the trickery, betrayed treaties, and the move to "Old México." I am the seventh generation of the people who prayed me into existence. The fact that I am here with them hums through my bones. The elders say that the old ones have prayed us all back.

"Ancestors, I am here. Your daughter has returned," I announce myself with the sunrise.

I had asked my Apache brother, Gregory Gómez, for some songs to sing them. After we prayed, he told me, "Little sister, the best songs are your own." But I worried they wouldn't know me. "You're Kikapu. They will know you," my spirit sister Catherine (sister in the Indian way) told me.

So there I was in prayer for three days. I prayed in Nahuatl and read Cuauhtemoc's words to them about how our families would be our teachers and our homes our sacred house of prayers, and songs came to me. The ancestors spoke through the land. Butterflies surrounded me and golden lights and a family of red-tailed hawks that guard the trees followed me. When I woke up to the ceremony of the sunrise, a great sorrow had lifted. Some part of me had returned. Songs have come to me ever since. And more stories about where a river was born.

Talking Indian

Years ago, in a sacred ceremony, something emerged from deep within and spoke, "I want to pray in my own native language." That prayer led me to recover my indigenous languages, to feel my throat vibrate and my spirit cleanse as ancestral words course through my body, healing some cells waiting for me to remember.

A ceremonial leader told me that learning to pray in an indigenous language is the quickest way to learn the language. It grounds us, and our words, in spirit.

I was forever changed when I saw Hawaiian youth salute all visitors to their schools in the traditional call-response welcome songs of their islands. I saw language make their spirits strong as their sacred taro plant. They were fluent in their native tongue, which had almost died among the Kanaka Maoli. I thought then that those of us who have been forcibly separated from the indigenous communities, languages, and traditions of our ancestors could also one day recover our languages.

I embarked on learning Nahuatl as a family legacy and a form of community healing. It's a journey that anyone can make who wants to return to her source. I chose Nahuatl because, though my ancestors were Kickapoo and Comanche, they married into Mexican Indian peoples. More than a decade ago, I started to learn Nahuatl in Mexico

City while I researched this book on spiritual change. But our lives must be ready to carry such knowledge; mine was not.

In our Nahuatl collective at Kalpulli Izkalli in Albuquerque, we had much discussion about language use, how words have an energy, how language contains instructions about culture and the land, how our ancestors respond to the energy of those words.

"We are an earth-based people and culture who are rooted to the land. Culture comes from the idea of what we cultivate, and language evolved from our ancestors' understanding of the land and ceremonial ways," the kalpulli wrote in a Nahuatl book that we created as a result of our learning. "These teachings and words were cultivated through traditions that venerate and give thanks for everything that has been given to us for survival."

My friend and Nahua teacher, Mapitzmitl Paz, says language is learned "in three spaces": the everyday, the philosophical and the ceremonial/energetic. We sought to balance our thirst for a philosophy that would place us and our role in the natural world–such as how energy changes within a day or night and in a particular season and how that affects daily life–with learning to greet people and welcoming them into our homes.

Because I knew only a few words in Kickapoo, when I went to our former Grand Village, I read from a great teaching in Nahuatl–and my ancestors recognized me. I believe that in the spirit world they hear all prayers in the language of the heart. They know us even when others might question our authenticity. Because the effort of learning an ancestral language is so sincere, intense and energy-giving, the universe responds in kind. So my ancestors speak to me in their languages. My dreams have changed. "They're calling you back," Marvin said.

This has been my own journey back to my ancestors, my own root healing. Each time, I name myself as an indigenous woman, I name my ancestors; and they walk with me. It is my own honoring song for them. They become part of my material world through my words, my language, my prayers. It has helped me back to the meaning of our names. Kikapua, loosely, means the people who keep moving or who make a place sacred because they have been there. And so I have tried to be a good person, to tell these stories in a good way, with a good heart.

As I speak words I have never known, it is as if they are an energy circling within my being, re-ordering some genetic memory to return me to my origins. To return me to the energy I've always been, untouched by forced separations, to Creation itself.

Retoño, Regeneration

I am in another circle, a circle for women leaders. We have made an altar. We name ourselves from our female ancestors. We call them in…I am the daughter of Martha Maldonado Dickinson; granddaughter of Vicenta Gonzales and Carmen Arteaga Maldonado; great grandaughter of Irinea Muñoz and Rosa Aguilera, Demetria Cruz and Concha Flores; great-great grandaughter of Mama Mencha and Tomasa Fernández. Sheepherders, women who drank scalding coffee, picked la pisca faster than their boys, curanderas, parteras, yerberas, women who "know" herbs.

And I remember again through the ellipses…as a girl, I used to stay up late into the night wondering who made God. If God made the world, then who made God? And who made Who made God? Those questions and my vivid dreams shut down, for the most part, after I was molested. My spiritual life would not reawaken until I had to heal from the rape. My dreams would only come to me throughout the years, when I really needed them.

Twice, I've dreamed that men I loved had married. I found out a few days later it was true. I've dreamed of people's deaths and of others' salvations. As I began to heal, the dreams returned more frequently. Or they returned so that I could heal. At first they were nightmares, for a long time they were so. And then the grandmothers came, the medicine people. They would scold me sometimes. They would tell me, "Eat broccoli and cauliflower." They'd show me my gallbladder point, or the meridian that affects the ovaries. Your stomach is all twisted; you need mustard; go to so and so doctor yerbero. I would follow their advice and work on these things. The herbalist would tell me that they were right.

I believe that we are a people of oral memory. I have seen it in women's circles, how when we are making a remedio or a shampoo, some little story comes out of us, as if from some cultural DNA. A long forgotten story of our abuelas appears from our cells in these circles of memory, these communities of memory. Once, while we were making soaps and talking kitchen talk about recetas and the weather, my mother remembered how my grandmother would cut a storm's path with a knife and a "Padre Nuestro." The storm would move in another direction. She'd cut the energy. Each time I'm in a healing circle, the talk brings out the remedio of memory.

One of the creation stories tells how Quetzalcoatl created humanity from a bag of his father's bones. I believe we must have that sacred creation in our bones–that none of what's been physically destroyed is lost. It will return and present it to us, in prayer, as we heal and for us to heal.

The Starlight Ballroom

I have helped with writing/healing circles. Numerous times I've drawn a codex of my life, kind of a spiritual map of the memory written on my body–organs, tripas, beauty marks and wounds. In August of 1999, while in a circle of indigenous women, I realized that I drew blue stars to symbolize my rape. Some 15 years after the rape, I realized that I could not physically have seen the stars. I was raped in a dark bedroom. But when I remember that night, I remember seeing stars, as if the ceiling opened up and the sky came into the room, like where my mama went dancing at the Starlight Ballroom.

It dawned on me that my prayers traveled there to the stars, and my prayers were answered. I had prayed to them that night, "Please, God, please don't let me die." At that moment, I found my courage. At first, after the rape, I felt terror in seeing the stars, feeling the dark surround me. Later, I began to see differently. Those stars that night led me back to the path of prayer and faith that I had lost as a defenseless child, when I had no words for what had happened, only an ugly feeling. Today, I'm no longer a rape survivor. I transform rape. I've transformed that violence. I've called my spirit back from the space of violence, left honey and flowers, and coughed and cried into the earth. Thank you, Madrecita. Thank you for my life.

I have walked the cycle of life and death: birth, transformation, rebirth, manifestation, and "the return." Joy Harjo, in Reinventing the Enemy's Language names this cycle: genesis, struggle, transformation, and the returning. When I first wrote "Memoria de los Agravios," I was still clawed by pain and suffering. Now I am living the re-creation of my life, the reconstruction de la vida, my regeneration. Mi retoño.

Welcoming

I show the elder Chakuka the photo of Mama Mencha. "Esa sí es india. Ella sí es Kikapu," says the spiritual leader. War Chief George White Water tells me, "You belong to the Vermilion band." It is good to come home.

I'm reunited with my people at a time when all the Kikapua have come together to help the Kickapoo Traditional Tribe of Texas (KTTT) take back its government. The nation eventually receives a court ruling that recognizes the authority of traditional Kickapoo practices to make legal and social contracts. On the way back from the court hearing, I see Tesquequite Creek on a road I had never traveled. Tequesquite is a natural sodium that forms from sweet waters. It is used as food and medicine.

A year earlier, I dreamed a river. A grandma is swimming inside it. I'm instructed to talk to the water spirit. "You have to call the spirit. Hay una planta en el río que cura." I see a water root, dark green and mushy, rise out of the water. The root was called Tesquequite.

In a low, baritone voice, it asks me, "Who goes there? ¿Qué es lo que quieres?"

Mama's Bones Remember

The stones are rocking
Coatlique is in the fire
Puke Vomit Fart Cough Cry
Mocos
I'm clean inside
My tongue has grown back
The corn and beans have been thrown
the future known
Turn the ground over, release the worms
clean la concha
el guerrero shakes his bones
las nanas, los tatas
are calling
ven, ven pa'ca, ven pronto,
ven, ve, verás
vas a ver

An Ant Elder

Guardian of Mother Earth

Chapter 11: El Ombligo de la Tierra

Many times, I went to the Place of the Flowers, the chinampas of Xochimilco and San Geronimo, in search of ombligos in the watery mirrors of the floating gardens, the place of never conquered blood where homes reflect upon liquid green and silver. In the ejido adjacent to the floating gardens where Maria Candelaria fell in love and our parents spread honey on the moon, the government tried to build a "Tenochtilandia," a tourist resort in the last remaining green lungs of Mexico City, an emerald in the biggest city in the world.

The native sons returned to fight for their land, doctors and nurses and artists, the children of people who walked barefoot, who prayed to the fields. Those now-grown children remembered that not even one corn seed do you waste. A single seed is sacred. When the bulldozers came, they stood side-by-side with the elders as those monsters tore down the corn. Goons beat the old ones because they remembered that not even one seed do you waste. Brother betrayed brother, son and father, as ejido officials bribed people to falsify documents so as to sell the land. They did not remember that you do not betray the land, not even one single seed.

> mud [Middle English, prob. < a Low German source as in mudde, IE meut, base meu-, wet, musty > moss, mother]
>
> – <u>Webster's New World Dictionary</u>

In 1989, Mexico City's government expropriated thousands of hectares of ejido land won through the Mexican Revolution for a master ecological plan for the greater Xochimilco area, which included an amusement park similar to Disneyland. The planners say it would have led to the urbanization of what is considered an agricultural province within the city, where Zapata and Villa met in a place that is now a storefront, and where you can still get the sweetest corn.

The Natural Law

"Never make a law against the spiritual law because you cannot prevail; never make a law against nature. Remember that you cannot and will not prevail. You will be defeated every time. It may not be your generation that sees it, but you will be defeated." – Chief Oren Lyons, Onondaga Nation.

The 1000-year floating gardens of San Gregorio and Xochimilco are the last living monuments of ancient México. They are the green lungs of the most populated and polluted city in the world, providing oxygen and water to 20 million people. Natives say San Gregorio Atlapulco, land of ejido-communal farms and flower isles within an ancient lake, has never been totally conquered. It was the last indigenous group to resist the Aztec empire. It was a way station for Zapatistas during the Mexican Revolution, and centenarian soldiers still come out to honor "mi general" on Emiliano Zapata's birthday. It still has a communal form of government and has no local police.

Mocosa

There is snot in our mother's rivers. Our mother, she always loves us, she never rejects us, no matter what we do to her. She always gives us her absorbing madre energy. The next time you've got snot in your nose, or vomit, now you know how Coatlique feels.

In many ways, the people of the Xochimilco area, living on the outskirts of Mexico City, have always confronted "progress." They protested when Porfirio Díaz tapped the area's spring to provide potable water for the expanding city; they protested in the 1950s when the government drained the lake to feed the city and then filled the canals with black waters of untreated sewage, killing off much of the fauna. Later, land expropriated for an ecological reserve became luxury housing.

Human Nature

"Las plantas quieren que tengamos fe." The plants want us to believe in them–maestro Madrigal.

When the Eurpoeans came, they disconnected us from our land. When they disconnect us from the land, they disconnect us from our body, from life itself. The church taught us that to know our herbs and our energy was brujería. We were conditioned to believe that the energies in life–and our own hands–were not natural, not part of our natureleza. Yet our medicine ways continued, in secret. Everytime we eat food or drink water, we connect to Grandmother. They are our medicine. As a Diné elder once told me, "Taking care of the earth is traditional medicine."

UNESCO named the area of floating gardens and agricultural islands patrimony of humanity. Fishing communities began gathering there 5,000 years ago, eventually developing the chinampas, by gathering water lilies and mulch into floating islands. Agroecologists say this technology contains 22,000 years of the evolution of humankind. Islands of compost: Tlazolteotl.

Mud Pie

The Yuchi-Creek tell how when there was nothing but water Crawfish dove down to the bottom and found mud. He stirred it up and took some. This made the Mud People angry. "Who is stirring up our mud?" they demanded. Crawfish moved so fast and stirred up so much mud that the mud people could never catch him. He kept bringing mud up from below, making more and more land. – The Mythology of North America by David Leeming and Jake Page

The chinampas, which at the time of the Spanish Conquest yielded crops all year long, was one of the great technologies "discovered" by the Europeans. However, ignoring the ancient technology, the Europeans imposed their own ways, leading to floods and the death of thousands of Indians. The old technology continues to be studied today. In their contemporary struggle, different groups received different concessions. In the end, San Gregorio landed a training center for new farming technology to help them compete in free trade. The government agreed to replace some of the expropriated ejido land, reforesting land to prevent squatting.

They Speak the Justice of Grandmother Earth

Toci makes the earth rock and roll when we don't listen. Consejos: "We are one body, human beings, plants, animals. We share the same history with Mother Earth. There are spirits of plants that want to be heard," says Doña Enriqueta Contreras, Zapotec partera. "Tell them to take care of the water," the Santa Clara elder Jose Lucero tells me. "Always pray for the water," says Shoshone elder Corbin Harvey. I know women who take care of the water; they know its songs. Others take care of the fire. The water is sacred because that is where we live until we are born, Grandma Emma. Como dice mi Roberto, "La educacción es la tierra."

In Xochimilco, some of its leaders were beaten after they fought off machinery that bulldozed the corn fields. In the end, only five families persevered. They lost most of the land, but their tenacity led to a federal decree this year for a 2,000-acre ecological preserve and other ecological measures. It's a tenacity that is an ancient force. "Sometimes I feel as if I am living in the wrong time, as if I belong in the past," the 25-year-old leader Andrés once told me. Sometimes we have no choice but to let Great Mystery work through us.

There are times when we must defy the unnatural order of things and other times, when we must trust the energy and form that creation takes. Tenacity creates a space for itself. Like the old man Zapatista, 104 years strong. He begins telling us his life–from age three. He asked us to tell Cárdenas to give him back his pension. "This land was watered with the blood of our ancestors," said Lucas Godoy of San Gregorio's Frente Zapatista. "We know that this is not the last fight for our land. It is only one–that we are living–but more will come and the struggle will continue."

La Flor: Symbol of life, creativity, beauty, our ultimate end, creativity that inspires science, the last of the day signs on the Aztec day count

And I think to myself, in 22,000 years of human evolution, when did they stop being Indian? When did they emerge mestizo? Was this the resistance of mestizos? As Zapata's struggle was one of Indios. Or did the memory of a corn seed make them Indian? Or listening to the stories of the 108-year-old Zapatista? Or their ritual to Xochiquetzal la flor hermosa and the beautiful flower's "seeds of love and beauty," as are worshiped behind the robes of the Virgin?

Perhaps only the monas that hang from the spindly ahuejote

trees could tell me. They are being strangled from the pollution. I found no who knew how the hanging dolls got there. Some say they are protection against bad spirits. (The ahuejote tree grounds the chinampas to the earth and its foliage allows the sun in but detains the wind and evades erosion.)

The guardian of the ancient pre-Hispanic treasures of Xochimilco died without telling the people where they were buried, somewhere deep within the floating aisles. Perhaps he buried them within the heart of struggle, inside an ombligo.

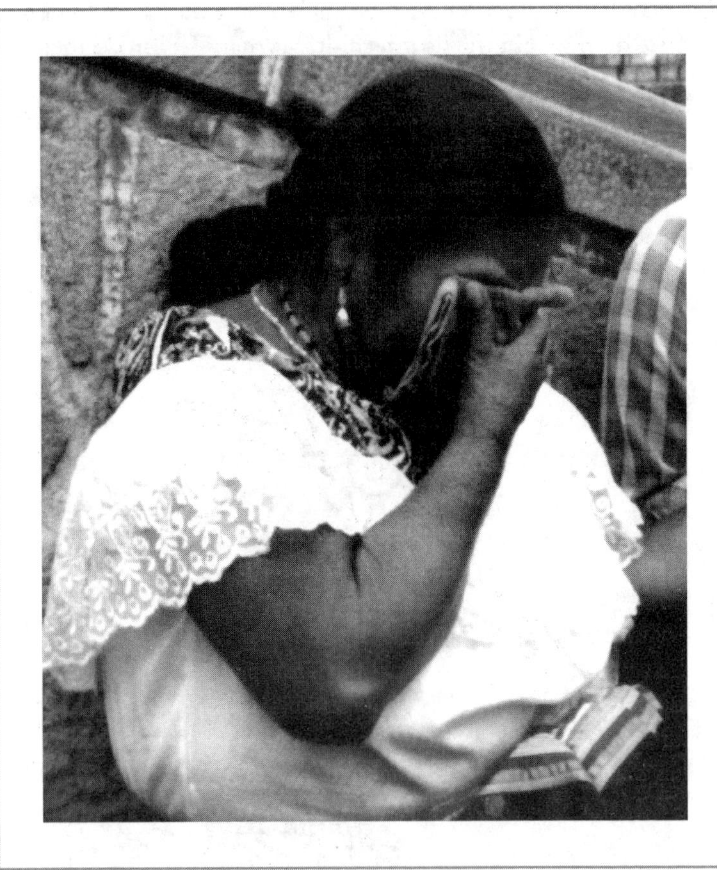

Abuela Pascuala, Chol de Tila

It is said in "el libro del consejo" that the people prayed to the Life Giver, the Creator, the Former. "May there be not disgrace nor misfortune. May no deceiver come behind them nor before them. May they not fall or be injured…nor be seduced…. That they not fall while traveling downhill nor uphill. That there be no obstacles behind them nor before them, nor things that will hurt them. Grant them a good road, beautiful flat roads."

In 1992, Mayan Indians led an historic march across México. It was known as the march of Xi' Nich' –the Ant. Xi' Nich'–men, women, and children sent as envoys from their communities–set out from Palenque, Chiapas, March 7, 1992, after people were jailed December 1991, following a peaceful sit-in in front of Palenque's municipal palace. Nine remained in jail, charged with terrorism and sedition. Eight were granted "conditional" freedom 40 days later, following the protest of 1,500 indígenas. The ninth man, falsely charged with homicide, was released over the course of the march, following negotiations with the government.

The Ant People Rest

Chapter 12: The Offering of An Ant

In the year of luto, the Mexican government stepped on the descendants of Chacmool and Kulkulcan in the municipality of Palenque. In the year of el luto, la hormiga picó al gobierno. The Ant bit the government.

The Ant precedes los enmascarados with wooden rifles. Both asked for the same things: clean elections. A hospital. Land.

Perhaps the March of the Ant began when an ant spent four days in silence; perhaps it began when the prayers to the milpa stopped or when 103 Mayans were arrested December 28, 1991, thrown into a Solidaridad truck, like costales. Corn sacks. Or perhaps it began when Ant helped Quetzalcoatl find food for the macehuales. Or when the ants helped defeat the 400 muchachos in the struggle between the forces of the earth and the forces of the heavens, perhaps. Or when they stole the flowers in the tests of Xibalba underworld. Or when Hunahpu and Xbalanque slept unhurt on an anthill. Or was it when the cardinal cried when it sang and the white and black jaguars lost their red spots?

They called themselves Xi' Nich', ant in the Mayan language of Chol. Four hundred indigenous people walked more than 1,000 kilometers across México, asking for roads, potable water, clean elections, an end to land disputes, and the right to maintain their customs. They asked to be judged in their own language, to live in peace, and to be afforded the universal rights of human beings. They asked to obtain birth certificates and to be able to pray to their cornfields. They bore the march of 500 years. This was the burden year of 1992.

Following the "route of Cortés," the Ant walked the path where the conquistador made his way to another world, an event feted in 1992 as the triumph of civilization.

The elders gave the líderes naturales, or natural leaders, the right to speak with a thousand tongues. In their feet marched many.

"Palenque was the house of the ants," said Manuel Pérez Constantín, one of Xi' Nich'. "They tried to stamp us out. At first we were hundreds, then a thousand. One ejido alone, one man alone, one woman alone, we are nothing; but together we are a force; together we are Xi' Nich'."

Indígenas from around the republic joined the march. They offered copal and prayer for its success, saying that Xi' Nich' had awakened their conscience, restored pride in being Indian, and diminished their shame in a country where being called indio is one of the highest insults of backwardness.

Along the March of the Ant, people offered their homes, their bathrooms, tortillas, taquitos, pesos. They greeted them with marimba bands and mariachis. Indians accustomed to being spat upon by mestizos were greeted with applause.

"Chiapas is like a big farm and the government is owner of life and death. It has its captains that are the lords of the people–the police," said Jesuit human rights activist Jesús Maldonado. "But now they use rifles and clubs instead of whips."

Even officials from the government's Instituto Nacional Indigenista (INI, National Indigenous Institute), one of México's more respected institutions, were unjustly jailed in Chiapas during the span of the march.

To many indigenous people, Xi' Nich' fulfilled a prophesy of the ancestors that some day their people would once again unite. Mexican intellectuals borrowed from the title of the book Visión de los vencidos, chronicling the conquest through the eyes of "the conquered," saying that the beginning of the next 500 years would be a departure point for the "vision of the defeated" to rewrite history.

In the country that termed itself the land of the "cosmic race"–of black, yellow, red, and white–an ant returned the bones of memory; and the so-called defeated were "welcomed to history."

They marched from México Profundo, from the house of the Ant, for 50 days. The doctor from Palenque joined Xi' Nich' with his wife and son. El doctor Hugo pulled his son out of school to walk with the Ant. "You will learn more about life from this march than in school." Things such as geography, history, politics, and endurance. They will see el pico de Orizaba.

As the Ant walks across México, it is joined by Lacandon Alta, Lacandon Baja, San Cristóbal de las Casas, Xochimilco, Tabasco, Sinaloa, Sonora, Chihuáhua, Oaxaca, Guerrero, Morelos, Tlaxcala Nahuatl, Otomí, Chol, Tzeltal, Zoque, Chontal, Mazahua, Mixe, Mexica, El Milky Way, El Tlaxcalteca, La Morenita, El Michoacano de Veracruz. Los muy sabios. Hijos de las hierbas, las selvas.

De donde vienen: la Cascada, Palenque, Ococingo, Chilón, Salto de Agua, Tila, Bachajón, Citala, Panetelo, Escuintla, UCISECH (Unión de Campesinos de La Selva de Chiapas), and CDLI (Comite de Defensa de la Libertad Indígena), Tsoblej-Yu'Un ocoltic, an assembly of Tseltales, campesinos from el Exodus para la Democracia.

¿De dónde vienen? el lugar de abundancia. Hay caminos en la selva tirados con memoria.

The Ant walked for 115,000 people from three municipalities. The municipality of Palenque alone has 90 ejidos. The Ant wonders why are its communities so divided by the regional authorities of Palenque and Ococingo, which create a political "zigzagdeo" like a game of checkers. One community will be in Palenque's jurisdiction, then Ocosingo's, then Palenque's. It is hard for the elders to travel so far. Sometimes 10, 20 hours away. The Ant asks why it cannot vote as regional autonomies.

They earn 20 cents per kilo for maíz and beans. Three out of 10 homes in Chiapas have an indigenous speaker; 63.3 percent of Chiapas is bilingual; 32 percent monolingual; 30 percent can't read.

They wear T-shirts: de Chiapas a México. They carry clothes in bundles, so many people are sending them clothes and blankets along the way. The Ant wants to carry it all. They send back bundles to their people.

Los agravios, según la hormiga

People have been assassinated by the police and los verdes. It was at a fiesta. Police went in, and on the third day, Eugenio Aguilar Sánchez, 28, died in '90 at 11:30 p.m. In another case, police say José Moreno had a .22 caliber gun. They killed him while attempting to detain him.

Era un judicial who killed José Daniel López Cruz. THEY say he had 300,000 pesos in his pocket when he went to buy a Coke, and the judicial killed him by busting his guts in 1986. They fired three shots, and he rolled down a slope. They stepped on his chest so that he would die. He died within 20 minutes.

February 1991, ejido Nuevo Francisco León, Ococingo municipality: Municipal police stopped a land invasion by the Cortés Mercado family. Three dead, four detained and 31 orders of apprehensions. "Y nos los castigan."

Many mestizos despise los indios. A man could be 50 years old and still they will say, "Ay viene ese muchacho. No tiene nombre ni siquiera. You could work with him, you could live with him and you'll still be 'boy' to him. Los inditos no saben–it's a national mentality. Es una indignación que revienta." – Padre Xel

Tomás Niño Arteaga, 25, Acacoyahua, Palenque municipality: "We came here because on December 28 we were evicted, 500 of us. They beat up old men and women and took four people prisoners for 40 days. They put in a different municipal president whom the people did not support."

They planted themselves in front of the municipal palace with 12 petitions: an end to corruption, provision of civil interpreters in their native languages, running water and roads. The government sent 200 police. They surrounded them and hit their legs. "A garrotazos, a purotazos."

I ask una mujer hormiga: From what people are you from?

– Oh no! I am not an Indian. I am a campesina–de raza española.

Era una noche de "hidalgo violines." The violins sounded beautiful and noble that night. "It started to rain. We went to sleep in the basílica. Others went to the kiosk. We were thrown into a Solidaridad truck as if we were sacks," says Efraín Gutiérrez Gómez, 39. "Todo eso nos ha pasado."

Some 93 were later freed; eight were accused of charges that would leave them in jail 10 to 40 years, accused of treason and attempting to disturb the peace of the State: "Atenta contra la paz and la integridad corporal y patrimonial de la colectividad y del estado." Terrorism.

Eight were gravely wounded. The group was tortured, beaten with macanas, and told they would be thrown into a river while being transported in the rain for 16 hours through the mountains. They received other threats and were not fed for two days. They forced them to change into clean shirts, said Padre Xel. Then they took photographs and a video of them to show the ants were treated well.

Efraín, one of the eight leaders, wrote his wife Concepción a letter from jail in 1992: "The children are helping, the women, the old people. These are your sons, your brothers. I am not only Efraín. Efraín has produced many sons. You should be happy. I march for them. These are your sons and daughters, your pride."

Concepción planted the maíz. She took it to the market.

The eight were freed after the Comisión Nacional de Derechos Humanos investigated and ruled the men had been detained "arbitrarily." A ninth man of Xi' Nich', Manuel Martínez Pérez, is accused of murder and treason. The government's National Commission on Human Rights rules that there is insufficient proof to detain him. Pero no lo sueltan. Five thousand Indians are jailed all over México. "The jails are filled with poor people. Por eso la hormiga se levantó." – Efraín hormiga

"The idea of the ant is of something small and insignificant that confronts something powerful, big. The ant is despised and small but has a collective purpose that acts communally, constantly working and well organized. It's small but can carry a tree. An ant can be crushed with a finger. But if that enemy doesn't know that the ant is not alone, he will be in for a surprise. He tries to kill the ant, but an ant's nest appears. I believe in the symbol of the true ant."

"I believe this is a noble march, a march of great nobility," says Padre Xel, otherwise known as Father Geronimo Hernández López, with the Centro de Apoyo de los Derechos Indígenas.

Padre Xel would later be accused of being Marcos. They both have big eyes and a big nose.

No sólo esta la hormiga. Not just one man, not just one house, but all of us. – Alberto Gonzaléz Armendáriz, 48, Ejido Emiliano Zapata, municipio Amaton

Two compas were jailed in 1978, accused of murder. Santiago Gómez Moreno was jailed 11 months. A group of 60 did a sit in; then 3,000 people gathered to see what the indios would do. The streets were filled, the churches. A judge freed him after they occupied the offices for one week in February, 1978. Officials kept asking them, What do you want? They wouldn't talk. They spent four days in silence.

At 13, Efraín started as a catechist with Padre Lucio. He heard him talk of liberation theology and God's social contract. He prayed in chapel pyramids. He prayed in the great church of Mother Earth. At 18, he realized he did not believe the words he spoke. He saw too many indígenas hungry, sick from something missing in their lives. It bothered him so much that he was hospitalized for eight days from fatigue. He stopped eating. He had so much hate he wanted to kill someone, "con un tiro me lo acabo." In the end, he knew he must serve his brothers and sisters. He organized a coffee cooperative in Xacala. Efraín met Padre Xel in the 1980s while organizing a coffee cooperative.

Efraín ran for local council in 1986. He lost by 600 votes. In 1988, he won the judgeship. Following "el fraude burdo" in 1988 in which Cárdenas lost as president, Efraín started going to the communities to teach human rights. The sites of the booths were changed at the last minute and names were not found on the voter's list. The Frente Cardenista, an oppositional party, later gave them the missing voting documents, which had been stolen and lost by the thief while he was drunk. Someone from the front returned them to Efraín.

He was named a local representative, but in 1992 PRIistas wouldn't recognize his victory. The Ant was born. "It's part of la lucha that someday, one day, the people must govern. It will be a continuous fight, we won't see the triumph. Yes, the Ant began with two or three. Sale, Sale. More and more come out. Here the people have come out like an ant." – Efraín ant

"Somewhere in the intentions come the changes." – Efraín

Efraín and others began to organize their communities. They divided the southeastern selva into three regions: el fuego nuevo because this effort was a new fire; los tres huerfanitos because the Indians always feel like orphans against the government; la base because that is where the 60 food cooperatives began, that is "where they were liberated," says Manuel Pérez Constantín.

25 January 92 – Officials from the CNDH met with local legislators without telling the Indians installed in front of the municipal palace. The meeting was suspended.

Chiapas Governor Patrocino González Garrido told La Jornada he would free the eight if the human rights commission rec-

La March de Xí Nich´

ommended so; but as far as he was concerned, "pues que estaban provocando a la comunidad, atosigando al turismo." No one was hurt, he said. All their belongings were returned to them in front of journalists, along with 50,000 pesos. "Si hubo violencia no la recibieron ellos," he told La Jornada. "The government is ready to participate in negotiations if, and when, ultimatums are not given."

– We can't let the people out of jail every time four groups start yelling.... Because el chiste will be to join an organization, violate the law, and then pegarse un grito, the governor says.

On the same day, headlines from Jalapa,Veracruz, and Oaxaca announce other native struggles. Con violencia, pistoleros ocuparon un ejido: UGOCP. "Una banda encabezada por Timoteo Díaz Palmero que se encuentra ligado al narcotrafico."

Another headline: Retira el MULT su plantón de la alcaldia de Juxtlahuaca, Oaxaca...el movimiento de Unificación y Lucha Triqui levantaron plantón en demanda de libertad de tres militantes....

On March 7, the Ant leaves Palenque.

7 March 92 headline in La Jornada: Police threatened campesinos of Hidalgo. Six organizations vow to march to the Zócalo April 10 after police evicted them from 80 hectares. Many have outstanding claims to land since 1932. One ejido, which has had possession of the land since 1953, is told by agricultural officials that its group does not exist in the books; another case since 1953 involves 355 campesinos and 1,600 hectares.

The Ant stopped and saw the ocean where Cortés arrived by Veracruz. They prayed. They stopped at a river and said, "Cortés stopped here. Y todavía estamos aquí."

As they walked, they became the mountains, they became the rivers, los llanos, las avispas, las abejas, el jaguar, el serpiente. They became the green of volcanes y aguacate. They became México. As native people often say, we are earth people. This is our ancestral memory. Our memory breathes in this land. It holds our mother's breath.

The elders say the traditions are dying. Who will pray to the corn? Who will offer scented prayers of copal? Who will make smoke? Who will talk to the water spirits? To Heart of the Sky, Heart of the Earth? Who will carry our prayers?

The Ant walks 12 hours a day, 24 kilometers. Their feet are a thousand miles of México, blistered maps as cracked as the earth that receives their steps. Their feet are stiff as amatl paper. Their footsteps create the road. What memory is written on their feet that plant barefoot words? Their feet do not hurt because they walk a long way. They hurt because they carry the burden of memory. Feet that always touch the memory of the earth. Perhaps feet are like cucarachas and hormigas. They must carry long memory to still be here. The Mam say a wise person is one who remembers something. This is a good person from which to seek council.

They are used to walking. They walk six hours to get to the nearest pueblo. Three miles to fetch water. Eighteen miles to a doctor. Sometimes women have their babies along the way. That's why they are on this long walk. The women are tired of having babies on the road.

The keepers of the mat leave tiny footprints across México, like the codex of migration. Uncured feet begin to burn between the fourth and sixth hour. No one complains. They burned copal, copal precioso.

"This is their flower wars."

People wave at the Ant. They throw them money. They throw them fruit. They offer their drinking wells. They greet them with marimbas. Police wave at them. The train blows its whistle. "¡Duro. Duro!"

Others yell, "Indios."

They were surprised by the support. They wondered if it was out of pity por los Indios patasrajadas.

– Porque no somos los perfumados, según una hormiguita.

They pray to the milpa. They pray to the harvest. The old ones go to the milpa to die. The abuelos son aguas manantiales, manan. Pure springs. Ya no se aguante pues el sufrimiento. This is why the people came. Who will take care of the milpa? Pray to the milpa? – Efraín

Efraín's wife saw him on television. "Why am I not walking with him?" she asked. She cried all that night and started to pull at frijol. She remembered their abuelos. But the 72 days in plantón had prepared her well. She fears Efraín would be taken. She joins the march. If he is abducted "aquí estamos nosotros." She will be joined by his brothers, his primos, his parents, a son and daughter, and a godson. Efraín's mother and father are on the march to support his "suffering."

Se movieron por "el clamor de la justicia. El clamor del pobre."

This is not something that can be learned in books. They threw gritos to the road. These are the customs of the Tzeltales, says Armando Aguirre, who wears a PRD tejano.

They are told Secretary of State Fernando Gutiérrez Barrios will not negotiate with an ant.

On 21 March 92, in Minatitlán, Veracruz, the Ant received an offer to negotiate from President Salinas de Gortari on the condition that the Ant suspends the march. Lo mandaron a la fregada al del PRI.

The indios walk into the conscience of México, where Indians are alive in the past and festoon the present with feathers and beads. "Todos somos los hijos de Cuauhtemoc," justify the mestizos. It is as if the spine of a great cornstalk sprung from the feet of the Ant like an ancient root. The first mazorca is saved for good fortune.

In 1992, there are 56 Indian groups; 12-20 million indígenas, depending on how you define who is an Indian. Those who speak the language? Those who live and work the land? Those who live with their communities? Those who still wear their traditional clothes? The two million plus who have moved to the city are not Indians to the government.

"A Mexican cannot explain what it means to be Mexican, but collectively Xi' Nich' awakened what it means to be Mexican. It connected them with their Indian roots," said the mestizo, Oscar Rodríguez, who helped in the caravan. All we Mexicans have denied our indigenous roots. With this experience, something was moved collectively with our own indigenous roots, although from a mestizo identity."

Someone from San Luis Potosí told the Ant, "Nos cortaran las ramas, nos cortaran el trunco; pero nuestras raíces jamás."

On the tenth day, they stay in casas ejidales of Palo Mulato, sleep six hours and walk another 22 kilometers. On March 17, Father Francisco Prieto, headquartered at ejido Palo Mulato in the parish of San José y los remedios en la rancheria Plátano y Cacao, tells the Ant: "Xi' Nich' is another sign of the people's desire for democracy, for an end to corruption and the prepotencia of the authorities, and a struggle so that society in general treats them as people." – La Jornada

March 25: After 18 days de marcha, the Ant arrives in los

Tuxtlas. This is the land of the colosul heads of Tres Zapotes in Veracruz that seem to grow out of the grass.

A group marches toward them. The Ant does not know if they will be greeted by friends or machetes. The group approaches the Ant, shaking the hand of each marchante, and they join the march. They clap. There are firecrackers. The march makes a half moon across the federal highway in the middle of the road. They stop traffic and do a danza indígena, danza con plumas de Quetzales y violín antiguo. The dance of Quetzal is a special Chol dance.

In April, the question becomes whether to enter Mexico City or not? The government has made promises on the condition that the Ant does not enter the city. The Ant says the government does not want it to ruin Manuel Camacho Solis' fiesta, the continental festival of government Indians to show que los Indians are happy.

The majority quieren cumplir la marcha and arrive in Mexico City. About 50 are willing to return; but if Manuel is not released, the government must take them back where they were.

The commission has recommended that the Ant not march into México.

"Esta marcha va a llegar al palacio nacional, to the very entrance. We want liberty.

¡A huevo!"

"We will write to Manuel and explain."

– Even if Manuel is in there a year, pero que Manuel se aguante because the march must continue.

"Hay que negociar con corazón." – el doctor Hugo

"¿Vamos a regresar?"

"NO."

"Al Palacio Nacional."

"A México."

– No se trata de ser una hormiga that marches by day and another that marches by night.

"Que promesas. ¡Van a burlar sin soluciones!"

"It is they who negotiate with heart and intelligence."– el doctor Hugo

Efraín hormiga tells Patrocino, regarding the compañero Manuel's release, "You want me to sign the papers without seeing the bride."

On April 10, the Ant stops to conduct a short act of homage to Emiliano Zapata in Jalapa, Veracruz. To everyone's surprise, el compañero Manuel walks into the crowd. As it turns out, Manuel was released by the government.

The Ant Continues Toward México.

Chol Benjamin Pérez Vázquez carries the sacred fire, the same torch he has lit since the Ant began to walk. They walked in the rain of our mother's tears por ser tierra lastimada. Maestro Gigante Relámpago greets them, Huella de Relámpago, Esplendor del Relámpago.

At el Puente de Jula in Veracruz, dicen que Patrocino is here. He has offered to release four prisoners who are members of various groups marching with the Ant and who have been jailed on various charges, if the Ant signs a piece of paper and agrees not to enter Mexico City.

"Era no mas por la burla." – Efraín hormiga

The Ant bathes in public showers on the plaza. Their feet are cracked like a dry riverbed, their skin split open. They sleep on concrete, with hammocks of food overhead. The Ant holds a meeting until 10:00 p.m. They rise at 5:00 a.m. to walk another 12 hours. The Ant eats bolillos and pozol, hominy muelle. "Díos es un caminante con nosotros."

The Ant is high-tech Mayan. Padre Xel has a laptop computer he uses daily throughout the march. The brothers and sisters of the Jesuit order have organized food and clothes donations. A caravan follows the Ant. The media covers its move daily. Some people say this is the protest of Archbishop Samuel Ruíz because the Ant has a well-coordinated network of human rights activists in the Christian-based communities. Later, others will say it was the first march of the Zapatistas.

"I do see that as an error on our part, that the indígenas could give us too much power over the direction," says Oscar, "because they trust us a lot. But one margin of certainty we have is that when they agree to something they say yes; and if they don't, they won't say anything. Something will happen, and they won't follow you. The kitchen will break down. That indicates something is not well. People who are manipulated may follow you for two days, but not forty."

A commission goes to Palenque to give information to the people. The local radio has scared the supporters at home with wrong information. They think people are hurt, that Xi' Nich' is going hungry.

La ofrenda: The ant elders arrive at the Basílica. They bring offerings of chocolate, sopa de arroz y miel, their food, 30 velas. They pray before the earth outside the church with jewels of copal. They offer their foreheads to the earth. They have advanced to see la virgen while the negotiating team meets with officials in Mexico City.

At the Basílica, Moros y Cristianos are dancing.

Santa tierra, señor de la cuenta. They offer honey and chocolate and mole and march to the iron monument of "la ofrenda" with 30 candles. They bow their heads. The candles drip on their hands. The women wear tennis shoes. They pour chocolate from tiny clay cups. They pray for their people's strength, to give them strength to arrive to México. The negotiating team is meeting with Mexican officials. The women are crying. They spoke to a Cuban woman who told them the poor are taken care of in her country. Una doña luchadora, Pasquala, Chol de Tila, hits her forehand on the ground and asks: "We are all of the same blood. We follow the same laws. We are all one with each other. Then, why do we have to suffer?" Pepe, the priest, holds her and consols her.

Prayer: First you give praise to el Señor, esa musica es alegría, so he will give his blessings. La bendición: You pray to the virgin, who gives us the strength. Virgencita venimos caminando, venimos a ofrecerle un regalito.... This is the way of our antepasados, pues la carne fue tierra, mi carne se va a volver a tierra, a gift for more strength, mas fuerza, so that we may all arrive here in Mexico City, so that the authorities won't deny us to live in peace, so that we will have more life. Forty-five days it has been through the force of la virgen, because el pueblo de Chiapas, el pueblo de Chiapas is suffering. Esta torturado. We need help now. You pray, pues a el díos, la virgen, despues a la tierra. This is the way of our antepasados. "Vinimos con Xi'Nich' con el hambre, con la conciencia, Díos de la luz, ilumina el camino, la luz, eso es que nos hace ver todo. Vino ser muy pequeño el animal. No era uno, no era dos. El indígena esta en movimiento. No somos ni uno, ni dos, que ya esta viendo que somos muchos."

The grandmothers and I go to the metro. The ant women fear the Mexico City metro. They are afraid to board. We hold hands and giggle. We are a Casasola photograph, Adelitas looking out the train. We all hold hands and board, y no se nos pasó el tren.

My friend Leopoldo walks with the Ant. We visit. Leopoldo is a Mayan spiritual leader from Guatemala. "In Guatemala, you can find people named Juan Xi' Nich'." Quetzalcoatl is also a surname. If someone is named hormiga, this does not mean that they are less than someone named lion or someone named coyote, because if we all coexist, if we respect animals this way, how can we not respect human beings?

Xi' Nich' also equals the number 20. The number 20 is Kukumatz (Gucumatz) or Quetzalcoatl. It is also a rayo. When it rains, the serpiente from below is united with Quetzalcoatl above; and they produce a rayo, se truenan. "When it rains, it is said that Kukumatz is hitting the clouds so that it will rain."

"For me, the rayo represents action, effect," I tell him.

"Sí, just as the atmosphere has rayos, so does our physique. The human being is a universe en chica. Do you know how we represent the rayo inside our body? Kumatz: lightening inside our bodies."

"Leopoldo, cuentame algo."

– In a sacred book of the Maya, it is written that when there was no corn, Quetzalcoatl saw an ant carrying a grain of corn on its back. Quetzalcoatl asked him from whence it came. He told him he found the maíz inside a rock. Quetzalcoatl wondered how to get it from the rock. He asked the rayo to open the rock. And though the rayo was big, it left only a small opening. So he called upon another rayo, and the rock opened a little bit more. A third rayo opened it even more. The first rayo was so strong that it burned the corn black. The second rayo left the corn red. Under the red corn was yellow because there was less heat, and it fell along the way. At the very end of the corn was white corn because the heat did not touch it. This is how the four colors of maíz were born. And this is how the culture of humans was born, thanks to the ant, thanks to the rayos. This the story of humanity and the four colors of corn. And that is how, in the Chol legend, the four colors of the world were created, the four races. Do you know how to tell when it will rain? Ants always disappear into their ant home two hours before it rains.

There is a word, vinac (also winic) for time and the universe. The number 20 represents the universe and the human being. They are the same. The human being has 20 fingers and toes; 13 is the number for men. Twenty times 13 is the gestation time of a human being. "My people make a ceremony to corazón de la fuerza o la energía, offerings to the heart of the force." – Leopoldo

There are always people in march in México. To walk across México is a long prayer. The petroleum workers, the auto workers of Monclova, the indígenas and campesinos of Guerrero en la marcha por la democracia.

An INI official and two collaborators were arrested February 29, 1992, without cause in Chiapas. People asked for their release throughout the march.

"Since I was 10 years old, I began to see my mother suffering, my father suffering. When I went to school, we didn't have money for my notebook, my clothes, or my shoes because we couldn't get the price we asked for our products. My father had to walk six hours with his bag of products and my jefa had to walk 500 meters to fetch water. Or when she sold her pigs, it was for a miserable price. We didn't even eat meat once a month because we had to sell our stock." – Francisco Guzmán Vázquez, 23, would have liked to attend a university. He lives in the town of Progreso–that is six hours by bus from Palenque, plus four hours on foot.

24 April 92: It is the first time the Ant did not walk as it waited for negotiations. Resting on the grounds of the Universidad Autonoma de Chapingo, they have arrived in Mexico City but not the Zócalo. "Estos indios no vinieron a bailar."– La Jornada

Headline: Xi' Nich' vino a resolver no a llegar al D.F., dicen los marchistas.

Xi' Nich' stays the night at the Universidad de Chapingo. They debate whether to take the government's offer. They hold council until late into the night, 300 people. "If we return with nothing but promises, the people will make fun of us. If we return without solutions, the caciques will continue to repress us. Se van a burlar de nosotros."

They agree to give the negotiating team a vote of confidence and entrust them with the final decision. The team decides to pause the Ant march until they can examine the details of the agreement.

The Ant sleeps on petates and serapes. The Ant gazes at a Diego Rivera mural in which the natives are painted naked. The people sleep. All is quiet. El tambor is silent. Hugo's son Francisco, "who likes these kind of things," is asleep. The girl with a dolly the size of a child with pink skin, maybe two feet, is asleep.

The accord is read at Chapingo in all the tongues of the Ant; the government agrees to free 10 compañeros and 151 orders of apprehension are suspended.

27 April 1992 – The goverment agrees to 377 public projects. The National Indigenous Institute promises 200 million pesos for water, electricity, schools, clinics, and birth certificates, among other things. The 10 compañeros will be freed, including three from CIOAC, Central Independiente de Obreros Agrícolas y Campesinos, says Mexican officals, after CIOAC lifts its "sitio" in Simojovel.

Their petition: Loans forgiven for five ejidos charged between 36 to 49 percent interest by Banrural; training and technical support so that the indigenous communities may use their forests more rationally and in accordance with their customs; technical support and credit to initiate commercial projects; 190 agricultural cases involving land disputes; 327 public works projects, including roads, potable water, schools, electricity, clinics, ball courts, casa ejidales and interpreters; and the cancellation of 151 orders of apprehension and the investigation of public officials (five agents in the public ministry and four judges in the civil registry).

The government does not agree to prosecute upper-level government officials whom the Ant says give the orders of generalized repression. Nor does the government agree to a statement about the general conditions and racist perceptions of the Indians. "Patrocino said the indios got more than they deserved." – Concepción

The Ant does not arrive at the Zócalo. It does go to Neza inolvidable. Painted in red, next to the statue of el rey poeta, is the word, Xi' Nich'.

"Xi' Nich' bienvendios a la colonia El Sol y a la historia."

"In November 1991, quedó plasmado la historia y el descontento del pueblo…voy a cantarles un corrido compañero. Ponga mucha atención…y ahora si las hormiguitas salieron. Se pusieron como campion."

Asi cantó el José Luis Muñoz Rodríguez, el michoacano de San Andres Tuxlta, de 57 years, orphaned since 13 of his mother, at age 11 of his father, after which the people became for him father and mother when his parents were killed by pistoleros for fighting for the land in Michoacan. His parents death se vengó because the pistolero Manuel Cuevas was killed when el señor Catalino Tapio "vengó la sangre de mi padre y mi madre." Then he was later killed by a teniente coronel who paid Tapio's compadre 20,000 pesos. "Eso valía la muerte del compañero Catalino Tapia." El michoacano has lived to tell it because one February 4, 1980, he was left for dead in a trash can by PRIistas, envuelto en un petate. At 5:00 a.m., he was discovered with a bullet wound to his head, all for defending his people, the Indian people, though he has forgotten somewhat the language of his people, "los Tarascos." He fights not for himself but for indigenous people because the animals are worth more to Mexicans–a cow, a horse, a burro–than an Indian.

Efraín's children have chapped cheeks; their lips are cracked. Efraín hugs baby Efraín and plays with him. A corrido is sung in the distance: "Vengo del pobre."

– "No llores," the People shout.

24 April 92: The Ant wears straw hats, saying: "Xi' Nich' vamos a México."

Says a man in Chol: "We are not going to be callados anymore."

Five hundred years y la fiesta for us was not a fiesta but la miseria. We live la guerra. Our children are living with parasites in their bellies. For us it is death. What lacked was enough pain so that we would stand up with amado sangre. – Efraín, who holds a bouquet of fragile, white flowers

"The earth for us is the mother of indígenas. Indígenas will go without anything but the earth, even if it's only a little piece of land." – Efraín on the 150th day of the Ant

How can the event be celebrated as the triumph of a civilization? Father Xel asked.

A sign: IMICHI: La hormiga esta brava.

We will take back the support of the people, which is what brought us here. – Efraín

La ofrenda final: 30 women, 20 children, 1,200 kilometers. They arrive for the first time. Xi' Nich' hormiga, Xi' Nich' de Chol, Xi' Nich' de Tzeltal. A violin and two guitars greet them. They call upon Pacal with six candles and copal. The grandfather touches his heart with scented fingers and walks to see the virgin. Pacal holds an hormiguera, an ant's nest.

They are reviving their traditions, las fiestas de alegría. Danza con plumas, con palmas, sones de pluma y palma.The tambourines play as Concepción Cruz Martínez speaks. "Efraín always likes to walk with justice. I have 11 children. (She is 33) I want to fight because I have children so that it won't happen to them as it happened to me. (She does not want them to bear babies on the road.) We are following truth. That is why they follow us."

The Ant wears T-shirts with ant antennae. Some wear little antennae on their heads at the Basílica.

– Son de naturales, con plumas, con plumas.

The Ant arrives with a rose and an orange in their hands, having walked 24 kilometers from la colonia el sol in Nezahualcóyotl. They march in a circle outside the Basílica, 400 tzotziles, tzeltales, zoques, tojolabales, choles. They pray on their knees con un jicara celeste with the virgin and her skin of wilted roses and yellow flowers. Otomí spiritual leader Thaayrohyadi Bermudez tells them that the elders of the different Indigenous nations have all been praying for them so that their voice is heard all over the world.

"This is the real encounter." Our ancestors are with us. They touch their foreheads to the ground. They drink from an olla. They are given flowers, flor de perico y ruda. "Ésta olla y la luna por la noche velo por ustedes," Thaayrohyadi tells them. Blessed be the old people.

Ninety-five Indian prisoners were on a hunger strike for 100 hours in Cerro Hueco prison.

–Porque vino una hormiga.

They carry signs that speak for them. "Municipio: Abasalo, Acacoyagua, Amatan, Bochil, Comita, Chilón, Escuintla, Jitotol, Ocosingo, Palenque, Pantelho, Salto de Agua, Simojovel, Sitala,

Tenejapa, Tila, Yajalón." Etnias: Tseltal, Chol, Tzotzil, Tojolabal, Zoque, Nahuatl.

Someday will they find a codex that says this was the year of the Ant. Will they know here walked an Ant?

"I know the martyrdom of many years. It is an honor to be with Xi' Nich'. Xi' Nich' is history that will arrive to our grandchildren. They will read it in a book of a time when the Mexicanos resisted to defend their lands." – a marchante known as El Milky Way

The Ant marches into the Basílica. The mass is said in three Mayan tongues and Spanish. The Ant offers guaraches to represent the sacrifice of their feet. The Ant offers up a lasso. The Ant holds the lasso in the air, unties it, and proclaims: "The Ant is set free."

In the plaza of Palenque, 5,000 Mayans celebrate. Inside the Basílica, Xi' Nich' leaders are seated with the priests. Women, children, old people–the grandfathers and grandmothers, the elders. The mass is said in Chol, Tzeltal, and Zoque. Three minutes of silence to reflect on what Xi' Nich' and its march has to do with Díos. A few people speak among themselves. Others look lost. (Whispers: How many days was it?) Eso es el triunfo. As is the custom in Chiapas, following the private reflection is group reflection. A woman with a baby strapped to her back with a rebozo: "The word of God is now a reality."

Padre Xel: Xi' Nich' is the force of el Pueblo.

"The greatest thing there is, is freedom," says Bishop Arturo Lona from Tehuantepec, who in 1995 will survive an assassination attempt.

"God walks with us. We have a life as sons and daughters of God, a God of struggle."

En voz lirica: ¡Una vals por Nuestra Señora! Xi' Nich' begins dancing on the altar as an offering. A hat is offered.

"For in Chiapas, brothers and sisters look for justice; they look for peace. Ya pues a Díos como ofrenda."

"The march of Xi' Nich' has canceled the orders of apprehension. We offer this hat, sandals, lasso, and shirt as symbols of the light that guided us from Palenque to this city."

Concha walks up and offers her two children.The Mayans walk around the church, praying with incense. Concha speaks: "We didn't want to bring children, but we did in solidarity to fight. We, as mothers, want to defend our people. And as mothers, we want to teach our children it doesn't matter even when they are so little. Thank you for the medicine of medicine. We came without a lot of sickness." Children, mothers, musicians, all approach the altar with the bishop and bless the hosts in their languages. "The Eucharist has ended."

– Buenos días paloma blanca.

"Foreigners are welcomed in our country, but not those who see us as a circus," says Víctor Guzmán López, Chol, from Nuevo Betancia ejido, 26 years old, at age eight orphaned. An ant brother brings him a soft drink. "Gracias. Gracias, hermano hormiga." Víctor hormiga continues, "I decided since I was 12 that they can even kill my son in front of me. I have made up my mind. El enemigo de todo es capaz. Si me matan bien. We are all going to die. If they want to kill my children, I say to you, con todo corazón, I have buried dead. I have touched dead brothers. We will continue caring for the milpa."

– Porque se le dio hormiga.

Una reflexión: Salio esto when they kicked us out last December. We found a nest of ants. We came out like ants after that. – Efraín hormiga

"Democracy? Here, it does not exist in México. We must create it." El pueblo, la gente humilde, la gente conciente, los pobres.

– Democracy, for me, must be from the bottom up because on top it is corrupt, sick, maleado. That democracy that is so spoken of ya es un arbol que se necesita ponerle hacha–it needs to be torn down because it is rotten. You can't fix it with fertilizer. It needs to be burned down. – Efraín hormiga

"This is a libratory psychology."

"We overcame tension with the group…" said el mestizo Oscar, who helped the caravan.

There were conflicts over such things as who would make breakfast, who would break down the camp, and gather food and wood. Sometimes such things would just break down.

There were differences between the two major groups, Chol and Tzeltal. Each spoke their native tongue, the mestizos in Spanish. There were differences of religion–cursillistas, comites de base. "But we learned from the march to be more sensitive to others, not to take things so seriously nor want to hurt others."

"We became more open and learned to live, play, joke. It shows that the struggle unites. The democratic life is essential in communal life. It is like negotiations. To derail the negotiations, this expression is to attack that participatory life and communal life, which when it manifests, it struggles for very concrete demands to live that participatory life. This is not a struggle of rancor nor of revenge." – Oscar Rodríguez Rivera, 32

> Heart of the Sky, Creator, Former spoke to the deer and the birds,
> the lions, tigers and serpents: Talk, scream…call out, talk with
> each other according to your species….
> So it is written in the Popol Vuh

During a teachers' march from Oaxaca, it became so bad that people stopped eating communally, each fending for themselves. Some started catching rides, advancing 100 kilometers over the others. People began to call it the march of the venados (deer) because they got to México so fast. So when federal police showed up with a flatbed trailer and offered Xi' Nich' a ride, "Get on because it is raining, and you're getting wet," some got on. The Ant told them, "Compañeros, we said we would arrive on foot, and on foot we will arrive."

Question: Is what you lived a democracy in progress?

Answer: I understand that far from these things such as elections, far from these decisions, I believe esa democracia should be much closer. I believe that it is the way of living, the way of making decisions, where you find freedom. I believe that is where you find democracy. I don't accept to only speak of elections, of decision making. Without democracy, or, to live democracy, in that, todos estamos en la misma, in the same condition of life. I am talking about life and that search for that democracy.

Consejo: "When that freedom to participate freely is granted, it makes people feel that whatever they do, even if they don't understand it, it is positive. It gives them a political space to not personalize things. It's to share completely what you know, little-by-little, from what we learn from all around us, that idea that all of us are capable, that there is nothing we can't realize in this life. It's a matter of agreeing to learn along the way. He who does it, not because he knows but because he knows the opportunity is valid. Not only one truth, or only one road, or only one way of marching."

The Mud People

Our lessons: "We were a small group who could fashion a meeting. The path became clear along the way. We were preoccupied with the dynamics of negotiating. Who would take my place? You saw others could, and others would, come later." – Víctor

"The Mayan people are like a mother with many children. There are other democracies–we call ours Mayan democracy or indigenous democracy. Participatory democracy. Knowledge is communal." – Leopoldo

What do I understand about democracy? Well, democracy is one man in Xi' Nich.' – Manuel hormiga

"Xi' Nich' has captured the best sons and daughters of the people, not as individual people, but as representatives of the community. It has heart."

"Ustedes tienen mística."

Newspaper headline.... Xi' Nich' showed: QUE NO ESTAMOS SOLOS

"Truly, we give thanks two times and three times.
We have been formed, we have been given
a mouth and a face,
we speak, we listen,
we think, we walk,
...we know.
what is far and near.
We see what is great and small
in the sky, on the earth.
We give you thanks for having created us,
Oh Creator and Former!
For having given us our being,
Oh, Our Grandmother! Our Grandfather!..."
Popol Vuh

  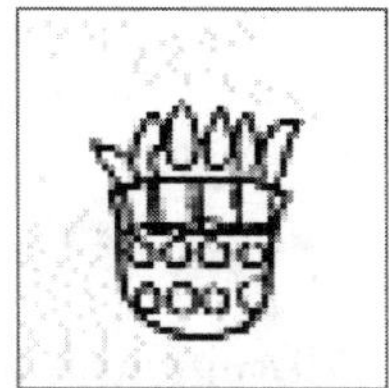

Since 1992, the people of the Ant have suffered numerous persecutions, including golpes, secuestros, and jailings. Much of the issues that inspired the march remain unresolved. Many of them are protaganists in the fight for indigenous autonomy and are Zapatista supporters.

Xi' Nich' was honored by the French government in 1999 with a medal for its work in social justice. In an interview with La Jornada, Magdalena González, who along with Víctor Guzmán traveled to Paris to receive the award, said this of the Ant: "Ants work in the subsoil. All that is seen is the nest, a little mound of earth. If someone tries to destroy it, it is not known how, but the ants come out. They multiply. They are everywhere. And then there are more nests."

When Quetzalcoatl went looking for food, he came upon a red ant that carried corn. He asked Ant where he got that food. Ant said he got if from sustenance mountain. So Queztzalcoatl changed into a black ant and followed red ant to the food mountain. There he found the corn.

In 2002, I returned to México for the first time after becoming ill in 1994. I sat at a sacred site of the Tlahuicas in Cuernavaca, Morelos. As I looked down at my feet at the base of a pyramid, I saw a black ant carrying a black feather, the size of my pointer finger.

"It was Quetzalcoatl," a Tlahuica told me.

A year later at Nahuatl Unviersity, Roberto and I saw red ants carry kernels of corn.

Ollin: Movement, Not Endings

Otomí Ceremonial Center, Temoaya, México, October 12, 1993 – The sacred fire stood watch over an altar of plumes that contained 45 staffs of Indian nations. We felt its warmth.

The sound of the drum greeted Father Sun's rising. We danced. And we prayed…with Mayans, Chichimecas, Quechuas, Aztecas, Otomies, Pueblos, Mapuches, Kunas, Xicanas and Chicanos.

Our red-brown skin spoke of our relations with the other nations. It also spoke of spirituality long ago taken from some of us but now recaptured in our hearts on this freezing mountain morning that gave way to the warmth of the rising sun.

A generation. Seven generations. Perhaps more than 500 years removed from our grandparents' spirituality. The elders, our abuelos, came to lead us back. The fire still spoke to us. The people fed the fire and the people spoke. The abuelos said it was not us speaking. It was the Great Spirit.

The arrows came from the four directions to revisit the force that has brought us here for the next 500 years, the spirit that led our grandparents for thousands of years. More than 500 of us came to this Second Continental Encounter of Indigenous Nations, Peoples and Organizations "to have truth and heart." We were part of this great gathering high up in a mountain forest in the state of México.

The peoples gathered around the elders in the circle of the prophesy and the abuelos said we are the prophesies. When we prayed to the Four Directions, the winds began to howl to the mountains that protect the sacred place that looks like an Indian city with great painted walls and tall, twisted stelles, perhaps 30, and stone, tipi-like structures that touched the sky. The abuelos said our ancestors were with us. Sometimes we could not hear what they said because the wind spoke so loudly. We understood. There were no words, only spirit. The land has a way of talking, of healing.

"This is a sacred circle. This circle has been called by the Great Spirit, the Creator, the Mystery," said an abuelo Maya.

Raza with indigenous hearts came for counsel with the abuelos.

The sage needs a fire to burn. That fire is called the spirit, and somewhere fly eagles. In 1992 there were protests, there were marches. People tried to destroy Colon's statue. They demanded the return of Moctezuma's Quetzalcopilli or headdress. Protesters were killed in Santo Domingo. Hundreds of thousands marched throughout the Place of the Wide Mother Earth: America. As mestizos looked on from the sidelines or marched as part of a popular movement, Roberto and I and many Chicanos marched as part of the Red Vein of our indigenous family. We felt strong. For us, there was no question where we belonged. A day before, Roberto and I exchanged rings from México antiguo at the pyramid of the Sun, on the anniversary of the last day before Cortés.

Later, Alfonso Pérez Espindola Tenoch, a ceremonial leader of the Lakota tradition who lived in Laredo, Texas, was put in a Mexican jail for transporting peyote because the government declared he was not an Indian. He had helped lead a prayer run, an ancient ceremony, across the Americas. Later he would lead sweats under the watchful eyes of his jailers.

Alfonso had carried one of the principal staffs, the one with the most prayers and many feathers. He endured the run through North America as they ran in the desert, as they ran sometimes 50 miles a day. They traversed sacred places, Wounded Knee and other sites of resistance. In Minnesota, a child runner was hit by a car. Unscratched, he later continued the run. In small Mexican towns, they were greeted by hundreds of children and blessed by elders. They also were regularly questioned by Mexican security agents. In some places, they saw the rivers were poisoned; at others, the rivers were dry. They noticed the deer were gone.

On October 11, 1992, we saw Alfonso and the runners enter the great pyramids of Teotihuacan, which the runners call the bones of their spirituality. The elders said the prophecies had been fulfilled. The eagle and the condor, the symbols of North and South America, had united in the people. An injury to a Lakota became an injury to a

Mapuche. "The prediction of our ancestors is completed." – An elder at Temoaya

A year later at Temoaya, again we saw many of the runners in ceremonial circles at an indigenous summit in a forest south of Mexico City. Tupac Enrique, a Chicano sun dancer from Phoenix, was keeper of the fire. He guarded the 43 staffs of nations, representing a federation that later clamored for Alfonso's release.

The abuelos said October 12 should no longer be called el Día de la Raza, when it is a day of mourning. Instead, participants proposed a Day of Dignity, Unity and Resistance; Indigenous Peoples Day. Even then, three months before Chiapas, there was the sense que algo se iba a soltar, that something was breaking. Los que todos somos los hijos de Cuauhtemoc were content to debate the past, but the uprising was about the present tense. It was about government officials forcing people to sign away their ejido land and families betraying their own for the right to sell the collective small farms. It was about mass graves in Morelos. It was about remembering, grieving, and anger. It was about the Old Talk, the huehuetlatolli, "great, great word" or the Ancient Word of the Elders. Several of the leaders at Temoaya received threats or were put on death lists following Chiapas. Of course, all the peoples of Chiapas are now suffering through the violence. They have forever changed the way we look at the idea of sovereignty and autonomy. As comandante Ramona has said, there will never again be a México without Indians.

In writing this, I remember people like Reyna Gómez Hernández, crazy Genaro Dominguez and los "indios canijos" de CNPI (Consejo Nacional de Pueblos Indios), and the lost codex that saved their communal lands from being converted into weekend homes for government officials from San Cristóbal. I would pray with them when the moon bit the sun, as danzantes made the Zócalo tremble. They would take me to see the piedras at Tres Zapotes.

I spent months with Genaro, who led a movement of Chicanoized Indians, indigenas such as Demetria, whose husband disappeared in 1991. She had been ashamed of being Mazahua. Genaro's movement attempted to re-Indianize the indios, preserving the language, customs and land rights. Genaro, who had been sequestered several times and led numerous hunger strikes in the plaza, was a man of enigmatic history. It was the people who slept in Genero's law offices on costales; indigenous women like Demetria who cooked for him, starved with him in the Zócalo; the people often kidnaped by pistoleros; the rock throwers in confrontations with goons; people like Reyna, a rock thrower, a bread baker, a woman who could defend herself with sticks; and her husband, Sabino, who was permanently brain damaged from a confrontation with government authorities. It was they who were the popular heroes.

As Reyna and I walked among wild alcatraz outside San Cristóbal de las Casas, below sacred rock temples on a cliff in San Felipe Catapec, she spoke of nights spent sleeping outside government offices and the days without eating, even when there were no hunger strikes. "You give your life to this struggle." It is no longer yours or mine. It belongs to the people, to the earth, to the chamacos, to the future. The future creates us.

At Temoaya, Roberto and I saw an old woman climb a tree three stories high, as if she were a girl of 10. She took from it branches with lagrimas de copal. She prayed to the tree. She prayed to the river. She prayed to the rocks. "I don't know what I will do when I am old and can no longer climb trees," said Doña Margarita. She has lived more than 60 years on this land with the blood of Chichimeca and Huichol in her veins.

Then she walked to the prayer circle where she offered the branches to the fire–fire that was lit during all six days of the summit. There she gave thanks to Father Sun, Mother Earth. The elders said the fire is unity. It is sacred. It is our grandfather. He is life.

She said the buffalo prayer. She said the prayer to the bear. To the eagle she prayed. "These staffs have life. Here is the feather of the eagle that will carry us to freedom," said Doña Margarita. "You all have indigenous blood in your veins and the blood is telling us to come back. These feathers will carry us to freedom."

At the altar was a bear hide and a buffalo head, eagle feathers, hawk feathers, that the Peace and Dignity runners carried high in their prayer run from Alaska to Chile. Among the staffs was that of the Chicano nation, carved with the eagle of the United Farm Workers.

Later, the participants at Temoaya issued an official declaration: "The mestizo, the majority of the time, is an acculturated, indigenous person who has stopped recognizing himself as such. Many of them, made desperate by an assimilation that is not real and leaves them not one benefit, retake their roots and come to be the best fighters of our cause because they know the pain, the humiliation that it means to lose identity."

In the United States most Mexican Americans are called mestizos, or oft-called Hispanics or Latinos. The message was for them, too. We sacrificed to take the pain from the future. This is what we are planting now to the Four Directions.

I came to México as a Xicana Indian. Detribalized Indian. I have worn many skins. Prior to coming to México, I had lived in Philadelphia and kept wondering what I was doing there with the Liberty Bell and Valley Forge, where the smallpox blankets were dispensed. I returned to México to heal and re-member who I was. This book became my prayer.

In writing this book, I prayed to know what action to take and to be in rhythm with Great Mystery, with the great law of the universe, so that the justice of the universe would flow through me. Now, everywhere I walk is a sacred place, sacred ground. Campo santo. Me sanó. To paraphrase the legendary Luis Leal, me hice piedra y mata de la tierra.

It was at Temoaya that I was inspired by the "little grandmother," Laurie Weahkee of the Diné and Cochiti Pueblo Nations, who now fights to save the petroglyphs in Albuquerque. "It is our responsibility to protect all the spirituality for the future. The decision and prayers you plant today are really for the generation to come. Generations before did their dance and prayer for us today and they're still alive today. We must look into ourselves…the life we live belongs not to ourselves but to the community."

I once asked my Buddhist elder in faith, Nancy Ali, why I had to struggle so much. "Because the common people's struggle is too hard. Ordinary people can literally change their entire destiny. Without this experience you can't accomplish what you want in this lifetime." My suffering, she said, would allow me to know their hearts and to write with conviction. How could I write about spiritual social change and not struggle?

Now, after many years of birthing this book, I see why I came. I came to alter the meaning of my life. I came to become stronger, mujer molcajete. I have healed in relationship and stained my heart with flowers. I have entered the Maguey House. I have emerged from the mud.

One afternoon a couple of years ago, I saw Mud Head walking to fulfill his ceremonial dance. It was a wet day in one of the Pueblos. I knew I had received a blessing. Recently one morning, I emerged from lodge with the sandy earth of South San Antonio covering me like a second skin. I looked in the mirror, and I saw Mud Woman. I thought of Josie's mama, Doña Alejandrina Mendez: "Que no te deshaces con agua." Just because you are the color of mud doesn't mean you will dissolve in the rain.

Through the people in this book, a part of me has been completed and part of their work completed in me. My memory called me, my night messengers, my conscience. The people in this book. Abeja called me. Hormiga called. The Great Mystery. The Mystic Law.

This book is not only about politics, or only about popular history, or only about social change. It is about a people's spiritual history, the recovery of their soul. One cannot be separated from the other. They are one. Spiritual matter. The material is spiritual. "Only when we respond to this material struggle spiritually, will we have a complete struggle." – Valerio Grefa of the Quichua nation in Equador in an interview in Abya Yala News

In fact, what I lived in documenting this book was the emergence of a people, our creation story. The creation story of anyone who decides to struggle with all the sufferings and opportunities that life presents, the creation story of the indocumentado who trusts the river with his life. Or she who trusts the desert. Human rights activist Victor Clark Alfaro calls the indocumentado the true anonymous hero of both countries.

People have asked who would read my book. What was the connection. It is the land and it is the ancestors. It is the migration story of Mónico's grandchildren in San Diego; Benita's stepson in Los Angeles; the abuelita's children in California and the Southern U.S.; the relatives of the guerrillero, "el flaco," aquí en el otro lado; or of tipos como Osorio. They carry the legacy for our culture of creation.

Journal entry 1991: "Stained glass lunas, black shiny nights… moral history is written with the blood of the people. Dar la vida para que la vida nos de pa'tras…the cardinal points are the expansion of the soul. Heroism is a process and a choice. Even when history is thrust upon you, it is still a split-second choice. Each person is a tide in the universe, great tides that pour one into the other, the wash of the universe. Rich men and the privileged, indios, campesinos. We all are born, and we all die. How we emerge from the earth of our existence, of our suffering, of our own adversities is what differentiates the mighty. We are all common people at the moment of death. What matters is to believe, hasta creer moriendo."

When I wrote this ending, Chiapas had once again bled at the hands of paramilitary. Mostly women and children were killed in Acteal. Even pregnant women were given a coup de gras. Later, in another liberated village, the people found brains in the fields. In others, the women were threatened that they would all be raped if the men did not come out of the jungles. It is the government who commits human sacrifice. These are the people of the group Las Abejas. They took the name of the bees because bees do not allow anything unclean in their hive; and their work makes pure, sweet honey.

When marchistas of Xi'Nich' and Las Abejas arrived in México December 12, 2000, they issued this statement: "…Largas caminatas hasta el palacio del señor que gobierna con poco oído y mucha lengua. Muchos pasos para que escuche nuestra palabra antigua…."

I remember the words of Daniel Molina, when I asked what inspired him to continue. "Because the last thing to leave Pandora's box was Hope."

I wrote this book so that those who read it will understand México through its people, the ones who never get on TV; the ones who rarely are heard by positional "leaders" who have power based on rank and decide to make war, send helicopters, or look the other way. I wrote this because it is the creation time for the Eagle and the Condor to unite in the people. I wrote this because in the process of la vida, la ví dar.

This has been my creation story. As Rudolfo Anaya writes, we want to prove life right. Most of all, I wrote this because I love my people.

This book is done. My heart is in it.

Nimiztmo tlazocamatilia no Ometeotzintli.

I thank you, Ometeotl

Viva México

Acknowledgments

In 1990, I began to research this book as part of my fellowship at the Center for International Journalism (University of Southern California). Having lived in México and having covered it as a journalist for a significant part of my career, I knew I wanted to convey how Mexicans dignify their lives. I had seen it countless times. Some people may take issue with my use of the word "heroes." I have wrestled with this dilemma, too. Unfortunately, I was hard pressed to find another noun for those who act heroically.

I took an extended leave of absence from the Philadelphia Inquirer and then, finally, a buy out to finance my research. During this time, I met my husband, Roberto Rodríguez, and he moved with me to Mexico City and participated in some of the interviews. Most occurred between late 1990 through October 12, 1993. The time I write from is prior to the uprising in 1994 that was at the crest of many movements. Though I had heard rumors of the guerrillas in the jungla, I knew little of what was about to happen on January 1, 1994.

Because of my limited budget, often I traveled three hours by public transportation within Mexico City and the people I was going to see were not there. They had no phone. Sometimes, I traveled two days by bus, not knowing whether the people I found there would be documented in this book. Sometimes, they were too busy to meet with me. Also, about the time I decided to do the book, I contracted an auto-immune disorder. Then, Roberto and I became nationally syndicated columnists in 1994 and my writing time was curtailed. I continued in spite of all of these challenges. It has taken me over 10 years to fulfill my promise to myself.

Please note where I developed personal relationships, I refer to my collaborators by their first names. Also, Mocehual or Nahuatl words are generally written without accents, in accordance with the way traditional Macehual people use language today. In addition, this book is written in a literary journalism genre. No footnotes are used but general citations are included. The change in tenses is in keeping with the literary tradition of South America.

Tlazocamati

Gracias a Sandina, Fernando, Carmen, Lía y la señora Juana, my neighbors and friends in México; a special thanks to Sandina, Elaine and Bibi, for sharing their resources, contacts and musings. Gracias tambien a Anibal, Beto, Juan Manuel, Irma, Javier, Rosie (of the Seminario Permanente de Estudios e Información Mexicano-Chicanos y de Fronteras) y a Primo and Sergio Aguayo. Gracias a toda la familia de Mónico Rodríguez (Beta, Marina, Judith, and Renato), Juan Anzaldo Meneses, Raul A.G., Andres Najera, Doña Rosario, and Elena Poniatowska for her graciousness. Gracias a mis compas Raquel y Ward, Sylvia Ledesma, Teresa Cordóva, Darla Morgan, Theresa Melendez, Octavio Romano, Teresa Carrillo, Ana García, Elba Ríos, and Alma Cervantes, Antonio Ríos-Bustamante y Yolanda Bernal. Thanks to my mother Martha Maldonado Dickinson and Francesca Hernández Prewitt, who helped me type my manuscript when my hands gave out, and to Norma Cantú and Josie Méndez-Negrete, who helped me find clarity. Mil gracias to my mother for her drawings of Tlazoteotl and to Deborah Vasquez for her artistic rendering of the book cover. Many thanks to my elders, teachers and friends John Kaskaske, Picajana, Martha Ramirez, Gregory Gomez, Mapitzmitl (Paz), Enrique Maestas and Martha Many Grey Horses, Nancy Ali. Gracias a Rudy Anaya for the use of la casita, where I wrote the chapter on the mothers of the disappeared and let go of demons along the Jemez river; and thank you to Rudy Acuña, who long ago told me that the thread to this book was my life.

A special thanks to the people in this book and to the people in México, from the bus drivers to the strangers who gave me directions. Gracias for the generosity and kindness. I thank Great Mystery for having known them and for having been able to write these words.

All my relations,
Patrisia Gonzales

The Woman Who Fell From The Sky

It is said a long time ago, so long not even the Earth existed, there was only water. It went on forever, and it stretched and stretched. And in that water were birds and animals swimming. And far above in the clouds there was a Sky Land; and in the Sky Land there was a great, big beautiful tree. It had four wide roots, and the four roots stretched to each of the sacred directions. From its branches, all kinds of fruits and flowers grew. In the Sky Land lived an old chief. He had a young wife and she was expecting a child. One night, she had a very strange dream. She sees the tree has been uprooted. When she was finished telling him the dream, the chief tells her, "I'm sad you had this dream. It's a very powerful dream, and, as it is in our way, when we have a powerful dream, we must do all that we can to make it come true." So the old chief came to the tree. He wrapped his arms around it, bent his knees, and pulled. At last, with one strong effort, he uprooted the tree and placed it on its side. Where the roots of the tree had been, now there was only a giant hole. The wife of the chief got close to the hole and she leaned forward to look down. She held one of the giant tree branches to steady herself and she thought she saw something far, far below, something that looked like water. She leaned out to look. As she did, she lost her balance and fell into the hole. And her hand slipped from the branch and the only thing she brought was a handful of seeds.

As she was falling down and far below, some of the birds and animals in the water heard a noise, and they looked up. "Someone is falling towards us from the sky!" They saw it was a woman. "We must do something to help her!"

Two swans flew up and caught the woman in their wide wings and slowly they begin to bring her down to the water.

"She doesn't have web feet; she's not like us. I don't think she can live in the water," they said. Another of the water animals asked, "What can we do?"

Then one of the water birds said. "I've heard there is earth far below the water. We can dive down, and she will have earth. Then she will have a place to stand."

Some say the duck was first to go down.... The swan.... The

beaver tried and went even deeper.... They all failed. And then a small, little voice was heard.

"I will bring up the earth or die trying." They all looked around to see who it was. It was the tiny muskrat. She was not as strong or swift as the others, but she was determined. And the farther she went, the darker it became; but she still kept swimming. She went so deep that it felt like her lungs would burst, but she still kept going. Just as she was becoming unconscious, she reached out one small, little paw and grasped at the bottom. She barely touched it. She floated up almost dead. When the others saw she had come to the surface, they thought she had failed. They saw in her right paw that she held it tightly shut. "Look, she has earth! And where can we put it?"

Just then a deep voice said, "Put it on my back." It was the Great Turtle who had come up from way down below. So they brought muskrat to the Great Turtle and placed her paw on his back. Even today, the marks of Muskrat's paws are on Turtle's shell. As a tiny bit of earth fell on the back of Turtle, immediately it began to grow larger and larger until it became the whole world.

Then the two swans brought Sky Woman down. She stepped onto the new earth and opened her hand, letting the seeds fall on the soil. From those seeds the grasses, the flowers and the food sprung up.

"Life on earth had begun."

– The Onondaga creation story of Earth on Turtle's Back as told to me by Grandma Emma Ortega, Apache-mestiza legend keeper.

Bibliography

Alvarado Peralta, Felipe. 1992. Ce-Acatl Topiltzin Quetzalcoatl. Mexico City.

Alvarez, Daniel Molina. 1986. Tlatelolco Mi Amor (antología homenaje, 1335-1985.) México: Editorial Antares.

Americas Watch. Human Rights in México: A Policy of Impunity. 1990. Washington, D.C.

Anzaldúa, Gloria. 1987. Borderlands La Frontera: The New Mestiza. San Francisco: Aunt Lute Books.

—1990. Making Face, Making Soul/ Haciendo Caras: Creative and Critical Perspectives by Feminists of Color. Edited by Gloria Anzaldúa. San Francisco: Aunt Lute Books.

Anzures, María. 1991. Coyolxauhqui: Nuestra Madre Cosmica. Mexico City. Consejo Nacional de la Cultura Nahuatl.

Balderrama, Francisco E. and Rodríquez, Raymond. 1995. Decade of Betrayal: Mexican Repatriation in the 1930's. Albuquerque: University of New México Press.

Bartra, Armando. 1985. Los Herederos de Zapata: Movimientos Campesinos Posrevolucionarios en México. México, D.F.: Ediciones Era.

—1985. Regeneración. Edited by Armando Bartra. México, D.F.: Ediciones Era.

Batalla, Paula. 1988. Donde Quiera Que Me Paro, Soy Yo (Autobiografía de una Jaramillista). México: CIDHAL Libros.

Bonilla Macharro, Carlos. 1981. Ejercicio de guerrillero. Gaceta Editores.

Brotherston, Gordon. 1979. Image of the New World: The American Continent Portrayed in Native Texts. London: Thames and Hudson.

Brundage, Burr Cartwright. 1979. The Fifth Sun: Aztec Gods, Aztec World. Austin and London: University of Texas Press.

Brushwood, John S. 1966. México in its Novel: A Nation's Search for Identity. Austin and London: University of Texas Press.

Camín, Héctor Aguilar. 1991. La guerra de Galio. México, D.F.: cal y arena.

Campbell, Howard. 1994. Zapotec Renaissance: Ethnic Politics and Culutral Revivalism in Southern México. Albuquerque: University of New México Press.

—1993. Zapotec Struggles: Histories, Politics, and Representations from Juchitán, Oxcaca. Edited by Howard Campbell and others. Washington and London: Smithsonian Institution Press.

Campbell, Joseph. 1949. The Hero With a Thousand Faces. Princeton, New Jersey: Princeton University Press.

Carrasco, Davíd. 1990. Religions of Mesoamerica. San Francisco: Harper & Row.

Carrillo A., Rafael. 1983. Posada y el grabado de temas populares hasta los artistas contemporáneos. México, D.F.: Panorama Editorial, S.A.

Carrillo, Teresa. Gendered Unions: The Rise and Demise of the Mexican Garment Workers Movement. At press. University of Texas Press.

Chan, Román Piña. 1990. Quetzalcoatl: Serpiente Emplumada. México, D.F.: Fondo de Cultura Económica.

Córdova, Arnaldo. 1989. La Ideología de La Revolución Mexicana. México, D.F.: Ediciones Era.

—1990. Chicana Voices: Intersections of Class, Race, and Gender. Edited by Teresa Córdova and others. Albuquerque: University of New México Press.

Ce-Acatl. 1992. Quetzalcoatl, su concepto y el hombre Tolteca. Mexico City. Number 27.

Dalton, Roque. 1984. Roque Dalton Poems. Translated by Richard Schaaf. Willimantic, CT: Curbstone Press.

Deleón, Arnoldo. 1992. They Called Them Greasers. Austin, University of Texas Press.

Deloria, Jr., Vine. 1994. God Is Red: A Native View of Religon. Golden, Colorado: Fulcrum Publishing.

—1992. Las Flores de la Muerte: Ensayo sobre la floricultura mexicana. Edited by Justus Fenner and Thomas Gebauer. México: Ediciones GEA.

Equipo Pueblo. Ed., Crónica del nuevo méxico. Edited by Equipo Pueblo. 1989. Mexico City. Equipo Pueblo.

Florescano, Enrique. 1994. Memory, Myth, and Time in México: From the Aztecs to Independence. Translated by Albert G. Bork. Austin, University of Texas Press.

—1990. Popular Movements and Political Change in México. Edited by Joe Foweraker and Ann L. Craig. Boulder and London: Lynne Rienner Publishers.

Freire, Paulo. 1990. Pedagogy of the Oppressed. New York: Continuum.

Galeana, Benita. 1990. Benita. México, D.F.: Lince Editores.

Galeano, Eduardo. 1987. Memory of Fire: Faces & Masks. New York: Pantheon Books.

—1992. We Say No. Translated by Mark Fried and others. New York and London: W.W. Norton & Company.

—1988. Memory of Fire: Century of the Wind. Translated by Cedric Belfrage. New York: Pantheon Books.

García, Mario T. 1981. Desert Immigrants: The Mexicans of El Paso, 1880-1920. New Haven and London: Yale University Press.

Gilly, Adolfo; Córdova, Arnaldo; Bartra, Armando; Mora, Manuel Aguilar; and Semo, Enrique. 1979. Interpretaciones de la Revolución Mexicana. México, D.F.: Nueva Imagen.

—1989. Cartas a Cuauhtémoc Cárdenas. Edited by Adolfo Gilly. México, D.F.: Ediciones Era.

González de Alba, Luis. 1971. Los días y los años. México, D.F.: Ediciones Era.

Graham-Yooll, Andrew. 1982. A Matter of Fear: Portrait of an Argentinian Exile. Westport, CT: Lawernce Hill & CO., Inc.

Griswold del Castillo, Richard and Garcia, Richard A. 1995. César Chávez: A Triumph of Spirit. Norman and London: University of Oklahoma Press.

Gutiérrez, Arturo Meza. 1997. Calendario Mexicano. México, D.F.: EDAMEX.

Gutiérrez, Marcela Tostado. El álbum de la mujer: Antología ilustrada de las mexicanas. México, D.F.: Instituto Nacional de Antropología e Historia.

Harris III, Charles H., and Sadler, Louis R., 1988. The Border and the Revolution: Clandestine Activities of the Mexican Revolution: 1910-1920. Silver City, N.M.: High-Lonesome Books.

Hart, John M. 1978. Anarchism & The Mexican Working Class, 1860-1931. Austin: University of Texas Press.

Hernández, Delfino Hernández. 1959. Anahuac Itlamatiliz: La Filosofia de Anahuac. México, Monterrey: Material Didáctico, S.A. de C.V.

Hodges, Donald C. 1995. Mexican Anarchism After the Revolution. Austin: University of Texas Press.

Inclán, Jesús Sotelo. 1991. Raíz y razón de Zapata. México, D.F.: Cien de México.

Jaramillo. Ruben M. 1981. Autobiografía. Mexico City. Editorial Nuestro Tiempo.

Jörgensen, Beth E. 1994. The Writing of Elena Poniatowska. Austin: University of Texas Press.

—1990. Revuelta, Rebelión y Revolución: La Lucha Rural in México del siglo XVI al siglo XX. Edited by Friedrich Katz. México, D.F.: Ediciones Era.

—1995. First World, Ha Ha Ha! The Zapatista Challenge. Edited by Elaine Katzenberger. San Francisco: City Lights Books.

Klein, Cecilia F. "Fighting with Feminity: Gender and War in Aztec México." Estudios de Cultura Nahuatl. Vol. 24.

Leeming, David and Page, Jake. 1998. The Mythology of Native North America. University of Oklahoma Press.

León-Portilla, Miguel. 1983. Los Antiguos Mexicanos: A traves de sus cronicas y cantares. México, D.F.: Fondo de Culutra Economica.

—1991. Toltecayotl: aspectos de la cultura náhuatl. México, D.F.: Fondo de Cultura Economica.

—1988. Time and Reality in the Thought of the Maya. Norman and London: University of Oklahoma Press.

—1989. Visión de los vencidos Relaciones indígenas de la Conquista. Edited by Miguel León-Portilla. México, D.F.: Universidad Nacional Autónoma de México.

—1989. Por La Regeneración de Xochimilco: Memoria del Encuentro Regional de 1986. Edited by Alfonso González Martínez. Ursula Coapa, D.F.: Grupo de Estudios Ambientales.

Martinez López, Felipe. 1985. El crespúsculo del poder: Juchitán, Oax., 1980-1982. Oaxaca, Oax. Instituto de Investigaciones Sociológicos de la Universidad Autónoma Benito Juárez de Oaxaca.

Men, Hunbatz. 1990. Secrets of Mayan Science/Religon. Translated by Diana Gubiseh Ayala and James Jennings Dunlap II. Santa Fe, N.M.: Bear & Company Publishing.

Momaday, N. Scott. 1976. The Names: a Memoir. Tucson and London: The University of Arizona Press.

Manjarrez, C. Froylan. 1981. La matanza de xochicalco. Mexico City. Editorial Nuestro Tiempo.

Monsiváis, Carlos. 1970. Días de guardar. México, D.F.: Ediciones Era.

—1977. Amor perdido. México, D.F.: Ediciones Era.

—1987. Entrada libre. Crónicas de la sociedad que se organiza. México, D.F.. Ediciones Era

Montemayor, Carlos. 1991. Guerra en el Paraíso. México, D.F.: DIANA LITERARIA.

Olivas, Abel Gamiz and Martinez, Alejandro Gamiz. Quetzalcoatl en la leyenda y en la historia. México, D.F.: Editorial del Magisterio "Benito Juárez".

Olvera, Silvia Limón. 1990. Las cuevas y el mito de origen: Los casos inca y mexica. México, D.F.: Consejo Nacional para la Culutra y las Artes.

Piña, Antonio Velasco. 1987. Regina. México, D.F.: Editorial Jus.

Poniatowska, Elena. 1980. Fuerte es el silencio. México, D.F.: Ediciones Era.

1988. Nada, nadie: Las voces del temblor. México, D.F.: Ediciones Era.

Ravelo, Renato. 1978. La Guerra de Liberación del Pueblo Maya. México, Ediciones Servir al Pueblo.

—1978. Los Jaramillistas. México, D. F., Editorial Nuestros Tiempos.

Reina, Leticia. 1980. Las Rebeliones Campesinas en México (1819-1906). México: Siglo Veintuno.

Rutherford, John. 1978. La Sociedad Mexicana Durante La Revolución. México, D.F.: Ediciones "El Caballito."

—1964. El Libro del Consejo. Translated by Georges Raynaud and others. México, D.F.: Universidad Nacional Autónoma de México.

—1986. Popol Vuh: Las anitguas historias del Quiché. Translated by Adrián Recinos. México,D.F.: Fondo de Cultura Económica.

Salas, Elizabeth. 1990. Soldaderas in the Mexican Military: Myth and History. Austin: University of Texas Press.

Séjourné, Laurette. 1962. El Universo de Quetzalcoatl. México, D.F.: Fondo de Cultura Económica.

Semo, Enrique, et. al., 1983. México un pueblo en la historia. Mexico City. UAP-Nueva Imagen.

Silko, Leslie Marmon. 1996. Yellow Woman and a Beauty of the Spirit: Essays on Native American Life Today. New York, NY: Simon & Schuster.

Sheridan, Thomas E. and Naylor, Thomas H., editors. 1979. Rarámuri. Northland Press.

Schroeder, Susan; Wood, Stephanie; and Haskett, Robert. 1997. Indian Women of Early México. University of Oklahoma Press.

Soustelle, Jacques. 1986. El Universo de Los Aztecas. México, D.F.: Fondo de Cultura Económica.

Suarez, Luis. 1978. Lucio Cabañas, el guerrillero sin esperanza. Mexico City. roca.

Taibo II, Paco Ignacio. 1991. 68. México, D.F.: Planeta.

Talavera, Fernando and Muñoz, Francisco. 1992. La organización de las costureras II. Taller de Economia del Trabajo, Facultad de Economia UNAM. Mexico City.

Tezozómoc, Fernando Alvarado. 1975. Crónica Mexicana/Códice Ramírez. Ed. Manuel Orozco y Berra. Editorial Porrúa, México.

Tibon, Gutierre. 1981. El Ombilgo, Como Centro Cosmico: Una contribución a la historia de las religiones. México, D.F.: Fondo de Cultura Económica.

Thomas, David Hurst; Miller, Jay; White, Richard; Nabokov, Peter; and Deloria, Philip J. 1993. The Native Americans: An Illustrated History. Alanta: Turner Publishing, Inc.

Timerman, Jacobo. 1981. Prisoner Without a Name, Cell Without a Number. New York: Vintage Books.

Todorov, Tzvetan. 1984. The Conquest of America. Translated by Richard Howard. New York: Harper & Row.

Tompkins, Ptolemy. 1971. This Tree Grows Out of Hell. San Francisco: Harper Collins.

—1972. Aztlan: An Anthology of Mexican American Literature. Edited by Luis Valdez and Stan Steiner. New York: Vintage Books.

Vázquez, Angélica Cuéllar. 1993. La Noche es de Ustedes, El Amanecer es Nuestro. México, D.F.: Universidad Nacional Autónoma de México.

Waters, Frank. 1975. México Mystique: The Coming Sixth World of Consciousness. Athens: Swallow Press/Ohio University Press.

Whitecotton, Joseph W. 1985. Los Zapotecos: Principes, Sacerdotes y Campesinos. México, D.F.: Fondo de Cultura Economica.

Zermeño, Sergio. 1978. México: Una Democracia Utópica El Movimiento Estudiantil Del 68. México: Siglo Veintiuno.

—1990. Movimientos Sociales en México Durante La Década de Los 80. Edited by Sergio Zermeño García Granados and Jesús Aurelio Cuevas Díaz. México, D.F.: Universidad Nacional Autónoma de México.

Zurda. A 20 años del '68. Volumn 1/Number 4. Mexico City.